POLITICAL AWAKENING IN NEPAL
(THE SEARCH FOR A NEW IDENTITY)

POLITICAL AWAKENING IN NEPAL

(THE SEARCH FOR A NEW IDENTITY)

PREM R. UPRETY
PROFESSOR OF HISTORY
TRIBHUVAN UNIVERSITY
KATHMANDU

COMMONWEALTH PUBLISHERS
NEW DELHI INDIA

Political Awakening in Nepal

Edition : 2022
ISBN 81-7169-190-0

Published by :
COMMONWEALTH PUBLISHERS (P) LTD.
4831/24, Govind Lane,
Ansari Road, Darya Ganj,
New Delhi - 110002
Ph. : 23272541, 23242541
e-mail : commonwealthpublishers2016@gmail.com

Distributed by :
ARJUN PUBLISHING HOUSE
4831/24, Govind Lane,
Ansari Road, Darya Ganj,
New Delhi - 110002
Ph. : 23272541, 23242541
e-mail : arjunbooks2001@gmail.com

Laser Typesetting by :
Dimple Computers
Delhi

Printed at :
Milan Enterprises
Delhi

DEDICATION

This study is dedicated to Krishna Lal Adhikari, Shukra Raj Shastri, Ganga Lal Shrestha, Dharma Bhakta Mathema, Dasrath Chand and Krishna Prasad Koirala who sacrificed their lives so that others may live with honour and dignity that were denied to them.

ACKNOWLEDGEMENTS

A study of this dimension, obviously, cannot be the work of a single individual. Many institutions and friends have made this research fruitful and rewarding. I would first of all like to thank Professor Yugeshwar P. Verma of Tribhuvan University for going through the pages of this manuscript and offering valuable suggestions and comments. I am indebted to my esteemed colleague Dr. Chandra B. Budathoki, Professor of History (T.U.), for providing not only valuable hours of fruitful discussions, but also a wealth of materials without which this study would have been incomplete. While working in the National Archives, New Delhi; India Office Library, London, the Foreign Ministry and the Army Head Quarters at Kathmandu, the help rendered by Shri S. Sircar, Miss. R. Wilkie, Shri Hari P. Chetri, and Shri M. Sapkota was extremely valuable. The information supplied by the archival sources have been supplemented by a series of interviews with the principal figures in the Nepali revolutionary drama in the first half of the twentieth century. Their names and roles have been mentioned in the bibliography. I am indebted to each one of them for the time they provided, interest they showed, and the careful assistance they rendered when I intruded into their busy and happy hours. My grateful thanks also go to Shri Mukunda Raj Aryal, Dr. Gajanand Agrawal and to Shri Gyanendra Prasad Adhikari (better known as Hansen) for providing me valuable information on the intricacies of the period. I am also thankful to Dr. Rajendra Ram, Professor of History, Patna University for his thoughtful encouragement, and to Shri B.R. Verma for undertaking the publishing responsibility. Finally, I owe no little to my wife Shusma Devi Uprety : it was her counsel and companionship that sustained me throughout the research endeavour. While these persons may detect their influences in the following pages, I suspect that they will occasionally see my stubbornness too. However, the incorporation of their suggestions ought in no way shift to them any errors and inaccuracies: they lie with me alone.

Tribhuvan University, Kathmandu — Prem R. Uprety
1st May, 92

PREFACE

The primary aim of this work is to place in its proper historical perspective one of the most significant and portentous events in the history of Nepal — the end of Rana oligarchy. This is of fundamental importance not only in the study of the evolution of Nepali polity; but also in the understanding of the intricacies in the process of development of a third world country. It was in 1950 that Nepal emerged from her self-imposed isolation and became an increasingly active member of the international community. As the modern concept of nation-state began to develop Nepal started to experience two levels of changes simultaneously on the domestic and the international fronts. The first level of change can be labeled as "modernization" or "westernization" or even "anglicization". At another level she became one of the chief spokesmen of the non-aligned movement and began to speak with confidence on world politics.

It was on February 18, 1951 the Rana autocracy was confined to the pages of history books. This change can be taken as a watershed in the history of modern Nepal. Both politically and intellectually the post-1950 Nepal was never the same as the pre-1950 Nepal. But even in 1950 a contemporary observer could see the Rana regime clinging desperately to life.

The word "regime" in modern times implies a system of government under a certain individual. But when we talk about the Rana regime we are speaking about a peculiar political culture that was in operation in this part of South Asia for a little more than a century. Besides, for a proper assessment of the Rana regime we will have to add the social and economic components to the political. The Rana regime, thus, may be defined as the way of life which the "revolution" of 1950-51 destroyed. The regime that the "revolution" destroyed is significant not only as a prelude to the revolution but also it possessed a phenomenon of its own. It was, in fact, the culmination of the splendour of the feudalistic era that could never be revived again. The "revolution" erupted from the conditions that preceded it among which the political awakening of the Nepali intelligentsia constituted a major factor.

The concept of political awakening in Nepal can often be misleading. It could be construed to mean that traditional Nepal was either dormant or devoid of politics. But this is far from reality. Traditional Nepal was not devoid of politics; rather on may occasions it was more alive and dramatic. But, it is the nature, style and objective that distinguished traditional Nepali politics from that of our times. Traditional politics in Nepal consisted of inter-family and intra-family feuds for the exercise of the sovereign power. It was characterized by sinister plots and counter-plots, ghastly murders, and wholesale massacres. The object was always the same, namely, the attainment of political supremacy without the involvement of the masses. The short, the traditional politics in Nepal was not the agitational politics of the twentieth century brought into focus with organization of political parties and equipped with modern tools of political agitation like mass-communication and *satyagraha.**

The absolute, arbitrary nature of the Rana Government in the first half of the twentieth century prevented the early

* *Satyagraha* is a technique which operates within conflict of situation. It consists of adherence to stated truth by behaviour that is non-violent; but which involves suffering. For more on the concept of *Satyagraha* as applied social political action see M.K. Gandhi, *An Autobiography or the Story of My Experiments with Truth*, trans. Mahadev Desai (Ahmedabad: Nava Jivan Publishing House, 1972 (reprint), pp. 239-40, 328-329, 332-333; Joan V. Bondurant, *The Conquest of Violence, the Gandhian Philosophy of Conflict* (Berkeley: University of California Press, 1969), pp. 15-105; Krishna Lal Sridharani, *War Without Violence* (New York: Harcourt Brace, 1931), pp. 315-316; Bondurant and Margaret Fisher, "The Concept of Change in the Hindu Society and Neo-Gandhian Thought" in Donald E. Smith (ed.), *South Asian Politics and Religion* (Princeton: Princeton University Press, 1966), pp. 235-248.

political mobilization within the boundaries of Nepal. Thus, political mobilization and the creation of voluntary associations by Nepalis occurred first in the North Indian cities like Banaras, Patna, Calcutta, Darjeeling, and Dehradun. The participants in this new politics were the Nepali elites domiciled or living in self-imposed exile in India. They were, in fact, by and large western educated Nepalis who came from the ranks of school teachers, lawyers, and social workers who drew their inspiration either from Gandhiism or the Arya Samaj. It was the collective efforts of the different groups of Nepali revolutionary intelligentsia that made the "revolution" of 1950-51 possible.

During my research I have almost exclusively relied on the semi-official records, secret registers, abstract translations of the conversations and radio broadcasts preserved in the Ministry of Foreign Affairs, Kathmandu; National Archives, New Delhi; and India Office Library, London. English as well as the vernacular periodicals and newspapers have frequently been used. Besides, interviews with persons who were active in Nepali politics during the 1930s to 50s have been extremely valuable.

Scope and Limitations

It is true that Nepali history in the eighteenth and the nineteenth centuries have been subjected to exhaustive study while the history of Nepal in the first half of the twentieth century has drawn little attention of scholars. The reasons are not far to seek. Most of the documents of this period fall in the restricted period in the archives of both India and Nepal. I am, however, extremely grateful to the Ministry of Foreign Affairs at Kathmandu, for permitting me to scan through the documents of this restricted period, without which this study would not have been possible. In addition, many of the documents of this period are in the personal collections of the individuals waiting to be brought to light by the diligence of researchers. Besides, since we are so close to these events, it is difficult to pen this period with absolute accuracy and precision. Still an honest efforts has been made to speak on the episodes that even today rouses so much passion and feelings. If this study provokes more research into this area I will feel my efforts have been amply rewarded.

The political history of Nepal, specially that which is associated with the political awakening in Nepal has been little academically documented. I have tried my best to do so with the help of archival records, personal interviews with the actors of the "Great Drama" and the other revolutionary episodes.

The basic thrust of this study is to see how the political culture of the Rana era collapsed due to the combined force of the internal contradiction of tradition and the external contradiction introduced by the conflict between tradition and modernity. The internal contradiction is symbolized by the institutionalization of "Kingship" within Kingship. The *sanad* of 1856 brought this contradiction into the forefront. Furthemore, the Ranas who had attempted to liberalize the social and educational structure of feudal Nepal through their socio-educational reforms, without liberalizing the political instruments of power ran into immense problems. Besides, the traditional Rana polity based upon absolutism, hereditary bureaucratic apparatus, isolation, and personalism were incompatible with the secular culture on which modern human civilization is based. The revolutionary organizations and political parties that sprouted in and outside Nepal during the 1930s and the 40s did bring the Rana regime to a close.

Organization of Study

The introduction sets the tone for the entire study by analyzing the foundations of the political culture of the Rana oligarchy under different headings like leadership, bureaucratic apparatus, and isolation. The second chapter discusses the role of Nepali revolutionary intelligentsia in the first half of the twentieth century. This revolutionary intelligentsia not only provided the spark for the "revolution" of 1950-51 but were very much in the center of the drama. It was these Nepali elites who helped to establish revolutionary socio-political institutions, which besides rousing socio-political consciousness among the people launched anti-Rana agitations in India and Nepal. This constitutes the theme of the third chapter. The fourth chapter is an analysis of the oppositional politics from 1941-1950. This was a period when secret underground politics was replaced by mass politics brought into focus by modern tools of communication like political parties and *satyagraha* movement. The fifth chapter, which concludes this study gives the dynamics of the "revolution" of 1950-51. Each chapter takes the theme of the "revolution" a step forward until we find ourselves right into the whirlpool of the "revolution" itself.

Prem R. Uprety

ABBREVIATIONS

AIR	All India Radio
FMAN	Foreign Ministry Archives, Kathmandu, Nepal
GI	Government of India
GN	Government of Nepal
IOL	India Office Library, London (Now Commonwealth Relations Library)
MAN	Military Archives, Kathmandu, Nepal
NAI	National Archives, New Delhi, India

CONTENTS

1

FOUNDATIONS OF THE POLITICAL CULTURE OF THE RANA OLIGARCHY

> Absolutism at the top implies hundreds of thousands even millions of large, small autocrats that monopolize all means of life and expression, work and pleasure, reward and punishment.... The machine of power becomes an engine of oppression. Where there is only one Employer, namely the state, meakness is the first law of economic survival.
>
> **Eugene Lyons[1]**

Culture, which in fact embraces life of a nation in totality in material, intellectual, and spiritual forms can be studied in two functional perspectives: the working of a society and the operations of a government. The inter-relations between the government and society or to put it in a different perspective the extent of government's control over society and *vice versa* varies according to time, periods, and regions. In short, one may say that while often the government serves merely as an instrument in the legitimization of the norms and values of a society; but at other times it even becomes a change-agent in the process of institutionalization of a new political behaviour. Thus, the

1. Eugene Lyons, quoted by Bertrand Russell, *Power : A New Social Analysis* (London: George Allen & Unwin, 1957), pp. 304-305.

inter-play between the government and society helps in shaping the political culture of a nation. So the political culture of a nation can be said to constitute a very wide range of beliefs, thoughts and symbols codified into a set pattern of political behaviour so as to enable us to understand the working of a political process.[2]

The real problem in analyzing a political culture is to explain why one group of people give orders and others obey. This problem can be analyzed in a fairly simple stimulus-response model. The command is, thus, the stimulus and the response the action that follows. Two examples can be taken from traditional and modern Nepal. First, one can visualize a village *mukhiya* (chieftan) giving orders and his faithful, brave countrymen following them. Second, one can also observe the *Rastriya Panchayat* (National Legislature) voting for an increase in land tax, the Ministry of Finance issuing orders and the millions of Nepalis lining up in the innumerable *malpot karyalayas* (land revenue offices) to pay the increased land tax. These two kinds of action-stimulus and response generate a set of conventions of their own, thus, giving rise to a pattern of "ordered system and symbols".[3]

The political culture of a people gives them an orientation toward their polity and its operation procedures. The term being "politically oriented" would, thus, mean the familiarity with the two sets of ideas: understanding how a polity operates and second knowing how it ought to operate. When people share with each other these two sets of cognitive and normative

2. Lucian Pye, Sidney Verba (eds.), *Political Culture and Political Development* (Princeton: Princeton University Press, 1965), Chapters I, II; Lucian Pye, *Aspects of Political Development* (New Delhi: Amerind Publishing Co., 1972), pp. 104-107.
3. Samuel H. Beer, *Modern Political Development* (New York: Random House, 1974), pp. 24-26; Apter David, *The Politics of Modernization* (Chicago: University of Chicago Press, 1965), pp. 1-80; C.E. Black, *The Dynamics of Modernization* (New York: Harper & Row, 1966), pp. 1-90; Prem R. Uprety, "Nepali Bureaucratic Culture: Few Dominant Features", *The New Horizons,* Vol. I, No. 1, 1981, pp. 1-7.

values everything works in balance and harmony. But as people cease to share these two sets of values the socio-political equilibrium in the system and sub-system is destroyed and a revolution occurs.[4] This prelude forms a perfect backdrop for the scrutiny analysis of the foundations of the political culture of the Rana oligarchy.

DOMINANT FEATURES OF THE RANA POLITY

Institutionalization of "Kingship" within Kingship

The advent of Jang Bahadur in the political horizon of Nepal created an unique political tradition which may be labeled as the "inauguration of `Kingship' within Kingship". Thus, a parallel line of hereditary structure, along with the monarchy, was created which deprived the latter of all his power, authority, and responsibility. So the Shah monarchs, henceforth, continued to exist as "Living museum-pieces" till the first half of the twentieth century. They simply survived; but neither ruled or governed. It was by the royal *sanad* (charter) of August 6, 1856 that Jang Bahadur was able to dry completely the fountain of authority that resided in the hand of the monarch. The *sanad* not only gave Jang Bahadur the `Kingship' over Kaski and Lamjung but also absolute power over the entire country, thus, reducing the Shah rulers to virtual non-entities. To distinguish these two parallel lines of authority Jang Bahadur provided the honorific titles of *Shri* 5 and *Shri* 3.[5] Literally speaking, the monarch was five times honourable while the Premier was only three times honourable. This important *sanad* in part ran:

> Should I anytime tyrannize over my subjects, the Sirdars or the army or wish to cause any dispute between the government of my

---

4. Samuel H. Beer, *Modern Political Development, ibid.*, pp. 25-26; Crane Brinton, *The Anatomy of Revolution* (New York: Prentice Hall, Inc., 1952), pp. 30-136.
5. The use of the expressions like *Maharajadhiraja, Maharaja* and the *Raja* and their inter-relationship can cause some confusion in the minds of the students of the Rana polity.

> country and that either of England or China you are free to prevent my doing so, and if I do not act according to your advice you are to enforce me to do so with my Sirdars and the Army if necessary, to both of which I have given orders to obey and assist you at such time.[6]

This was a total surrender of the monarch to Jang Bahadur Kuwar and his family. The language of the *sanad* can also be read as an indirect confession of the monarch of his "past acts of tyranny". The *sanad* was to prevent its future occurrence. Jang Bahadur was a man of the hour. He picked up his fortune by the point of his sword during the *Kot* massacre of September 15, 1846.[7] The way he was able to extract the *sanad* was a master-stroke of his craftiness and political wisdom.

Conspiratorial Violent Politics

It is true that Jang Bahadur did eliminate the inter-family struggle between the Thapas and Pandeys, the Brahmans and Chautariyas for the exercise of royal authority, by confining the royal prerogative within the royal family, yet, he could not do away with the intra-family feud within his own family. To prevent the succession of a minor to the office of premiership Jang Bahadur instituted the Agnate form of succession,[8] which confined the office of premiership within the Rana family according to seniority of age among the male members. This system though it succeeded in preventing the minor from succeeding, it converted the office of the Premier into a hotbed of intrigues among the incumbents, for, none could become a Premier until he was well advanced in age. Thus, throughout the Rana period one witness a series of conspiracies,

6. True abstract translation of the *sanad* by the Assistant Resident W.B. Irwin, *Foreign Secret Consultation,* August 29, 1856, No. 61, NAI.
7. For more on the circumstances surrounding the fateful event of the Kot massacre see Ludwig Stiller (ed.) *Letters From Kathmandu: The Kot Massacre* (Kathmandu: CNAS, 1981), pp. 320-369.
8. The agnate form of succession was in voge among the Persians.

assassinations, and forced abdications. The result: among the ten Rana Premiers only four died peacefully in office; others were either assassinated or forced to abidacte. The struggle for succession was further heightened by the high rate of fertility within the Rana family. Accordingly, by 1929 there were over 380 male members within the Rana family, thus, constituting "a serious problem socially, politically and economically".[9]

In an effort to narrow the list of aspirants for the office of Premiership the Ranas were categorized into three classes: A, B, and C class. It was only the A class members, who as claimants of "a pure breed" were included in the roll of succession.[10] This division, though it did narrow the list of aspirants for Premiership, yet, it could not prevent strifes, forced abdications and brutal killings inside the Rana aristocracy.* Thus, the first usual act of the Rana Premier after accession was to revise the roll of succession. However, in an effort to prevent the family feud, the nephews of Juddha Shumsher brought up a proposal, which would have limited the post of premiership to a period of five years. This important proposal in part ran :

9. Indian *Political Proceedings,* (Ext.), File No. 29/1928, NAI.
10. Scholars have not reached a concensus over the definition of the three categories among the Ranas. However, the simplest definition based upon the practice of inter-dining (eating of the boiled rice) would be sufficient in providing us at least one handle to unlock the issue. The A Class Ranas were children from wives with whom the taking of boiled rice was permissible. The B Class Ranas were born from wives with whom all levels of inter-dining was possible except the eating of the boiled rice. The C Class Ranas were those born from mistresses, thus, eating with them in public was not permitted. Premier Chandra Shumsher had officially removed the C Class from the roll of succession while the B Class was so further and further removed from the roll of succession that no chance was left for their succession.

* According to one hypothesis it was Premier Chandra Shumsher who was responsible for the division of the Rana family into the three categories: A, B and C Classes. See Dharma Ratna Yemi, *Nepal Ka Kura: Samichchhatmak Itihas* (The Happenings of Nepal: A Critical History) (Kathmandu: Yemi Prakasan, 1957), p. 172.

As Prime Minister (Shri 3 *Maharaja*) can rule the country for not more than five years: after the expiry of this period every Prime Minister shall be removed from office automatically.[11]

However, this valuable document even if it was duly signed by the Premier (though the evidences are to the contrary), remained a dead letter; while the conspiratorial violent nature of the Rana politics continued unbated till the twilight of the Rana rule.

Absolutism

Absolutism was the dominant feature of the Rana polity and "personalism" its driving force. Absolutism not only determined the entire political articulation but also helped to shape the social, economic, and intellectual milieu of the period. Absolutism presupposes a centralized autocratic rule with full despotic and arbitrary powers. The Rana bureaucratic apparatus consisted of a pyramid of graded officialdom ranging from the *Maharaja* and his council to the district officers (*badahakims*) with each layer suservient to the above and overbearing to those below. The bureaucratic structure devised by the Ranas, thus, became the symbol of ruthless oppression. So centralized

11. For more on the proposal see Sham Bhakta Pant, "Padma Shumsher's Succession to Prime Ministership", *Kasturi*, Vol. VII, 1978, pp. 66-67. The writer points out that Juddha Shumsher accepted the proposal to cement unity among the Ranas. He, thus, sealed the document by the *Khadganisana* (seal of the *Maharaja*). The signing ceremony took place in the presence of all his brethren, who were in the roll of succession. The writer continues to say that the document was also signed by all those who were assembled and they took their oath touching the sacred idol of Guheshwari that they would abide by the new regulation. Another source, however, indicates that Juddha upon being informed of the proposal that aimed at limiting his term of office was enraged. He, thus, called a meeting of his brothers in the roll of succession in the Gallery Baithak (Hall) while he took off to his pleasure resort of Godavari. He only returned in the evening to see the pale, yellow, and hungry faces of his fellow brethren. He then dismissed the distinguished gathering with a thunderous roar: "Some of you would like to unseat me from my *gaddi* (office)". Interview with a personal attendant of *Maharaja* Juddha, who also looked after the gallery *baithak*, April 25, 1985. His name is Ram Babu Dhakal.

was the mode of recruitment that all appointments including that of a peon or a turnpike needed the approval of the Premier. In addition, the system of *pajini* necessitated the reappointment of all ranks from the janitor to the Commander-in-Chief.[12] Thus, where there was only one Employer, the *Maharaja,* the citizens were converted into subjects and their rise within the bureaucracy became an act of patronage.

Since the *Maharaja* was the focus of all authority, even the smallest decision of the bureaucracy needed his approval; and he became the only spokesman on all state matters.

A couple of examples would not be out of place. During World War I, the stormy weather of the North West Frontier caused a severe damage to the Nepali tents; so Padma Shumsher, the General Officer in Command, allocated a sum of 1,200 Indian rupees to stitch the tents and then hastened to report the matter to *Maharaja.*[13] What the *Maharaja* had to say in this regard is quite interesting. He told his trusted nephew that if circumstances necessitated, he should even go ahead and buy tents, for as the Nepali proverb goes "in exigencies you should even break a diamond". "But never tell the British officers that you need my permission in such matters".[14] Again the British envoy, to Nepal, R.L. Kennion, was surprised to find that General Baber Shumsher, who came to receive him at Thankot, could speak on any subject except Nepal. The Envoy later made a note in his diary:

> I afterwards came to know that for Nepali officials (except the Maharaja) to discuss with the envoy and matter that had the very remotest connection with his official duties was a taboo.[15]

12. See *Gorkhapatra,* editorial column, Shrawan 20, 1970 (August 1914), p. 2; also *Gorkhapatra,* "Annual Pajini and Thaumati", Shrawan 23, 1979 (August 1923), p. 2.
13. A letter from General Padma to *Maharaja* Chandra, Jestha 1, 1972 May 1915), Book No. 195, sub-titled *Jangi Badobasta Ratna Grantha Mala,* pp. 1-13, MAN.
14. A letter from *Maharaja* Chandra to General Padma, Bhadra 10, 1972 (August 6, 1915), *ibid.,* p. 3, MAN.
15. R.L. Kennion, Diversion of an Indian Political (London: William Blackwood and Sons, 1932), p. 198; "Recollections from Nepal", Blackwood's Magazine Vol. I, CCXXIX, No. MCCCLXXVIII, May 1931, pp. 665-78.

A Reuter correspondent, being dazed by the might of the Rana Premier around the turn of the century describes him as "absolute as a deity".[16]

A corollary to absolutism within the Rana system was the fusion of the concept of paternalistic government in which authority came from above and confidence from below. The Rana Premiers did not have faith in the efficacy of franchise. Which they regarded as the source of great trouble in the country where the masses were ignorant, credulous, and superstitious. In addition, they were convinced that an average man should not meddle with state affairs which were very intricate and technical. Thus, it was quite natural for them to look upon political dissent to be an act of treason; and the right of public meeting or to form an association or to present a collective petition to be not only a disease in the body polity but also an anathema to public good. Thus, one can understand why *Maharaja* Chandra Shumsher looked upon the Congress led Indian National Movement in the subcontinent with serious misgivings. So it did not take a long time for him to develop a horror towards subversive mobs like the Bolsheviks, Communists and the Gandhites or the so called non-violent agitators.[17] Premier Juddha Shumsher also stepped into the shoes of his predicessor with a firm conviction that progress was not synonymous with democratic form of government nor did he see the agitation for Home Rule in India a spontanious desire on the part of the many for the good of the country, but "a ferment spread by the few who themselves wished to rule".[18]

The Ranas believed that democracy, which could be successful in the homogenous population of the West, was in fact totally unsuited for heterogenous population of South Asia. Under the hallo of absolutism the Ranas believed that among all the forms

16. *Evening Standard,* July 29, 1906, p. 4.
17. A letter from *Maharaja* Chandra to Viceroy of India quoted by L.E. Hunt. "The Road to Kathmandu", *Statesman* (Nepal Supplement), April 4, 1937, p. 3.
18. Ishwari Prasad, *The Life of Maharaja Juddha Shumsher Jang Bahadur Rana of Nepal* (New Delhi: Ashish Publication, 1975), pp. 369-70.

of government known to man the Rana oligarchy was the wisest and the sanest for Nepal.

Hereditary Bureaucratic Apparatus

The bureaucratic apparatus was the most important fortress of the Rana oligarchy. The absence of parliamentary and other secular institutions made the bureaucracy more important than anything else. Hereditary accession to the high-status positions in the state was the basic principle behind civil and military recruitment. This hereditary accession was based upon familial principle. The most glaring example of this principle would be the assumption to the high office of Premiership among the male members of the Rana family according to seniority of age. There were also other hereditary posts that fell on familial lines like those of the commander-in-chief, lieutenant general, commanding generals, other generals, and colonels. Again the position of the *Raj Guru* (Royal Preceptor) was held by one Brahman family throughout the Rana period. The same was the story of the *Raj Purohit* (Chief Priest). Another example would be that the *Jaisi Kothi Adda* (Foreign Department) was held by the Newar family for several generations.[19] Family background was very important for any appointment into the state services. When a student graduated from a school or a college, the head master or the principal used to take him to the Rana Premier for the purpose of recruitment into government services. There the Premier was more interested in hearing about the family background of the graduate rather than appreciating his intelligence as revealed by his transcript. To prevent the entry of a "rotten egg" into the well filtered Rana bureaucracy the family lineage of an individual was thoroughly checked and scrutinized. Individuals, whose families were even remotely connected with the "disloyal elements" were clearly kept away from state services. Thus, the family consideration remained a more important element in the process of recruitment than the capability of the individual to perform the job. So ascriptive principles and nepotistic norms together with narrow

19. For background see Prem Uprety, "Nepali Bureaucratic Culture Few Dominant Features", *op.cit.*, pp. 3-4.

parochialism had replaced achievement or merit criteria. Since state service was not a career open to talents, the Rana bureaucracy was slow and cumbersome and serving very little the needs of the common man. Further, incompetence among the bureaucratic personnel made the cost of error and misjudgment very high. The nature of the recruitment left little room for the Rana service-holders to bring any innovation or to deviate from the wishes of their masters. Thus, an administrator in the Rana regime signed a death sentence upon the freedom fighters in the same way he had done a thousand of other things in life, for, he lacked the courage that was needed to refuge. He could have refuged to do so if he had chosen; but he did not, for, the stakes were just too high.[20]

Casteism and Ethnocentrism

The hereditary structure of the Rana polity was further strengthened by the stratified hierarchical social order, namely, caste-ridden and priest-ridden social structure. Like in the folk society[21] the individual social and political status is fixed by birth; it changed as he lived but it changed in the ways which are foreordained by the sacred cannons.

The absence of modern cultural artifacts like the political parties, professional communicators, and legislative bodies strengthened casteism and ethnocentrism in the Rana polity. The Ranas were convinced that the hierarchical stratified society, which lacked change and mobility, was a true bastion of the traditional order. The legal code (*muluki ain*) of 1910 V.S. (1854 A.D.) gave the necessary legal sanctions to the social gradations based upon the principle of hereditary caste. The Rana oligarchy kept the priestly caste quite happy and used it as a vital supporting structure of the regime. The institution of *dharmadhikar* was built around the Raj Guru (Royal Preceptor). It had its own hierarchy and officialdom to administer the religious canons in

20. More on the Rana civil service see Bhim Bahadur Pandey, *Tes Bakhat ko Nepal* (The Then Nepal) (Kathmandu: CNAS, 2039 (1982)), Vol. I, pp. 153-174.
21. More on the folk society see Robert Redfield. "The Folk Society", *The American Journal of Sociology*, Vol. LII, January 1947, pp. 293-308.

all parts of the country. The priestly authority, thus, ran parallel with the temporal power to preserve and protect and at times even to redefine basic elements of Rana conservatism.

The closed society, which the Ranas were able to build and strengthen, gave rise to the nations of ethnocentrism at all levels and in particular within the Rana family itself. The Ranas felt themselves to be a superior breed of people who were "ordained" to rule and command; while it was the duty of the masses to obey and follow.

Singha Durbar, built on the Versailles model, symbolized the glory of the Rana oligarchy but through it also sprang the fountain of Rana ethnocentrism. Its cost to the poor nation is to be evaluated not only in the crores[22] of rupees that went on its construction and the lavish courtly life it supported; but also in terms of ethnocentric values it propagated and the ever increasing gap it created between the ruler and the ruled. While the rulers, sunk in ease and luxury, and were devoted to the pursuit of gain, the masses were reduced to the status of the newer of wood and drawer of water. The bright complexion of the Ranas was further enhanced by the colourful silky, satin garments they wore, the sparks of precious gems that decked their headdress and the spacious stately mansions (*durbars* or *mahals*) they lived in. Here they lived like proud divinities in sharp contrast to the poor earthly brethren who surrounded them. Even the priestly class and the nobility, the Thapas, Pandeys or the Basnyats, lived like "little Ranas" in their comfortable villas with numerous concubines and a train of attendants. They, like their masters, possessed all the splendor of the East and the comforts of the West. All this helped in more than one way to strengthen the notions of ethnocentrism in the Rana family as well as in the different clans of nobility.

Isolation

Isolation has been one of the cardinal elements in shaping the fabric of Rana polity. The Ranas kept the country virtually isolated from Western secular influences. They were also equally successful in checking the spread of ideas from one part of the

22. A Crore is a Nepali monetary unit denoting ten million rupees.

country to another. Thus, the shield of isolation was more or less complete from without as well as from within. However, this isolation was not new to Nepal. National isolation as a tool of foreign policy was used from Prithvi Narayan Shah onwards in varying degrees. Jang Bahadur, however, felt that it was not feasible or even desirable to maintain the point of isolation at the level of 1818-1836. It is true that the Ranas kept intact the policy of isolation for a little more than a century. Yet, it was diluted by the element of subservient friendship" with the British. So intimate and sincere was the bond of Anglo-Rana alliance that the new rulers of Nepal could continue the policy of isolation without making the British feel that their imperial interest demanded a change in its policy towards the Nepali Durbar.

The Ranas were more or less able to seal Nepal from the impact of two momentious events of modern times: the French and the industrial revolution. Both taken together constitute the greatest turning point of modern civilization. To contain the flood of Western impact that was sweeping in the subcontinent the opportunity for higher education was not introduced in Nepal till the first quarter of this century. Furthermore, in an effort to make the grip of isolation more complete and thorough, the Ranas tried to isolate Nepal from the physical contact of all foreigners. Accordingly, no Westerner in private capacity could visit Nepal. This curtailed the Western population in Nepal to those employed in diplomatic service or a few employed in the state services as consultants.[23] So if Nepal became "a sequestered

23. The European population in Kathmandu during the first quarter of this century were seven persons: the British envoy, his neice, an English electrical engineer in Nepal state services, his wife and two small children as well as a nurse employed in the Royal palace. E.A. Powell, *The Last Home of Mystery: Adventures in Nepal* (New York: The Century Co., 1920), p. 178. By 1950 only a few hundred Europeans had ever visited the city of Kathmandu and only a handful of them had been allowed to go outside the Valley. See Tony Hagen, "A Foot on Roadless Nepal" *National Geographic Magazine* Vol. 117, No. III, March 1960, p. 364; also Leuectagh Erica, "Erika and the King of Nepal", *Reader's Digest*, March 1957, p. 24.

kingdom",[24] then Kathmandu was to remain the "mystic Xanadu"[25] not only for the chosen few Westerners, who got a chance to peep into it, but also the greater majority of her own countrymen. No Nepali living in the plains could dream of entering Kathmandu without a passport. Likewise, a Kathmanduite was also required to show his passport before commencing his journey outside the Valley. It was true that the gates of Kathmandu were flung wide open during the Shivaratri festival to Hindu pilgrims and tourists for a week during the month of February. But the Nepali police and the *athpariyas* (spies) made it sure that none of the carefree pilgrims lingered on after the scheduled time had lapsed.[26]

The internal isolation of the country was further strengthened by the lack of professional communicators like the political brokers and journalists. Though there was only one state owned newspaper, the *Gorkhapatra*, yet, the state Radio channel as a media of communication was absent. The Rana rulers were agitated by any innovation that promoted "mass culture".[27] The foremost among them was the cinema, which presented the photographs of the actors in a swift moving succession. The Rana Premiers like Juddha Shumsher believed that the showing of the vivid scenes from the accidental way of life had a very demoralizing effect upon the Nepali populace. Nowhere is this psychology of the Nepali mind better manifested than in this remark made by P. Chetwode in 1935 :

24. Penelope Chetwode, "Nepal, The Sequestered Kingdom", *The National Geographic Magazine,* Vol. LXVII, No. 3, March 1935, pp. 319-352.
25. S. Dillon Ripley, "Peerless Nepal — A Naturalist's Paradise", *The National Geographic Magazine,* Vol. XCVII, No. 1, January 1950, p. 8.
26. Iswar Baral narrated to the author an episode in the 1930's during which a Nepali friend of his from Saptri was denied entry to Kathmandu even when he had a passport for he was either wearing the national dress or could he speak Nepali. Interview at JNU, New Delhi, May 8, 1985.
27. Raymond Williams, *Culture and Society: 1780-1950* (New York: Harper & Row, 1966), pp. 295-338.

> The charming son of the Nepali Envoy to India told me that one day he sent his Gorkhali servants to a cinema hall in Delhi. They came back horrified and exclaimed that the male actors they had seen could not possibly be men; if they were they did not deserve to be so. This is what the martial Nepalese think of the movie stars.[28]

Nepal was virtually roadless when the Ranas had left, yet, there were cars in the Kathmandu Valley. The sight of about hundred coolies carrying a car to Kathmandu was an unforgettable sight to the European travellers in the first half of the twentieth century. An American Naturalist, who visits Nepal in 1950 pours forth his emotions in these words "instead of cars carrying workers Nepal has workers carrying cars".[29] A similar outburst of feeling moves the mind of another Westerner. To quote, "Life goes on the reverse in Nepal where men carry automobiles".[30]

Leadership

A study of dominant features of the Rana polity would be incomplete unless we bring the human element into the picture: Jang and Chandra symbolizing the physical and mental prowess of the Rana system. One could also point out in the jargon of social sciences that systemic relationships are not sufficiently explanatory unless we take refuge to the human factor of leadership. The *Maharaja,* with his honorific title *Shri* 3, was the most pivotal point around whom the entire Rana polity revolved. He was the fountain of all legal and even moral authority in the kingdom. In short, the Rana polity rested on the personality, zeal, and courage of the individual Premier. So if on the one hand powerful and assertive personalities were the life and blood of the system; on the other weak characters proved to be a drag in the body polity. Far from being in the periphery of omnipotence, most of the Rana Premiers slided into the pool of incompetence; thus, eventually contributing in varying degrees to the extinction of Rana oligarchy.

28. Penelope, Chetwode, "Nepal the Sequestered Kingdom", *op.cit.,* p. 328.
29. S. Dillon Ripley, "Peerless Nepal — A Naturalist's Paradise", *op.cit.,* p. 35.
30. Penelope, Chetwode, "Nepal, The Sequestered Kingdom", *op.cit.,* p. 326.

But Jang Bahadur, whom one might describe in the phrase "he came, he saw and he conquered", symbolized the whole spirit of Rana leadership. He picked up his authority by the point of his sword and was able to expand and fortify it by the repeated, skillful use of the same instrument. The humiliation and defeat in the Anglo-Nepal war and the anarchic conditions that prevailed in Nepal during 1843-46 necessitated a person who could ride this chaos and bring some kind of peace and order. Jang Bahadur emerged as the man of the hour. The political stability he could provide through the instrument of absolutism was perhaps welcomed by the Nepali elites as a sigh of relief, for, they could tread on a more firm ground than the chaotic uncertainties of the past. Several events like his European travels, stories of the "Sepoy Mutiny", restoration of the *Naya Muluk* (new territories), "victory" in Third Nepal-Tibet war, together with the myths and legends associated with his name only enabled him to be the absolute ruler of the kingdom but also made him a popular figure among writers, researchers, journalists and story tellers. *Maharaja* Chandra Shumsher was another charismatic personality among the Rana rulers. His efforts to modernize Nepal, though, however, small as it might be, are seen in his social and educational reforms. Besides, the Treaty of Friendship signed between Nepal and Great Britain in 1923 is a triumph of Rana diplomacy.[31]

However, as week premiers succeeded to the *gaddi* of *Maharajaship* since Chandra Shumsher, the Rana oligarchy was deprived of the vision and political leadership to steer the ship of state through turbulent times that engulfed the second quarter of this century. Thus, an edifice that was built over a period of more than a century crumbled into pieces within a span of a few months during 1950-51.

31. For a full text on the Treaty of Friendship between Nepal and Great Britain in 1923 as well as the speeches made by the British Resident W.F.T.O., Corner and *Maharaja* Chandra during the signing ceremony see E. No. 1, *Poka*, No. 1; also *Gorkhapatra*, Poush 9, 1980 (Dec. 24, 1923), pp. 3-7.

2

NEPAL'S REVOLUTIONARY INTELLIGENTSIA IN THE FIRST HALF OF TWENTIETH CENTURY

Intellectual freedom consists of liberation from the belief in God, in the immortality of the soul, and in general of freedom from all kinds of idealism.

Michael A. Bakunin[1]

The intelligentsia are to be distinguished from pure intellectuals or elites, who constitute the artistic, social, and political vanguard of a nation, in their commitment to a greater cause or in other words in their conviction to change and transform the existing way of life for the betterment of the masses. They, thus, reject the idea of engaging in literary and aesthetic pursuits for its own sake. The intelligentsia, in fact, thinks and dreams, writes and composes, cultivates arts and sciences and engages in trade and commerce for a greater quest — for human fulfilment or for human salvation. It is for

1. Michael A. Bakunin see Vladimir Burstev (ed.) *Zasto let, 1800-1896: Sbornik po istorii politicheskikh i obshchestvennykh dvizhenii v Rossii* (London, 1897, Collection of materials concerning political and social movements in Russia), pp. 106-07; also see Iu Steklov, M.A. Bakunin: ego zhizn i deiatelnos (M.A. Bakunin's Life and Activity) (Moscow: 1927), Vol. III, p. 227.

this reason and this reason alone that they study history, aesthetics, physics and chemistry and even medicine. There are moments when the intelligentsia helps to revitalize or transform religious symbols and tradition to rouse the feelings of humanism, secularism and cosmopolitanism; but at times the intelligentsia in their pessimism and despair is even seen engaged in the task of merciless destruction. However, their vision is not only motivated by the sole purpose of destruction. Out of the destruction they hope to rebuild a society free from misery and exploitation.

The radical mentality of the Nepali intelligentsia in the first half of the twentieth century was a direct special response to the Nepali culture and society. But when viewed in a broader perspective, the appearance of the Nepali intelligentsia was a symptom of the changing political culture of South Asia.[2] The "modernization" and "westernization" process that had begun in South Asia was bound to have an impact on Nepal. Thus, like their counterpart in India, the Nepali intelligentsia was a product of the "westernization" process that had picked up its momentum in the second half of this century. However, in the South Asian context "westernization" means "Anglicization". It is true that the Nepali traders and merchants were exposed to the English language as early as the eighteenth century, yet, a systematic development of English education in Nepal began to take shape only in the second half of the nineteenth century. The story of the process of "westernization" in Nepal is, in fact, associated with the founding of an English school by Premier Jang Bahadur after his visit to the United Kingdom in the year 1850. The sapling of English education in Nepal grew into a full grown tree with the founding of a liberal Arts College in Kathmandu

2. More on the concept of revolutionary intelligentsia see Philip Pomper, *The Russian Revolutionary Intelligentsia* (New York: Thomas Y. Crowell & Co., 1971), pp. 1-157; Raymond Williams, *Culture and Society, 1780-1950* (New York: Harper & Row, 1966), pp. 265-355; Ronald Stromberg, *European Intellectual History Since 1789* (New York: Meredith Publication Co., 1966), pp. 113-133; J. Armbruster (ed.), *A Process of Global Enlightenment* (Washington: Bicentennial Committee, 1976), pp. 19-86.

in 1918. It was raised to a Bachelor status in 1924; and by 1928 there were 60 primary schools built over a period of three decades.[3]

One is at the outset tempted to assert that the Nepali intelligentsia was the conscious outcome of the decision taken by the Rana autocracy to introduce English education in Nepal. The credit of taking this important decision goes to the first Rana Premier. Though at the initial stage, English education was restricted only to the ruling family, yet, as time rolled on its canvas was broadened to include the commoners of the Kathmandu valley and beyond. It was, however, *Maharaja* Chandra Shumsher who opened the door to higher education in Nepal by inaugurating "graduate studies" in Kathmandu, immediately after the World War I. Here the medium of instruction and examination was English. But the Rana Premiers were not working in a vacuum. They were responding to a series of changes in the subcontinent after the consolidation of the colonial rule. Jang Bahadur had opted for the spread of English education in Nepal for he had come to the conclusion that the Britishers had come to India to stay and their exit in the near future was unthinkable. So it was imperative for the ruling class in Nepal to learn the language of the colonial masters of India.

Premier Chandra, however, had to reconcile himself with a different type of situation. He saw the Nepali youths in the Indian universities like Allahabad and Calcutta could be a serious threat to his regime for they were strongly under the influence of Bolshevism, communism and civil disobedience.[4] Thus, by opening a "graduate" college in Kathmandu, he hoped to check, at least to some extent the contamination of the Nepali youths from the "evil" doctrines. The Nepali Premiers

3. An Account the progress of Education in Nepal is given in Political Secrete Letters from India, Vol. I, 87, Reg. No. 293, also E.C. 8-21, Reg. No. 855/1930, NAI; *The Pioneer*, April 9,1978, p. 3; *The Independent*, October 22, 1920, p. 4; *The Leader*, Oct. 22, 1920, p. 4.
4. More on the impact of "left wing" political activities in Nepal see Prem R.Uprety, *Nepal: A Small Nation in the Vortex of International Conflicts, 1900-1950* (Kathmandu: Pu Gomi, 1984), p. 97.

while pursuing the policy of "westernization" were either responding to the administrative needs of the time or were attempting to perpetuate their arbitrary authority as long as possible. It is, however, the irony of history that the revolutionary intelligentsia they helped to generate did pave the way for their own overthrow.[5]

Intelligentsia at Home

In a modern nation-state it is the professional communicators like the political brokers and the journalists who perform the task of political reporting and the criticism of the government and society. But since the professional communicators were absent in the Rana period their task were performed by the writers. Many writers in the Rana period emerged out of their traditional role of composing prose and poetry just for the sake of asthetics. They rather wrote for the need for reforms in the society; but in a very subtle way. As emerging communicators, they began to disseminate a new vision of reality and awareness of potentialities of politics. They distinctly occupied the vanguard role in urging their fellow countrymen to widen their narrow horizon and absorb the spirit of the modern world. Their slow, yet, a gradual diffusion of new ideas and the stir of new emotions and feelings all had the ultimate consequences for politics.

The struggle between reason versus unreason is a never ending battle in the history of human civilization. It is a struggle that was faught by the ancients and is being faught even today.[6] It is, however, encouraging to note that even in the darkest and the most primitive age there were some *philosophes* who never hesitated to speak their mind. Thus, even the most despotic regime had its defenders of the oppressed and the champions of reason and humanity. They talked about freedom in diverse forms: freedom from arbitrary power, freedom of

5. The *Maharaja* is said to have confessed in private on the day of the inauguration of Tri Ghandra College which in part ran: "today I have cut my limbs with an axe". His remark, though short, was very prophetic.
6. More on the struggle between reason versus unreason see Peter Gay, *The Enlightenment — An Interpretation*, *op.cit.*, pp.212-401.

speech, freedom of movement, and the freedom to realize ones own talent.

Among the different arbitrary governments that existed in the world in the first half of the twentieth century none, perhaps, surpassed the Rana oligarchy of Nepal in its absolute control over life and property,[7] total censorship of ideas a strong vigilence on the entry of the foreign nationals, and the movements of her own citizens. So tight was the instrument of control that one got the feeling that not even leaves of trees dared to shake themselves without the command of the Rana Premiers.[8] An Indian newspaper during World War II while discussing the features of Nazism and Facism lists Nepal as the perfect specimen of both these twin doctrines. To quote:

> Here is our own borders is an administration more archaic in its construction, more arbitrary in its methods and more reactionary in its ideals than any other we can think of.[9]

However, even the darkest phase of the Rana oligarchy did have its own little flock of *"philosophes"* Madhava Raj Joshi, Jaya Prithvi Bahadur Singh, Krishna Lal Adhikari and Shukra Raj Shastri, to mention only a few — who devoted countless hours of their time and energy in trying to evolve ways and means to improve the socio-political conditions of the Nepali people. The Rana period was, thus, not all obscure or absurd. It had its luminaries, the defenders of the down trodden and the advocates of reason and humanity. Their cries, though they appeared to be cries in the wilderness of the Himalayas, yet, proved seminal. They resounded in the fertile Valley and the plains, with greater force.

7. A popular expression of the Rana period runs as follows: *"jiu dhan Sirkar kei"* or in other words "life and property belongs to the government".
8. B.P. Koirala in his "Mero Jivan Katha" (The Story of My Life) captures the stimulus-response factor of the period in these words "even the leaves of the trees of this country feared to shake themselves without his (Chandra Shumsher's) command". *Pragati,* Year II, No. 2, 2011 B.S (1954), pp. 123-32.
9. *National Herald,* November 20, 1940, pp. 8-9.

Madhav Raj Joshi, a staunch Arya Samajist, wished to build the Nepali society on pure Vedic percepts[10] tinged with western democratic values (equality, *shuddhi* and *niyoga*).[11] This objective was to be fulfiled by establishing two schools (*pathsalas*) in Kathmandu for boys and girls. To finance the operation of such educational institutions, he wanted the government to levy an annual or a monthly tax of one rupee on all the domestic animals of Kathmandu valley.[12] The Ranas were, however, not only alarmed by the radical concept of the education for the fair sex but were highly disturbed by the proposed innovative direct taxation system, which could pave the way for popular unrest and lead to the springing series of demands from the masses. So Madhav Raj was politely asked by the then *Mukhtiyar* (Commander-in-Chief) to withdraw his petition, for there was neither any such precedent nor was it possible to build one.[13]

Jaya Prithvi Bahadur Singh was another educator and a political cartoonist of the period. He, however, taught his countrymen no new path of heroism or enlightenment. He was no prophet or a religious preacher. But he was a humanist and talked about the virtues like courage, cleanliness, truthfulness,

10. To quote the founder of the movement, Swami Dayanand Saraswati, I regard them (Vedas) as infallible and of primary authority .... just as the sun and the lamp is self-luminous as well as light giver so are the four Vedas.
    See Dayanand Saraswati, *The Light of Truth: Satyatha Prakash* (trans.) Ganga Prasad Upadhyaya (Allahabad: Kali Press), p. 84.
11. *Shuddhi* involved the process of proselytization of a non-Hindu to the Hindu fold through a well publicized ritualistic ceremony; while the concept of *niyog* permitted temporary marriage for the widows and widowers and for the married couples who could not produce children.
12. See a petition filed by Madhav Raj Joshi to the *Mukhtiyar* Deva Shumsher during the closing years of his *mukhtiyarship* in Shukra Raj Shastri, *Sri Mahadev Raj Joshi Ka Jivan Charitra* (The Biography of Sri Madhav Raj Shastri) (Hindi) (Kathmandu: Publisher N.K., 2015 (1959), pp. 263-64.
13. *Ibid.*, p. 264.

charity, and services to the needy and the oppressed.[14] These concepts simple as they are, are as old as human civilization itself. However, the technique of fables, parables, and short stories through which he used to carry his message to the masses was innovative. He could narrate a simple story with hypnotic effect. This hypnosis was partly due the fact he talked sense and partly to the fact that he was in so close proximity with the language taste and intellect of the people. His stories were, infact, not intended merely for pleasure; but to fulfil his long term political objective. He desired to instill a new political courage or a new adulthood among the Nepali people. So that they could move with times like their fellow brethren of Asia. To arouse the social and political consciousness of the people, he published his monumental work *Sichya Darpan* (Mirror of Education) in three volumes.[15] The book, which was published in pocket edition, was to serve as a manual. It was small enough to be carried inside a pocket to the numerous villages where the literate could read from it aloud to the illiterate and acquaint them with its illuminating contents. Some of his advices like emphasis on cleanliness and exhorting the people to go to bed at nine and get up at five may seem to some very elementary; but were very instructive and pragmatic.

Specific Examples from Sichya Darpan

The first part of this treatise on education is a collection of short stories where characters are either human or semi-human creatures who speak with humour and delight about the follies of life, social prejudices; and the urgency to correct them. These stories, though, a very carefully selected sample from Eastern,

14. More on the activities of Jaya Prithvi Bahadur Singh as a humanist see Uttam Bahadur Singh, *Manatabadi Raja Jaya Prithvi Bahadur Singh: Ek Parichaya* (Humanist King Jaya Prithvi Bahadur Singh: An Introduction) (Kathmandu: Shri Mati Sabitri Singh, 2035 (1979); also Raja Ram Slubedee, "History of Bajhang (1503-1848)", (Doctoral Dissertation, Tribhuvan University, 1986), pp. 95-102.
15 Jaya Prithvi Bahadur Singh, *Sichya Darpan* (The Mirror of Education) (Kathmandu: Jaya Prithvi Bahadur Singh), Vol. I, 1962 (1905), pp. 84; Vol. II, 1964 (1907), pp. 132; Vol. III, 1964 (1907), pp. 110.

Western and Persian literature, not only divert our attention and amuse us as they were meant to do; but also go further and makes us laugh at the absurdities of the Rana polity.

The dialogue embodied in a highly visionary conversation between the Emperor of England and a few of his courtiers cannot deceive any one except those who chose to deceive themselves. As the mighty waves slash the English sea-shore we hear Oswald and Ova telling the greatest Emperor in the world that the sea was his subject and the waves were only unfolding themselves to carry out his commands. The British monarch, being blinded by the pride resulting from his absolute prowess ordered the turbulent waves to be tranquil. The "melodrama" then unfolds. The roaring waves, far from retreating to a point of tranquility in obedience further rose to engulf the whole camping site of the Emperor. This episode brings the Emperor back to his senses. He realizes the illusion of his absolute power and the frailty of his temporal authority over nature. He, therefore, offers his crown to the waves and retires to live the life of a commoner.

England has little to do with this story. Just as Persia has relatively little to do with the *Persian letters* of Montesquieu.[16] It is the cloudy oppressive atmosphere of the Rana period and the subsequent intellectual climate that followed that has much to do with it. The story portrayed in a very ingenious way the total blindness that accompanies absolute and arbitrary authority. In the story the British monarch decides to abdicate his throne as he comes to realize his limitations. But the then Rana Premier (Chandra Shumsher) is too dull and stupid to realize his follies or line himself with the spirit of the time. On the contrary, he continues to exploit the masses for his personal gain and pleasure. Thus, in a very witty and skillful manner he throws a "bombshell" against the Rana regime, without even mentioning the word Rana or Nepal. But the message is clear and the methodology unbelievably daring. This section concludes with a detailed account of the Nepali heroism and valor during the Anglo-Nepal war. But unfortunately patriotism had reached an

16. Robert Loy (ed.), *The Persian Letters: Montesquieu* (New York: The World Publishing Co., 1961), p. 47-296.

all time low during the Premiership of *Maharaja* Chandra Shumsher.[17]

The Part II of the pedagogical treatise narrates the fall of the Hindu rulers of India to foreign invaders, for, they were not united and sunk in the pursuit of personal gains.[18] The pedagogical message is clear: the Ranas were also highly divided and interested only in the accumulation of riches. If Part I and Part II of the *Sichya Darpan* serve as a diagnosis of the disease, then Part III is the prescription for the cure. At the outset the writer makes it a point to narrate two objectives of all mortals: first, to attain *moksa*[19] (salvation) from the bondage of the human existence and secondly, to improve the condition of one's fellow-countrymen by feeding the needy and the destitute.

National development should not be the concern of one individual only but a shared concern of all of us. To put it in a different perspective, one does not have to be a ruler or a *bhardar* (a noble) to initiate the process of development but all of us can be a catalyst in its initiation as well as attainment. In the modern world, however, development is contingent on two factors: capital (*dhana*) and the realization of its generation (*ilam*). The sum and total of the wealth generated by the individuals represent the real wealth of the nation.[20] He further stressed on the fact that the capital in the society must be invested in the multiplication of goods and services. To keep money in banks or safe-lockers is a misuse of money. Money should always be rolling to generate primary wealth of the nation. Jaya Prithvi Bahadur cites Japan as an example which has mobilized its resources and developed the country in a very short period. This has been possible because the Japanese people do not snoar with ease and luxury nor have they deposited their

17. Jaya Prithvi Bahadur Singh, *Sichya Darpan*, Vol. I, *op.cit.*, pp. 31-84.
18. *Ibid.*, Vol. II, pp. 66-84.
19. According to Hindu Social Psychology *moksa* constitutes one of the four *purusarthas:* the other three being *dharma, artha* and *kama.* See Padharinath H. Prabhu, *Hindu Social Organization*, Bombay: Popular Prakasan, 1963), pp. 73-100.
20. He, however, does not go into the two-fold character of labour embodied in commodities (capital) as vizualized by Karl Marx.

money in foreign banks. They are active and industrious as is manifested by the growing industrial complex and business. The author would like to see the Rana rulers of Nepal to follow the Japanese road to development and prosperity.[21]

The Earliest Burlesque of the Rana Regime

Krishna Lal Adhikari was a leading advocate of freedom — about all freedom : freedom from arbitrary power, freedom to think and freedom to express ones own opinion. His controversal little book entitled *Makei ko Kheti* (The Cultivation of Maze) published apparently in July 1920 was a perfect expression of this freedom.[22] It was the first in the series that was to appear under the general title "Krishi Sichyabali" (Education in Agriculture). The book had received clearance for publication from a government publication agency, the *Gorkha Bhasa Prakasini Samiti** and was printed in the Pasupati Press. The exact date of publication of the book has been debatable, though 1920 appears

21. Jaya Prithvi Bahadur Singh, *Sichya Darpan,* Vol. III, *op.cit.,* pp. 1-86.
22. Most scholars attribute the book to *Nayab Subba* Krishna Lal Adhikari, whose close association with Krishna Prasad Koirala was an eye-sore to Premier Chandra, for example, Bhuvan Lal Pradhan, "Makei ko Kheti: Lekhak Krishna Lal Adhikari" (Cultivation of Maize: Writer Krishna Lal Adhikari), *Madhuparka,* Year 9, No. 10, Falgun 2033 (March 1977) pp. 11-14; Krishna Prasad Upadhyaya, "Makei Parba ra 2007 Sal" (Makei Episode and the Year 2007), *Gorkhapatra,* Feb. 18, 1969, p. 15; Ganesh Bhandari, "Itihasik Makei ko Parba" (Historic Maize Episode). *Pragna,* Year I, No. 2, 2027 (1970), pp. 5-11. Ganesh Bhandari, however believes that though the prose portion of the book was written by Krishna Lal, yet, the poetry portion was penned by the poet Shambhu Prasad Dhungel. Others feel that the book was composed by Bhoj Raj Kafle, a student and a close relative of Krishna Lal. But since he did not have the guts to publish it in his own name it appeared in the name of his teacher. Apparently, he is said to have accepted the authorship of the book before *Maharaja* Chandra. See Bhuparihar Poudyal, *Itihasik Makei Parba* (Historic maize Episode) (Kathmandu: Dipa Jyoti Prakasan, 2040 (1983), pp. 113-115.

* The *Gorkha Bhasa Prakasini Samiti* was established in Poush 1972 (Jan. 1915) *See Gorkhapatra,* Poush 26, 1972 (Jan. 1915), p. 2.

to be more probable.[23] However, the controversy over the authorship, the date of publication has been further augmented by the fact that neither the book nor its manuscript is available for scrutiny and analysis.[24]

Though the book is entitled the *Cultivation of Maize*, yet, maize cultivation had little to do with the primary objective of the book. The book portrayed in a very ingenious way the nature of the Rana administration through a medium of satire and paradoxes. The policies and the personal life style of *Maharaja* Chandra Shumsher came under bitter criticism. The analogy from medical science is used to describe the Rana bureaucracy. The then administration is dubbed as *chandrodaya*. Then in a very skillful way the author asserts that *chandrodaya* is too strong a medicine for pediatric treatment of Nepali children. Then would rather prefer a rather simple remedy provided by the *dogare ko balamrita*. Further, the book also compares the enlightened administration of *Maharaja* Deva Shumsher to that of his successor Chandra. The message was more than clear to the Premier and it was quite natural for him to be irritated.

The personal life and the foreign policy of the Premier also came under severe attack. The *Maharaja* had a special affection for foreigners, in particular, the Bengalis. A Bengali professor of Tri-Chandra College, Otu Krishna Maitreya, had already become a close confident of the Premier. Chandra's attatchment to foreigners together with his contempt for the Nepalis forms the object of wrath of the author.[25] This anger is epitomized in a comparative analysis of the utility of a dog of an English breed

23. The dates 1915, 1918 and 1920 has been given by Krishna Prasad Upadhyaya, Bala Krishna Sama and Bhuvan Lal Pradhan respectively. Krishna Prasad Upadhyaya, *Ibid.*, p. 15; Statement by Balakrishna Sama in Bhupahar Poudyal, *Ibid.*, p. 80; Bhuban Lal Pradhan, *ibid.*, p. 11.
24. Out of the 1000 books that were published 999 were burnt by the Government. The one copy remaining apparently perished with the passing of time, See Sambhakta Sharma, "*Krishna Lal Adhikari ra Makei Parba*" in Bhupahari, Poudyal, *op.cit.*, p. 44. All we have with us today are the flashes of memories reported by those who saw the book or remembered the episode.
25. See statement by Bala Krishna Sama in Bhupahari Poudyal, *op. cit.*, pp. 80-82.

and native dog. To be more specific, the native dog (*bhote kukur*). which sleeps in the open air and feeds on the corn-meal-musk and wild vegetable stew, is far more useful in protecting the life and property of the Nepali people than the pampered English dog, which only eats rice-pudding and sleeps and snoars in sofas and couches of the rich and the nobility.[26]

The subtle irony of the passage has more than one meaning. Viewed from diplomatic perspective the allegory is a beautiful political satire on the pro-British policies of Premier Chandra Shumsher, who had developed an English taste, opinion and intellect. But when scrutinized from the domestic plane *Maharaja* Chandra himself symbolized the ease and comfort — loving English dog; while the ill-clothed, ill-fed and poverty striken Nepali people represented the *bhote kukur*. Again from a narrower perspective, one could also interpret the foreign dog to be the Bengali Professor Otu Krishna Maitreya, who was so much pampered in the court of Premier Chandra that his pride and paternalistic behaviour had soared to its apex: while the *bhote kukur* represented the Nepali people who did not have an access to the Rana court, yet, were far more useful to the society than foreign dogs.

Another interesting, yet, a pinching theme of this book is the deteriorating condition of maize cultivation in the then Nepal and subsequent sad plight of the Nepali peasants. The book not only appeals for the introduction of new techniques and methods in maize cultivation; but also advocates an equitable distribution of land to the landless and the destitutes. To quote:

> Jagga jorchchan dhanilae hartaragari ha!!! basai dukkhi janchhan,
> Kheti garchhan najani mala jala tarika ghatnago bali jhan jahan,
> Yesto chala hunalae jamina rukhinago bhaei sakeo kitana, bad jagga bhaeko kina yesari hare! dukkha khepchhan kisana.[27]

26. Statement by a contemporary of the author, Tara Nath Ghimere, Bhupahari Poudyal, *op.cit.*, pp. 83-84.
27. The passage can be translated as follows: "the rich accumulate land by all means as possible; while the poor leave their land and migrate to new places. The poor do not know how to cultivate their land so the yield of land is getting less and less. The land of the peasant is slowly turning into a semi-desert. So why don't we distribute land among the peasants and help in relieving the suffering of the poor souls." See Ganesh Bhandari, "Itihasik Makei Parba", *Pragna*, Year I, No. 2, 2027 (1971), p. 6.

The message of the book was clear. It was not only a bitter attack on the domestic and foreign policy of the Ranas but also a sober reflection on the increasingly growing peasant problem and its only possible remedy — a fair distribution of land.

Once a thousand copies of the monograph was published. Krishna Lal had planned to use the *sepoys* as convenient instruments to disseminate his ideas across the country.[28] Accordingly, he had intended to sit with a pile of books at Tundikhel and distribute them to the soldiers at the rate of five per district. He chose the soldiers as a vehicle to transmit his ideas, which would rapidly diffuse among different strata of the masses.[29]

But before his dream could be realized a sharp heavy axe of censorship fell upon him on Shrawan 17, 1977 (August 1921). Krishna Lal was sentenced for six years of rigorous imprisonment. All the books (except one) were brought before the Premier at Singa Durbar and burnt. But since one copy could not be detected, the author was given a further three more years of punishment, thus, making his term of rigorous imprisonment to a total of nine years. Altogether 36 persons were rounded up in connection with the episode. Many of them lost their job; seven of them were imprisoned from seven to fifteen days; and others had to pay a fine ranging from fifty to hundred rupees.[30] Krishna Prasad passed away before completing his fourth year of imprisonment at a youthful age of 36. The most notable feature of Krishna Lal was his youth and the new courage he had developed in himself. Today, as one vizualize tuberculosis bacillus consuming the frail body of Krishna Lal for four full years during his confinement we cannot help being stunned and speechless before so great and cruel a calamity.

28. It is to be remembered that human communication was and still is the most effective means of communication in Nepal.
29. Statement by the brother of Krishna Lal, Bhupahari Poudyal, *op.cit.*, pp. 83-84.
30. Bhupahari Poudyal, *Itihasik Makei ko Kheti. op.cit.*, 81-133; Bhuvan Lal Pradhan, "Makei ko Kheti", *op.cit.*, p. 13; Ganesh Bhandari, "Pandit Samabhakta Subedi", *Madhuparka,* Year II, No. 8, Jan. 1970, 66-67.

There were, however, other *philosophes* whose flashes of discontent against the Rana regime were not only persistent but also revolting and equally significant. The publication of *Chandrabadini* and *Chandro Daya Darshan* in 1971 V.S. (1914 A.D.) by Shambhu Prasad Dhungel is an example. The work, which was originally intended to eulogize the splendor associated with the accession of *Maharaja* Chandra served just the opposite. It rather exposed the luxurious and pompous life of the Ranas in general, and Premier Chandra in particular. Then in *Chandro Daya Darshan* the poet urges the Premier to follow the example of the moon and expel the darkness that was enveloping the nooks and corners of Nepal. The attack on the Rana polity was indirect; but the very idea that the whole country was enveloped in obscurity was enough to make the Rana Premier think twice about the real strength of their system.[31]

Another poem *Pijarako Suga* (The Bird in a Cage) by the poet laureate, Lekh Nath Poudyal narrates the sad plight of a bird in a cage. It was written in 1974 (1917). In fact, the poet is describing the fate of a political prisoner, whose lamentations remain chocked within the thick, lofty walls of the prison.[32] In the same vein the revolutionary poet Juddha Prasad Mishra in his poem entitled *Jabi ko Charo* (The Bird in a Net) talks about the great calaminity that has struck the mother bird when she has fallen into the net of the hunter. Her limbs had been torn and tattered during her numerous attempts towards freedom and safety. The allegory contained in the poem was shocking to the Ranas for the Nepali people also like the bird in the net were longing to stretch their weary, worn-out limbs as they yearned for emancipation from the iron clutches of the Rana autocracy. In the poem the poet makes an indirect appeal to the Rana Premier to release the political prisoners. The poem in part ran :

31. Iswar Baral, "Sambhu Prasad Dhungel", *Nepali,* No. 7, 2018 (1961), pp. 9-17.
32. The Royal Nepal Academy (ed.), *Adhunik Nepal ko Kabita* (Modern Nepali Poetry) (Kathmandu: The Royal Nepal Academy, 2028 (1971), pp. 14-16.

Kasari sahu maile aja yo bazrapat,
Nathicha timi binti pankha bigri sakechchan,
Rukha bicha priya bachcha launa ke bahirahechhan.[33]

Outpour of Revolutionary Literature in the 1940s

The Nepali intelligentsia was very productive in the 1940s as manifested in the banned tract literature, political pamphlets and revolutionary slogans. None, however, surpassed in volume and intensity than the revolutionary literature that poured forth from the *Raktapat Committee.* Neither the structure or the composition of this organisation can be detected, for, like all underground organizations it has left little records, and apparently even that has perished along with it. However, the meager literature it has left behind speak of the intimate contacts it had with the Bolsheviks of the Soviet Union and the *Kalong Samiti* of Japan. Three themes run parallel in the literature that has emerged from this group.

The first is the concept of the Republic of Nepal. The *Raktapat Committee* lived by the slogan "Long Live the Republic of Nepal". It is, thus, quite natural for the members of this organization to yearn for the inauguration of the Himalayan Republic. Nowhere does this sentiment find a better expression than in these words:

> It is high time that Cromwell should rise and give the nincompoo the example of Charles I then only this country can raise its head in the fast changing times.[34]

A second theme distinctly visible in these banned tracts and the pamphlets is the exposition of the Rana rule in general and the personal life of the Premier Juddha in particular. The most

33. The lamentations of the mother bird runs: "How is possible for me to stand the bolt from the blue? Please do not press me for my wings have already been shattered. I do not know what has happened to my little birds in the tree!" See Juddha Prasad Mishra, "Jabi ko Charo" (The Bird in a Net), *Sharada*, Year I, No. 12, Magh 1992 (1936), p. 5.
34. See the revolutionary leaflet issued by the *Raktapat Committee* in the month of February 1940. It is a direct challenge to all absolute monarchs and dictators as manifested by its very title "Long Live the Republic of Nepal". E. No. 6, *Poka* No. 11, File No. 11, 14, *Ga*, 1949.

moving and emotional tract was the one entitled "Nepal Under the Ranas: Atrocities Over Nepalese" issued by the *Raktapat Committee* on September 7, 1940.[35] The pamphlet opens with a naked statement that in the twentieth century there are not so unfortunate than the Nepali sisters. The reason is obvious: the ignoble Rana Premiers have sucked the life-fluid of the country. Thus, while the world is moving on the path of progress and enlightenment every day and every minute the Nepalis are rolling down the hill. The attack on *Maharaja* Juddha was the most severe and edging to virtual polemics. The following lines can be taken as being the most illustrative.

> Let me tell you one thing: you will not be blessed with peace and tranquility in this Hindu *Raj* as long as the reign of administration in this country is in the hand of this ignoble, outcaste, and disrespected *Raja* from whom according to the laws of *Dharma Shastras* we should not even drink or dine. His private life is equally detectable. He is one who loves to have incestuous relation with his daughter-in-law; one who after making his daughter pregnant secretly handed over the unwanted issue to a poor Bengali; one who lives in a world of gambling, music, mirth, and wine at the cost of thousands of his subjects; one who drives his own kith and kine through hills and jungles without any regars to religious canons; one who captures in his net the innocent, budding, beautiful Brahman damsels to quench his amorous thirst of sensuous living. If a person like that is not inflicted with leprosy who will be? You can imagine for yourself how can we be happy in the regime of this person?[36]

35. The records of the *Munshi Khana* (Foreign Department) asserts that the *Raktapat Committee*, whose headquarters was in Kathmandu, had posted at least 41 copies of the pamphlet to different high placed persons in the country. One of them is now preserved in the Foreign Ministry of Nepal. It was the one posted to *Maharaja* Juddha himself that describes his as *Joota* Shumsher. It was mailed to him from the post-office of Cwanpore in India in an open cover. The language is Nepali but the script is Roman. More on the pamphlet see E. 6, *Poka* No. 11, File No. *Cha*, 1997/1940. Also Appendix A.
36. See the proscribed pamphlet entitled "Nepal Under the Ranas: At rocities Over the People". The exact rendering of the pamphlet into English is very difficult due to several factors like the faulty sentences, faded obscure letters, the absence of diacritical marks and frequent shift of words and phrases from Nepali to English and Hindi. See E. No. 6, *Poka* No. 11, File No. *Cha*, 1997/1940. The translation into English is mine.

A last major theme of these pamphlets pertaines to the overthrow of the Rana regime in Nepal in a short span of time. This it hoped to bring about by increasing the membership of the *Raktapat Committee* and the cooperation with Japan. Japan was at the time heading towards South and South-East Asia as "a liberator" of her Asian brethren from the ugly bonds of Western colonialism. The peak of the zeal of the *Committee* is immortalized in these sentimental lines.

> The time is fast approaching when the high souled members of our Committee will be flying its republican flags in Singha Durbar, Lalitpur Royal Complex, Bhaktapur Palace Plaza and the streets of Kathmandu, in particular in the avanues of Indra Chowk Square — the very hub of national life. Then we shall, with our heads raised, narrate the atrocities of the Rana rule to the whole public very openly, and candidly from housetops.[37]

Another revolutionary literature of the period was a "book" entitled *Jagriti* by Agni Prasad Sharma (Kharel) towards the close of 1942. The "book" never saw the light of the day. Apparently, it was confiscated and destroyed by the Government of Nepal. From one reliable source one gathers that the "book" was devoted to the process of establishing parliamentary democracy in Nepal by uprooting the Rana aristocracy.[38] The introduction to the "book" was militant in style and content and was saturated with socialist percepts. It talked about the establishment of *Akhil Nepal Barga Mahasabha* to fulfil the stated objective. The "book" was divided into ten chapters. The first two chapters, which served as a prelude, set the tone for the entire "book" by assessing the social, economic, and religious structure of the Nepali society. The sixth and the seventh chapters constituted the very nucleus of the book as they gave a detailed outline of the secret organization and emphasised the need for military training of the members. The eighth chapter

37. *Ibid.*, p. 1.
38. See deposition by Narendra Keshsari Sharma, a resident of Dilli Bazar, Chaitra 20, 1999 (April 1943). He had read the "book" *Jagriti* and corrected it several times. He further narrates that the author kept the book under lock and key and allowed him to read with occasional breaks. E.No. 2, *Poka* No. 11, File No. A, 1945.

entitled "Politics" gave a bitter criticism of the government at times even leaning to the side of polemics. The ninth chapter was, in reality, a synopsis of the coming democratic rule in Nepal. The last chapter is a resume — a sum up of the writer.[39]

A little liberal atmosphere that prevailed in the country with the exit of British from the subcontinent and the accession *Maharaja* Padma Shumsher to Premiership enabled Agni Prasad Kharel to present a book in the form of a petition to the *Maharaja.* The book was entitled *Bintipatra: Prastabit Sasan Pranali ko Swarup ko Drishya* (Petition: A Glimpse of the Proposed Administration System) published in the year 1947. The book consists of a series of petitions relating to all-round development of the country with primary focus on political, economic and educational aspects of development. In the political sphere the book proposes the drafting of the future constitution of the country through a duly elected constituent assembly. It suggests that there should be a *Maha Sabha* in the Center where the supreme authority of nation should reside. The district affairs should be entrusted to the Councils and city affairs to the municipal boards. Again, to save the nation from the pangs and traumas resulting from the then *Satyagrha* movement in Nepal it asks the government to fulfil the demands of the workers and release all political prisoners.[40] The situation had not yet, gone out of control and the government by the use of its reason and political will could save the country from bloodshed and chaos.

On the economic front the writer advocates the concept of planned development, which implies a judicious allocation of the nation's limited resources for achieving specified targets and objectives. While setting up development goals it proposes to take the country through a rigorous period of 15 years pan. During this period great stress was to be laid in collectivization of agriculture. While in the Educational sphere it suggests the establishment of a university with an affliated agricultural college to train people in the field of agriculture. In addition to

39. *Ibid.*
40. Agni Prasad Kharel, *Bintipatra: Prastabit Sasan Pranali ko Swarup ko Drishya* (A Glimpse of the Proposed Administratives System) Banaras: Agni Prasad Kharel, 2004 (1947), pp. 25-81.

this, it demands the making of primary education free and compulsory.[41]

The Nepal Sahitya Parishad (Nepal Literary Council), which was established in the closing years of the 1940s helped in a significant way in arousing the popular consciousness of the people. The Parishad served as a forum for two conferences of poets in 1947 and 1948. Here the Nepali intelligentsia gathered together and discussed freely and candidly the political climate of the period. The poems recited in the Saraswati Sadhan of Tri-Chandra College was a reflection of their state of mind. The then administration was greatly agitated by the content of the poems recited by Gopal Prasad Rimal, Bijaya Bahadur Malla Purna Prasad Brahman and Lila Dhoj Thapa in the second conference. They showed their displeasure towards the Parishad in two ways. First, all the poems recited in the conference were confiscated and secondly, the Parishad was expelled from Saraswati Sadhan.[42]

Nepali Intelligentsia Abroad

The study of Nepali intelligentsia would be incomplete without the analysis of the activities of the Nepali intellectuals in India. This intellectual foment started with the arrival of ex-*Maharaja* Deva Shumsher in Mussorie towards the turn of this century. Deva Shumsher wanted to establish a school in Banaras, which could serve as a meeting point of Nepali intellectuals and students. Though permission to operate such an educational institution was not granted by the British government in India, yet, he did buy a house in Brahma Ghat of Banaras.[43] This mansion was the become the forum for Nepali intellectuals during the first half of twentieth century. The Nepali intelligentsia in India in this period drew inspiration from the revolutionary

41. *Ibid.*, pp. 8-32.
42. Hridaya Singh Pradhan, "*Nepal ma Jana-Jagriti ra Rana Sasan ko Anta*" (People's Consciousness in Nepal and the End of Rana Rule), *Jagaran*, Year I, No. 1, Falgun 4, 2007 (Feb. 1951), p. 12.
43. Bala Chandra Sharma, *Nepal ko Itihasik Rup Rekha* (An Outline of the History of Nepal) (Banaras: Krishna Kumari, 1977, p. 354.

movement in Bengal between 1906-1917.[44] It was in 1907 that Prithvi Man Thapa used his links and support of Bengali terrorists like Bipin Chandra Pal and Brahma Bandhav to start a Nepali newspaper. This paper took such a critical attitude towards the Anglophile Rana regime that the British Government was compelled to ban its circulation in India. The paper, thus, had a very short life. The strong arm of the British vigilence as well as financial exigencies of the time did drive the paper out of existence. It was in this period that *Maharaja* Chandra received several anonymous letters from India asking him to abandon his pro-British policies. The *Raja* was also asked to join his hand with the other rulers of the subcontinent (Bhutan, Kashmir, Gwalior, Jodhpur, Indore and Bharatpur) to overthrow the colonial rule from South Asia.[45] The Nepali intelligentsia in Banaras were also successful in publishing a feature article, which accused Premier Chandra of Nepal for having taken no interest in the development of the country. He was also charged for turning the clock backward by adhering to the concept of the *status quo.*[46] There was at this time a wide scale rumour that the Nepali intelligentsia abroad were in close alliance with the Bengali terrorists were engaged in the manufacture of bombs in the remote parts of Nepal; and were training groups of Nepalis for its use.[47]

In 1916 Subba Devi Prasad Sapkota conducted a ceaseless campaign of anti-Rana publicity through the weekly periodical entitled *Gorkhali* published from Banaras for full six years. The objectives of this paper were of two fold. First, to expose the obsolete character of the Rana regime, which was responsible for the social and political backwardness of the Nepali people. To remedy such a situation the paper demanded political rights

44. In Bengal alone terrorist activities were responsible for killing 82 and wounding 121 persons between 1906-1917. See *Sedition Committee: 1918, Report* (Calcutta: Govt. of India, 1919), pp. 15-21, 31-34.
45. India Foreign Political Proceedings, (Ext. B.), August 6, 1907, Nos. 340-48, NAI.
46. Indian Foreign Political (Ext. Section) August 1908, Nos. 253-254, NAI.
47. *Nepal Residency Papers,* No. 845, File No. 452 of 1909, NAI.

for the people and advocated social and economic reforms. Secondly, it asked the Nepali living or domiciled in India to join the *Satyagraha* movement launched by the Indian National Congress under the leadership of Gandhi. This appeal of the paper did not fall on deaf ears. Many Nepalis like Laxmi Prasad Sapkota, Man Singh Gurung, Dharanidhar Koirala, Dina Nath Sharma and Pandit Krishna Prasad Koirala joined the Non-Cooperation Movement of India.[48] Premier Chandra was well aware of the damage done to his regime by the paper and waged a battle against it on two fronts. First, he started a counter-propaganda against the paper and its associates among the pro-Rana elements at Banaras. His objective was to dissuade them from joining "the enemies" of the Nepali nation. Second, he was successful in persuading the Government of India to proscribe the paper. The British Government took actions against the paper in two stages: firstly by asking the paper to submit to the security bond as provided by the Indian Press Act of 1910 and secondly by banning the paper in 1922.[49]

Earlier in 1906, the *Maharaja* had prohibited the circulation of three Indian newspapers in Nepal on the ground that they incited the Indian people to revolt against the *Raj*. What he really feared was that the Nepali people might follow the suit. The Premier had also ordered all the foreigners employed by him, including the Bengalis, not to enter into correspondence with the Indian agitators on the pain of punishment he thought fit.[50]

Dharanidhar Koirala was another literary luminary of the period whose poems and songs successfully generated waves

48. D.R. Regmi, *Wither Nepal* (Kathmandu: Publisher, N.K., 1952), pp. 37-38.
49. See a letter from Chief Secretary of U.P. to Sec., Home Department Political, November 20, 1920, India *Foreign Political Proceedings* (Ext. Sec. B.), August 1921, Nos. 120-37, NAI; also D.R. Regmi, *A Century of Family Autocracy in Nepal* (Banaras: Nepali National Congress, 1958), p. 27.
50. The vagueness of the punishment is significant. Copies of the proclamation were posted all over Kathmandu. See "Sedition in India: Pro-British Attitude of an Independent State, *Evening Standard* July 29, 1906, p. 4; also *Observer*, Sept. 9, 1907, p. 6.

of fear and anxiety in the tranquil political horizon of the Rana oligarchy. As early as 1919, he wrote emotional pamphlet titled "*Jaga Jaga Aba Jaga* (Awake, Awake, Now Awake). It asked the Nepali elites of all shades to awake themselves from intellectual slumber, mundane affairs, and worldly pleasures. Again his song *Bidesh ma Janchchu Kulli Kam Garchchu Kasto Lajmarnu ni !* (What a Shame is it to Go to Foreign Lands and Work as Coolies!) on the other hand was meant to arouse the consciousness of the masses in Nepal to the fate of their fellow-brethren in India. Thus, if his poems were addressed to the Nepali elites, the songs were for the masses. He also had opened a Gorkha Library in Khurseong to arouse political consciousness among the Nepalis living or domiciled in India. In 1924 Premier Chandra chided him for asking people to wake up when the two met at Vichcha Khori in Amlkehgang. But the answer given by the poet, "we both are Nepalis and both seek national welfare", made the *Maharaja* sad and bitter and even vengeful. Chandra as the poet says "would have chewed him alive" had the British not given him protection in India.[51]

As the World War I came to a close, the war veterans brought a new element in Nepali revolutionary intelligentsia. The voices of the veterans, who preferred to live in India became extremely vocal. Accordingly, *Jamadar* Keshar Jang Gurung sent an open letter to Premier Chandra, which demanded for the establishment of a parliamentary form of government under the constitutional leadership of the monarch. His other demands included the dismantling of the hereditary structure of Premiership and the fixation of the annual salary of the Prime Minister. His letter concluded with a bold assertion that if his demands were not met he would approach the League of Nations on behalf of the Nepali people to redress their grievances.[52]

More tales of lamentations about the physical tortures, sufferings and misery of the Nepali people are contained in the essay entitled "Hamro Desh Au Jati ko Vartaman Awasta" The

51. Personal interview with the poet in Kathmandu in October 16, 1975.
52. A letter from *Jamadar* Keshar Jang Gurung, February 1919 to *Maharaja* Chandra. Its abstract is given in G.C. Shastri, *Freedom Loving Nepal* (Kathmandu: G.C. Shastri, 1960), p. 15.

Present Conditions of Our Race and Nation) by Khadga Bahadur Chetri, a Nepali domiciled in India. The writer has judiciously selected two important themes in his patriotic composition. The first is the diagnosis of the disease. He is sad because the rulers of Nepal, being unresponsive to the needs of the people, have closed all the gates of development of the country. The attack on the Ranas becomes even more severe when the essayist calls upon the Lord to purify Nepal from the sanguine spirit of the Ranas by preventing among our race the birth of individuals who are anti-national, selfish and devoid of intelligence.[53] Thus, while other countries are on the path of rapid progress and enlightenment due to the progress of science and technology Nepal is rolling down the hill. The result is that the poor and the destitutes of the unfortunate motherland are moving from door to door in foreign lands in search of food and livelihood. Here in search for a few hateful pieces of silver, they undergo humiliation and indignities. The second theme is the prescription for the cure. It invokes upon the All Mighty for a quick deliverance by giving birth to independent, freedom loving, and patriotic Nepalis individuals.[54]

Another important book is a work by Shukra Raj Shastri entitled *Svarga ko Durbar* (The Palace of Heaven) published in 1930. It was published by the author himself from Calcutta, which was the home of numerous secret clubs and terrorist societies. The book, though dedicated to the *Maharaja* of Nepal, was revolutionary both in its thematic structure and interpretation. The learned Vedic scholar goes at length to point out that one really does not have to travel to the realms beyond to discover the palace in heaven, for, it is located in our own motherland. But it is a pity that gates of this divine edifice has been closed due to the prevalence of social evils like polygamy, child marriage, un-matched marriages and wide occurrence of inter-family and intra-family feuds. Thus, a teen-aged widow-girls, with faces disfigured by the rolling of the rivulets of incessant tears, are a common sight in Nepal. They live, if you choose to

53. Khadga Bahadur Chetri, "*Hamro Desh au Jati ko Vartaman Awasta—Gorkha Sansar*, Year IV, Kiran 6, 1929, p. 10.

54. *Ibid.*

call that living, on a scanty diet of one meal a day of either a handful of soyabeans or a bowl of corn-meal-musk or a few balls of potato. Another chronic social disease flowed from her surplus population with the large-scale unemployment resulting from it. This is visibly manifested in the thronging of the Nepali youths as sweepers or watchmen in the major Indian cities. This fact, among others, has shattered to fragments the very bastion of Nepali pride and nationhood.[55]

A shower of anti-Rana literature that were printed in India and smuggled across the border into Nepal was a cause of much concern to Nepali bureaucracy and leadership. Thus, the need for a media for the Nepali elites to ventilate their ideas and opinions was felt by the Government of Nepal. The British resident minister played an important role in moulding the pyschology of the then Premier Juddha Shumsher.[56] He, therefore, decided to start a periodical in Nepali, which he hoped would go a long way in checking the flow of virulent anti-Rana literature that was flowing so freely out of "the gutter" of the India vernacular press. The Government of Nepal, thus, gave permission to start a monthly periodical entitled *Sharada* in 1936. All the writers in the journal *Sharada* in the pre-1950 era romanticized the past for they could either freely comment on the present or speculate about the future. However, the poems like *Jabi ko Charo* (The Bird in a Cage) or *Pravu Vedo banu* (God Please Make Me a Sheep) had strong political overtones.[57]

It is difficult to pen down with an element of certainty the precise relationship between the Nepali redical thought in the first half of the twentieth century and the political upheval of 1950. While it would be unjust to see the revolution of 1950 as the sole outcome of the propaganda literature of the first half of the twentieth century, it would also be equally unrealistic to

55. Shukra Raj Shastri, *Svarga ko Durbar* (The Palace of Heaven), Calcutta: Shukra Raj Shastri, 1986 (1930), pp. 80-82, 32-126.
56. For the abstract trans. of the conversation between *Maharaja* Juddha and Minister G.L. Betham on Jan 2, 1936 see E. No. 2, *Poka* No. 560, File No. 421 *Ka*, 1997/1940.
57. Juddha Prasad Mishra, "Jabi ko Charo", *op. cit.*, p. 5; Laxmi Prasad Devkota, "Pravu Vedo banu", *Sharada*, Year 13, Nos. 1-2, 2004 (1948).

deny the impact of banned tracts and proscribed literature of the period, which grew in intensity and at times even shaped the path and direction of the Nepali freedom movement. The truth lies probably somewhere in between these two dichotomous hypothesis.

However, the role of Nepali intelligentsia in the revolution was different from that of the French *philosophes* in the eighteenth century. While the French *philosophes* supplied only the doctrine and the revolutionary zeal to the actors of the Great Drama of 1989, without bring a part of it, the Nepali intelligentsia fulfilled both these difficult tasks. They were not only the fountain of the revolutionary zeal and propaganda but also its very actors. All the giants of the French Enlightenment like Baronsde Montesquieu (1689-1775), Jean-Jacques Rousseau (1712-1778) and Voltaire (1694-1778) passed quietly out of the scene before the French Revolution began. It was only Danis Diderot who lived till 1784. Had they lived longer they would, perhaps, have been the victims of the Great Terror itself, which came to a close in 1794.[58] But the Nepali intelligentsia like Madhav Raj Joshi, Krishna Lal Adhikari, Shukra Raj Shastri and Krishna Prasad Koirala not only supplied the revolutionary doctrine and the zeal but also constituted the very nucleus of the movement launched against the Rana oligarchy. Others like B.P. Koirala, Agni Prasad Kharel, Yuddha Prasad Mishra, Gopal Prasad Rimal, and Kedar Man 'Byathit' not only supplied fuel for the revolutionary Propaganda, but were also at the center of the revolution of 1950.

58. More on the French Revolution and the Enlightenment see R.J. White, *Europe in the Eighteenth Century* (New York: St. Martin's Press, 1965), pp. 112-139; Peter Gay, *The Enlightenment: An Interpretation, op.cit.*, pp. 31-94.

3

REVOLUTIONARY SOCIO-POLITICAL ORGANISATIONS : STRUCTURAL AND FUNCTIONAL ANALYSIS

> Our Organization, therefore, has not been destined to superimpose any system upon the people. The future order will emerge without doubt from the popular movement and from life itself. But this problem we leave to future generations. Our task is a passionate, total, universal destruction of this ugly system.
>
> **M.A. Bakunin, S.G. Nechaev**[1]

The dawn of the twentieth century caught Nepal by surprise in two ways: first, on the diplomatic front the rulers of Nepal painfully came to realize that her commercial privileges in Tibet had crumbled down and her political influence in the country had significantly eroded[2]: while secondly, in the domestic sphere, the Rana oligarchy slowly discovered that the anti-orthodox, socio-religious movement of the Arya Samaj besides exposing the socio-religious hipocracy of the regime had also generated social and political foment among the Nepali elites that had hitherto been the bulwark of the Rana system. The

1. Basil Dmytryshyam (ed.). "Catechism of A Revolutionary" (History of Nechaev Affairs) in *Imperial Russia: A Source Book* (1700-1912), p. 264.
2. Prem R. Uprety, *Nepal-Tibet Relations, 1850-1930: Years of Hopes Challenges and Frustrations* (Kathmandu: Puga Nara, 1980), pp. 119-120.

spirit of political awakening launched by the Samaj slowly developed into oppositional politics nutured by socio-political organizations built both at home and abroad.

SOCIO-POLITICAL ORGANIZATIONS AT HOME

The Arya Samaj in Nepal

The Arya Samaj, which began as a revivalist sect among the Hindus, borrowed its methodology and techniques of institution building and propaganda from the Christian missionaries. The founder of the Arya Samaj Movement in Nepal was Madhav Raj Joshi. He, having attended the frequent *shastarthas* (formal debates) of Dayanand Saraswati at Banaras from 1893 onwards became a zealous devotee of the Samaj. Accordingly, he sent his sons to the Dayanand Vedic Schools and commenced preaching the Vedas in Nepal by the turn of the century. This was the beginning of the tension between the Samajist[3] and Sanatanist[4] in Nepal, which continued till the early years of 1940's. The tension between the *Samajist* and the *Sanatanis* (was bound to be severe in Nepal for they stood at the diametrically opposite poles of the socio-religious spectrum. The emphasis of the Arya Samaj on Shuddhi[5] equality and

3. *Samajist* is an abbreviation used to denote an Arya Samajist, the follower of Swami Dayanand Saraswati.
4. The *Sanatanist* included a broad spectrum of orthodox Hindus who believe in preserving the *Varna* System and accept not only the authority of the *Vedas*, but also of the epics, *Smritis* and the *puranas*. Background see Indra Vidyavachaspati, *Arya Samaj ka Itihas*, Vol. I (Delhi: Savadeshik Arya Pratinidhi Sabha, 1957), pp. 190-201; also Prem R. Uprety, *Religion and Politics in the Punjab in the 1920's* (New Delhi: Sterling Publisher, 1980), pp. 16-18, 53-57, 72-77.
5. The word *Shuddhi* has come to denote a double meaning: purification of one's body from every-day acts of pollution through bathing and recitation of the *mantras* (sacred hymns) and in extreme cases through *praischit* (self-torture) or the *gaudan* that is, the offer of a cow to a learned Brahman; or the acceptance of an individual or a group of individual into the Hindu-fold through a well publicized ritualistic ceremony. For a detail account on *Shuddhi* see Prem R. Uprety, *Religion and Politics in the Punjab in the 1920's, ibid.*, pp. 71-77.

niyog[6] sent shock waves at all levels of the Nepali society.[7] Swami Dayanand had flung open the door of Hinduism to all mankind irrespective of his birth, religion and nationality. He had converted a Muslim and his zealous followers followed the suit. The Nepali Arya *Sanatanists,* who constituted the very bastion of Hindu conservatism in the subcontinent, not only refused to accept a non-Hindu member to their fold but were also unwilling to drink or dine or take a glass of water or a piece of sweet-meat from an Arya Samaj convert. The teaching of the *Vedas* to the *Shudras* and the *Udas*[8] did bring wrath of the high placed Brahmans and other Hindus of Kathmandu Valley. A petition signed by a group of Hindus in Patan in part ran:

> A person by the name Madhav Raj Joshi is disturbing the peace of the people by teaching the *Vedas* to the *Shudras* and the *Udas* — a class which does not have the right to study the scriptures. The Government must punish the trouble-maker.[9]

Madhav Raj Joshi took the liberal regime of *Maharaja* Deva Shumsher as a good omen to transplant the Arya Samaj in Nepal. It was on January 1901 Madhav Raj inaugurated the Arya Samaj in Nepal.[10] The 1901 house of a distinguished businessman. Lal Bahadur, of Kel Tole, Kathmandu, served as

6. The concept of *niyog* occurs in the *Satyatha Prakash,* which permitted temporary marriages for the widows and widowers and the married couples who are not able to bear children, Dayanand Saraswati, *The Light of Truth: Satyartha Prakash* (trans.), Ganga Prasad Upadhyaya (Allahabad: Kali Press, N.D.), p. 84.
7. Prem R. Uprety, "Communal Nationalism in India and the Arya Samaj", in S.A.H. Haqqi (ed.), *Democracy, Pluralism and National Building* (Delhi: N.B.O. Publisher, 1984), pp. 86-101.
8. The *shudras* and the *Udas* occupies the lower rungs of the Nepali social hierarchy.
9. Shukra Raj Shastri, *Shri Madhav Raj Joshi ka Jivan Charitra* (Hindi) (Kathmandu: Publisher N.K., 2015 (1958)), pp. 266. It might be interesting to note that the petition signed by the Hindus of Patan had the following names: Kancha Juju, the son of Khadga Narayan Sharma and a few others.
10. Balachandra Sharma gives the date of the inauguration of the Arya Samaj in Kathmandu as Marga 15, 1953 (Nov. 1896). *Nepal ko Itihasik Rup Rekha,* Banaras: Krishna Kumari, 1976, p. 399. But the date given by the son and biographer Shukra Raj Shastri is more correct.

the head quarter of this organization. The daily recitation of the *Styarthaprakash* became a regular feature of this Arya Samaj *Mandir*. Devotees flocked in good number to listen to the holy scripture. The athpaharyas (spies) of the Ranas occasionally did raise doubts over certain themes and issues in the discourses, but were quickly silenced by the sharp axiomatic reasonings of Madhav Raj. This success compelled him to open the Arya Samaj *Mandir* at Pokahra in Western Nepal.[11]

The growing popularity of the Arya Samaj was a clear threat to the orthodox priestly tradition of Nepal. The hill brahmans conspired to arrange a formal debate between the *Samajists* and the *Sanatanists* with (a view to bring the latter into disgrace before the Premier and the Monarch. Accordingly, a stage for *Shastartha* was set at Singha Durbar on Shrawan 12, 1962 (July 1905). Madhav Raj and his Punjabi colleague Guru Dayal spoke for the Arya Samaj while Pandit Jagannath Shastri and his associated took the bench of the opposition. Three knotty issues figured prominently in the debate : teaching of the *Vedic* scriptures to the untouchables, worship of idols, and the utility of the *Shraddha* ceremony (death anniversary). If the insistence on the teaching of the *Vedic* percepts of the *Shudras* was an anathema to the orthodox *pandits,* then the rejection of the institution of idol worship and the traditional *shraddha* ceremony made them emotionally unstable and even nervous. Finally, when Madhav Raj labeled the *linga* of Pasupatinath as an idol or at best a beautiful piece of sculpture, commotion and panic disturbed the thought provoking atmosphere that had prevailed in the *sabha.* The *Sabha* took a dramatic turn for the worse when Royal Preceptor, Prayag Raj Pandey, dismantled his sacred headdress and with tears trickling down his cheeks begged permission to strike a blow at the infidel who dared to call the linga of Pasupati Nath an idol. The *Maharaja* was, yet, hesitant to give such a permission; but when the Royal Preceptor announced that all the *Parbate* (Hill) *Brahmans* would leave Nepal if the permission was delayed or not forthcoming, he consented. As soon as the consent followed blows and buffets with sticks and clubs fell on the body of Madhav Raj. He would have, perhaps, been beaten to death had the better-wisdom of the

11. Shukra Raj Shastri, *Shri Madhav Raj Joshi ka Jivan Charitra, op. cit.,* pp. 275-76.

Maharaja not prevailed. He was, thus, kept in the *thana* temporarily for a few days. In the mean time, about 14 Arya Samajists were rounded up, including *Sahau* Lal Bahadur, whose dwelling had served as the Arya Samaj *Mandir* for the Valley people.[12]

How to punish the criminals of *shastarthas* posed a serious problem to the then Nepali jurisprudence, for, there were neither laws nor precedents? The *Maharaja,* thus, had to use his sixth sense to deliver a judgment that would not be too harsh, yet, at the same time be sufficient enough to cool the temper of the priestly class. Accordingly, Madhav Raj Joshi was given a rigorous imprisonment (with chains and leg-iron) for two years and then was to be exiled from Nepal. Pandit Janardan Jha and Kuldip Man were given short simple sentences; while others were either given five lashes or had to pay a fine that varied from 20 to 100 rupees.[13] In addition, the whole family of Madhav Raj was ostracized to such an extent that no one even dared to drink a glass of water or eat a piece of sweet-meat from their hands. Besides, Amar Raj and Shukra Raj were expelled from the Durbar School for according to the decision of the School establishment they had become untouchables. Thus, as living in Kathmandu became impossible for the family, they left for Birgang.[14]

After a lapse of eight years, Madhav Raj once again returned to Kathmandu Vally upon the invitation of the *Maharaja.* His aim was clear : to weave a secret net-work of the Arya Samaj in Kathmandu. *Sahu* Krishna Lal, the proprietor of the Cap Store in *Thayamdu* in Kathmandu, offered his house as the place for congegration of the *Samajists.* In the mean time, Shukra Raj came with his bachelors degree in Sanskrit from the Gurukul "University" at Sikandarabad, India. But to avoid suspicion he took a government job in Singha Durbar, the office of the Premier. Many a time, he was asked by the *Sanatanist* Pandits to enter into a formal debate with them; but he had declined. However, when he was assured that his independent views would to respected, he consented to participate in the debate on

12. *Ibid.,* pp. 275-344.
13. *Ibid.,* pp. 360-68.
14. *Ibid.,* pp. 360-390. Madhav Raj, however, escapes from prison in Chaitra 1964 (108) and lives in India for about eight years. Here he sends his sons to the Gurukul schools.

the subject of idol worship. The debates continued for quite some time and the Premier did appreciate them. But the Premier soon discovered that the debates in spite of their logical content had the potential to contaminate the simple-minded Nepali people.[15]

A second phase of the Arya Samaj Movement dawned in Nepal under the dynamic leadership of the two graduates of Gurukul "University" Amar Raj Joshi and Bakpati Raj. A key note of this phase is the absolute, underground nature of this movement. A secret Arya Samaj organization was established in Kel Tole, Kathmandu. The dwelling of Fateya Bahadur served as the venue for the *Samaj* and Amar Raj Joshi, Chakra Bahadur and Bakpati Raj Joshi were elected the president, vice-president and secretary of the Arya Samaj Mandir respectively. Here they began to preach the doctrines of *Satyathaprakash* under the cover of *Satya Charan Malami Guthi* which was an organization to relieve those who faced the problem of cremating the dead bodies. The organization, however, in an effort to maintain the secrecy of its activities moved its headquarters to the house of its vice-president in Pulchowk, Lalitpur.[16] A few days after this the four Arya Samaj leaders were arrested. They were: Amar Raj, Bakpati Raj, Chakra Bahadur and Tulsi Meher; and were collectively charged for propagating the heterodox doctrine of the Arya Samaj under the disguise of *Satya Charan Malami Guthi*.[17] The Ranas were annoyed for two reasons. First,

15. Chandra Shumsher wanted to bring Shukra Raj Shastri to his fold. Thus, wanted him to work in close association with Hem Raj Pandey. Hem Raj tried to take him away from the Arya Samaj faith; but was not successful.
16. Balachandra Sharma, *Nepal ko Itihasik Rup Rekha, op.cit.*, pp. 400-401.
17. The *Satya Charan Malami Guthi* was a social trust set up by the Nepali Arya Samajists with the objective to provide material and priestly assistance to the needy and the destitutes, who were faced with the problem of disposing their dead. The post-cremation rituals of the Nepali Hindus were not only expensive but continued for one whole year. Thus, when the year ended the bereaved family found himself broke both materially and psychologically. To prevent such a chaotic situation the *Arya Samaj* simplified death rituals and substituted the expensive gifts and sacrificial ceremony by a simple *home* (sacrifice to Gods) and eating of haluwa-puri (bread and sweet-spread) ad *prasad* (offerings to the deceased, *pitris*.

the democratic organizational structure of the *Samaj* with its duly elected office-bearers and governed by egalitarian precepts ran contrary to the ascriptive non-participatory polity of the Ranas. Secondly, the innovative ideals of the *Samaj* like *Shuddhi* and *niyog* brought a small earthquake in the Nepali society that was governed by rigid *sanatanist* ideals. The actions of the Ranas against the *Samajists* were dictated by self-interest as well as the need to keep the priestly class, the indispensible support of the system, in good humour.

During the initial stage the case was taken up by the Commander-in-Chief; but due to its complications it was quickly referred to the *Maharaja* himself. The *Maharaja,* after much serious thinking, thought it prudent to confine the three Arya Samajists for two years of rigorous imprisonment and deport them from the Valley of Kathmandu. The sentence in part ran :

> The triumvirate, Amar Raj, Chakra Bahadur and Bakpati Raj, have been expelled from the country for having disturbed the peace of the country by preaching the doctrine of Satya Charana Malami Guthi of Dayanand.[18]

A close scrutiny of the sentence is indicative of the utter inability of the Rana bureaucracy to distinguish between the *Satya Charan Malami Guthi* and the doctrine of Dayanand. The *Samajists* of Nepal had used the Trust (Guthi) only as a convenient cover to preach the Arya Samaj faith.

The three were taken round the city of Kathmandu for being culprits. But the people of the Valley weapt bitterly for the social reformers had been expelled for an indefinite period and had to pay a fine of 480 rupees each. They very well remembered how their father had been previously exiled for a period of 14 years. The payment of the fines came as a serious burden to the Joshi family. But it was the generous help of Sunder Lal that came for their rescue otherwise their jail term would have been further extended.[19]

A third phase of the Arya Samaj Movement began in Nepal after the passing of Premier Chandra Shumsher (November 24,

18. Shukra Raj Shastri, *Shri Madhav Raj Joshi ka Jivan Charitra, op. cit.,* p. 503.
19. *Ibid.,* p. 503-04.

1929). This phase can be said to have begum with the meeting of Shukra Raj Shastri with Mahatma Gandhi and Subhas Chandra Bose in India. This event, though simple as it was, became a talk of the town in Kathmandu for it was widely reported by the Indian press. The priestly class of Nepal was specially annoyed, for, the Indian newspapers depicted Shukra Raj as "a national social leader of Nepal". They, thus, left no stone unturned to tell the Nepali Premier Juddha Shumsher that Shukra Raj was an athiest, anti-national and a traitor. Upon his arrival to Kathmandu Premier Juddha summoned him to his office at Singha Durbar and scolded his for having met the enemy of the British — Mahatma Gandhi. Thus, Shukra Raj lost his job in *Gorkha Bhasa Prakashini Samiti* and was kept under Valley arrest, which was later turned into house arrest. The news of the fate of the Nepali social reformer immediately attracted the attention of the Indian journalists. The news that Shukra Raj had lost his job and was kept under house arrest for meeting the Mahatma in India drew headlines in the Indian papers. This punishment, they pleaded, was unjust. Even under such strong vigilence Shukra Raj and his colleagues were successful in setting up a secret office of the Arya Samaj in Bhotahity.

One fine afternoon at 3 p.m. in the month of Bhadra 1997(1940) Shukra Raj gave a *Gita Prabachan* (discourses in the Gita) to a crowd that had assembled at Indra Chowk. During the discourse he talked about marriage, polygamy and other evils in Nepali society. The themes he chose though were exclusively social did have political overtones. For example, the speaker while giving 50% credit to the administration for legislating against child marriage, took away 50% credit from the bureaucracy for they were not faithful in its implementation. A thunderous ovation rang across the spacious plaza of Indra Chowk when the Samajist leader uttered his first few words "people think that I have left the country but you can see me now! I am talking to you".[20]

The above show of popularity did prevent his immediate arrest. But this did not prevent the Rana Premier from arresting

20. See the diary from Chandra Kanta, *ibid.*, pp. 507-628; also interview with Kedar Man 'Byathit', August 16, 1985.

him and have him chained and leg-ironed the next day. He was then taken to the central jail to serve three years of jail sentence. The Ranas also remotely implicated him in the *Praja Parisad* movement and on Magh 9, 1997 (January 1940). He was brought before the tribunal where judgment was being passed against the *Praja Parisad* members. He did not ask for pardon and, thus, suffered the fate of the *Parisad* member. Thus at 4 p.m. Shukra Raj was taken from the prison cell. The year was Magh 9, 1997. He was then hanged by a *khari* tree at Teku, Kathmandu. His body was displayed throughout the day with a poster posted on his chest which ran : "this is how the Guru (teacher) of all those who are anti-national and tracherous and incite the people to revolt will be punished".[21] Thus, with the passing of Shukra Raj Shastri the Arya Samaj Movement that was inaugurated by his father and nurtured by his brothers came to a sudden and violent end. It had waxed and waned like the moon for a little over three decades only to be extinct once and forever.

Ekadasi Sabha

With the dawn of the twentieth century, a nucleus of opposition to the Rana regime was developing within the Rana bureaucracy and the Council of Nobility. When the Premier Chandra Shumsher introduced the proposal of helping to British during the Young husband's military expedition to Tibet before the Council of Nobility many of its members passed some adverse comments. In summary, they pointed out that such a step, besides jeopardizing Nepal's traditional political and commercial rights in Tibet, would also pave the way for another long and protracted war with Tibet, for, it would go against

21. See a memo prepared by General Nara Shumsher, the Director General of Police, entitled "The Following Judgment has been Passed against Conspirators, who are the members of Praja Parisad and the propagadists of the 'Zanata Paper' of Patna". The Memo is undated but the content shows that it was prepared immediately after the judgment was delivered: See E. No. 6, *Poka* No. 1, File No. 14 *na*, pp. 1-2; also Shukra Raj Shastri, *Shri Madhav Raj Joshi ka Jivan Charitra, op. cit.*, p. 650.

Nepal-Tibet treaty of 1856.[22] But the proposal of the *Maharaja* carried the day. However in retrospect, the Nepali Premier in a letter to the British Resident, is seen labeling his nobles who had opposed his plans "Little Nepalanders" as compared to the "Little Englanders" of British, whose ideas were narrow and limited to the personal experience of their country.[23] The Strongest opposition to the plan came from *Subba* Devi Prasad Sapkota, who decided to leave the country for Banaras early next morning in anticipation of a severe prosecution. His flight, though did save him from physical tortures, yet, all his property was confiscated and his family fell into disgrace for all times.

This arbitrary nature of the Rana regime was a cause of great concern to many open minded Nepali bureaucrats. The *Ekadasi Sabha* was the first organization formed in Kathmandu by the enlightened officers of the Rana bureaucracy to modify the techniques and methods of the arbitrary Rana rule. The arbitrary practices of the Rana administrators had brought much hardship to the life of the *rakami* bureaucrats,[24] who were handling the different departments like the judicery revenue and the customs especially outside Kathmandu village. It was a common practice among the Rana Premiers to send wealth

22. See Article 2 of the Treaty between Nepal and Tibet of 1856. A copy of the official Nepali text of the treaty is found in the archives of the Foreign Ministry, Kathmandu. See *New Unnumbered Poka* entitled "Chin Lhasa ko Lekhapadhi", *sub-poka,* No. *Bho* 5. The English version of the Treaty is found in the National Archives of India. See *Foreign Secret Consultation,* No. 27, May 30, 1856. See also the letter from *Raja* Surendra Bikram Shah to Governor-General of India, Calcutta, Shravan badi 14, 1913 (July 1856). This letter contains ten clauses of the treaty. The original letter is in *Farsi* (Persian script). An English translation of the Nepali version of the treaty is also fround in Prem R. Uprety, *Nepal-Tibet Relations, 1850-1930, op.cit.,* pp. 213-14.
23. See a letter from *Maharaja* Chandra to the British Resident C.W. Ravenshaw, July 25, 1905, *Secret External B,* Proceedings No. 188 of Feb. 1905, NAI.
24. Literally speaking a *rakami* is a term used to denote a person, who is well versed in the practical applications of the laws in courts. However, in this context the term *rakami* is used in a broader sense to include all "seasoned administrators" who know the intricacies of the laws of administration.

individuals as heads of different departments in the Terai; charge them for misappropriation of their authority and lock them up in the *Sadar Khor*,[25] where they served their term of

25. From a purely literary perspective a *khor* is an animal den. But since the conditions of the prisoners kept in the prison cells was no better than the animals kept in cages these prison cells were officially termed as *khors*. The prisons of Nepal in the Rana period were known as *kal kotharis* (a place where men waited for death). They far from being institutions of re-education and rehabilitation were "torture-cells" or "concentration camps". A nearest parallel to them would, perhaps, be the panopticons or "the Ghost Houses" of Jeremy Bentham. The Benthamite panopticons "with its attendant master, armed with whip and leg-irons its diet-sheet bread of gruel and potato and its pauper dead being carried for disection" shared much in common with the Nepali *khors* of the twentieth century. For more on the British Utilitarian Prophet Jeremy Bentham (1748-1842) see John Stuart Mill, *Bentham and Coleridge* (London: Chatto & Windus, 1950), pp. 39-168; Eric T. Stokes, *Utilitarianas in India* (Oxford: Clarendo Press, 1959), pp. 1-47; Raymond Williams, *Culture and Society, 1780-1950* (New York: Harper and Row, 1966), pp. 132-33. Interview with Nil Raman Upadhyaya, a *Subba* in Revenue Office in Biratnagar (1919-1920). He was charged for misappropriation of authority, had all his property confiscated and was confined in the *Sadar Khor* or Dillibazar, Kathmandu for one and half years. When he was set free he had already become a mental wreck. The interview was taken on April 7, 1955. In this connection see also a letter of appreciation from the British Resident W.F.T.O. Corner, to Nil Raman April 5, 1919, E. No. 2, *Poka* No. 65 *Ka*, File No. 9, 1919; The Sad plight of the Rana civil servants in probably best expressed in this emotional outburst of *Subba* Nil Raman Upadhyaya. To quote:
Tinka dillagi satha: niskane baeruju maha
Sabikai thhari paile insafa nahudai yaha
Gharabara lutilinu khor ma lagi jakanu
Kasto annaya ho Chowkako saktha nayaya ma ke bhanu

or

The misappropriation born form their laughter and delight,
Leads to punishment without a fair trial.
With all property confiscated in prison one lands,
Such are the injustices of the Chowk office and how?
What kind of justice is in wait for me now?
See unpublished autobiography of Nil Raman Upadhyaya entitled "Samchhipta Nil Jivani" (A Concise Nil's Autobiography), p. 10, author's collection. The trans. is mine.

rigorous imprisonment. Few returned from the *Khor* "alive" and those who did had already become mental wrecks. To save the Nepali officials from such traumatic experiences a few officers of the Rana Government set up a secret organization to facilitate the process of handing over the charges of one officer to his successor (*bajbujarath*). The architects of this organization were: Krishna Lal Adhikari, Rishi Bhakta Upadhyay and the chief of *Bandobasta Adda.*[26] They met once a month on *Ekadasi,* which was a national holiday to find out ways and means by which they could be useful to the *rakami* bureaucrat on whose head the axe of Rana tyranny was about to fall. This very useful and constructive organization suffered a natural death when Krishna Lal was sentenced for nine years imprisonment for writing the controversal proscribed tract entitled *Makei ko Kheti:* and Rishi Bhakta lost his job during the proceedings of the same episode.[27]

The Cult of Adambari Mat

The decade of 1930's though a period of relative lull in the Arya Samaj activities in Nepal, yet, a new social reform labeled as the *Adambari Mat* was on its making. The founders of the

26. Krishna Lal Adhikari and Rishi Bhakta Upadhyaya held the office of *Subba* in the Council and the *Mulukikhana* (National Treasury) respectively. *Subba* Rishi Bhakta was noted for his bold and frank expressions. Once when *Maharaja* Chandra asked his opinion on the state of the nation his bold and fearless comment shocked the Premier. To quote "the money being deposited by the wealthy Nepalis should be invested in setting up industries in Nepal. This will not only provide jobs to the people but will also prevent the flight of Nation's precious resources to foreign lands." See Krishna Prasad Upadhyaya, "Makei Parba ra 2007 Sal", *Gorkhapatra,* Feb. 18, 1951, p. 15.
27. In those days it was very difficult to seal an organization from Government spies *(Athpaharias).* One day Subba Krishna Lal introduced a new member, Bishwa Nath, to the organization. It was Bishwa Nath who presented a copy of *Makei ko Kheti* to the *Maharaja* and brought the politics of proscription to a climax. *Ibid.*

movement came from the Newar community[28] of Kathmandu Valley. The Newars with their trademarts extending from Lahore to Lhasa constituted a very affluent mercantile (vaisya) class in Nepal. They were the masters of the family guilds, book-sellers, and painters. Others were: *vaidyas* (physicians), *naus* (surgeons), professors school teachers and retail shop keepers. They led a comfortable life devoid of luxuries. One can hardly think of a profession they did not excell. They, thus, supplied the recruits varying from mechanics in factories to the advisors of the Rana Court in the capacity of *Kazis* and *Bada Kazis*. In times of emergency like the Third Nepal-Tibet War, they even advanced loans to the Government.[29] However, inspite of their immense wealth and even authority, they occupied a low status in the highly stratified orthodox Hindu society — only a step above the *shudras*, the untouchables. Above all, they hated the tyranny of the Brahmans, whose feet they had "to kiss" according to the social convention. The chief spokesmen of this movement were: Sapta Ratna Tuladhar, Jog Bir Singh, Manju Harsha Bazracharya, and Karuna Ratna.[30]

The cult of *Adambari Mat* drew its inspiration from the egalitarian concepts of the Arya Samaj as well as the stress on *ahimsa* (non-violence) of Mahatma Gandhi. The first major source of inspiration to the founders of this movement was the notion of equality propagated by the Nepali Arya Samaj leader, Shukra Raj, whose anti-Brahman stance was well known to the then Nepali elites. In the Third Anniversary of the Arya Samaj held in Darjeeling on December 1926 he bitterly criticized the Nepali Brahmans who considered themselves second to none

28. The Newars are not an ethnic community in the true sense of the word for they constitute members of the Indo-Aryan, Mongolian and other stock. They, however, dominated Kathmandu Valley in the medeival period; and developed a distinctive culture of their own with their own language and script.
29. More on the loans and donations during the Third-Nepal Tibet War see Prem R. Uprety, *Nepal-Tibet Relations, op.cit.,* pp. 67-68, also appendix K, p. 127.
30. The other members of the *Mat* were: Manik Man, Siddhi Ratna, Man Dass, Harsha Dass and Cittadhar Upasaka. See Balachandra Sharma, *Nepal ko Itihasik Rup Rekha, op.cit.,* p. 402.

except the creator. He further lamented over the fact that the Nepali Brahmans of his country had forgotten the sacred scriptures and were either living as cooks in India or were at home cheating the ignorant masses. Thus, setting forth a very unhealthy social atmosphere.[31] The second source of influence was the teachings of Mahatma Gandhi. Being under the "Magic spell" of Gandhi's teachings on truth and *ahimsa* the *Adambaris* advocated the cult of non-violence in everyday life by abstaining from meat and wine.[32] However, the inauguration of the so-called *Adambari Mat* did realize that *ahimsa* was something more than the negative state of non-killing; it was a positive state of love and doing good even to the evil doer. Mahatma Gandhi on many occasions goes at length to free his concept of *ahimsa* from the illusions that frequently obscure the understanding of the common man :

> Ahimsa is not a crude thing it has been made to appear. Not to hurt any living thing is no doubt a part of *ahimsa*. But it is the last expression. The principal of *himsa* is to hurt by evil thoughts, by undue haste, by lying, by hatred and by wishing ill to anybody.[33]

Since the positive concept of *ahimsa* was more difficult to translate into public life the founders of his movement stressed more on the negative side: that is the abstinence of consuming flesh and alcohol. This movement was directly aimed against the Brahmans. The *Adambaris* boldly told the common man that they should cease to consider the Brahmans as a "Superior breed of people", for, they were men just like every body else. Nor were they the "agents of God". If they represented anyone it was only themselves. This innovative social concept sent shock saves at all levels of Nepali "caste-ridden" and "priest-ridden" society — one which regard the Brahmans as sacred as the holy cow or the mother Ganga.

31. *Gorkha Sansar*, December 21, 1926.
32. Balachandra Sharma, *Nepal ko Itihasik Rup Rekha, op.cit.*, p. 402.
33. M.K. Gandhi, *From Yeravda Mandir: Ashram Observances*, trans. From original Guzrati text by Valji Govindji Desai (3rd. ed.) (Ahmedabad: Navajivan Publishing House, 1945), p. 13.

As the *Adambari Mat* picked up its momentum, the Government of Nepal had to intervene to safeguard the interest of the priestly class, which was so indispensable for the survival of the Rana oligarchy. The Ranas accused the founders of the movement for disturbing the peace and traquility of the kingdom. The founders were charged with henious crimes and were about to be expelled from the country. But due to the last minute afterthought the Ranas decided to let them go scot-free on the condition that they would never propagate the cult again.[34]

It is true that the *Adambari Mat* had nothing to do with politics, yet, it did carry political overtones. This movement, though was very shortlived, did provide a forum to attack the most privileged order in the society, which regulated the socio-religious life of the people from birth to death. Their immediate object of attack, though were the Brahmans, yet, the Ranas were also not free from criticism, for the priestly class constituted the very bastion of their oligarchic rule. In summary, the movement launched by the Newars of Kathmandu against the Brahmans was more directed against the Rana rulers of Nepal than the priestly community, for, it was the rulers who had patronized them.

It is difficult to understand why the Ranas cracked down the movement with such severity. It is quite possible that their apprehension of the involvement of the monarch in the movement could, perhaps, explain the psychological reflexes that was working in the mind of the Ranas, when they decided to end the movement once and for all. The aftermath of the *Adambari Mat* was rather cruel to the Nepali monarch. Even after the movement was crushed, the Ranas kept the monarch under strong surveilliance. His movements were restricted within the Narahity palace complex. He was either permitted to receive guests or visit those he liked without the permission of the *Maharaja*.

34. Chandra Bikram Budathoki, "History of the Democratic Movement in Nepal (1931-1951)", (Thesis Patna University, 1974), pp. 100-101.

Prachanda Gorkha : A Secret Club of "Revolutionary Conspirators"

There is hardly a major episode in Nepali revolutionary movement in the first half of the twentieth century which is not directly or indirectly associated with the foreign events in the subcontinent or abroad. The origins of the *Prachanda Gorkha* can, thus, be traced to the aftermath of the Great War and the Terrorist activities in Bengal that grew with an increasing momentum with the partition of Bengal in 1905.[35] During the World War I the Gurkha troops had defended, in the best way they knew how, the modern technocratic civilization that was crumbling to pieces under the pressure of blind nationalism and arbitrary power.[36]

It was in the European cities of Nauve Chapelle, Mersailles and Netby as well as Monte Cassino and Ypress that the Gurkha troops gained a firsthand knowledge of the Western industrial prosperity and an open political tradition. This exposer to political freedom and affluence, which stood in glaring contrast with poverty conditions and deprivation at home, helped greatly is shaping the radical sentiments of the Gurkha troops in the British army. When they arrived in South Asia the teachings of the Indian revolutionaries like those of Bipin Chandra Pal, M.N. Roy, Kamal Nath Tiwari and Kapil Deo helped to channelize the fiery sentiments of some of them into an open revolt against the Rana oligarchy. Thus, in the 1920s the Nepali youths drank deep from the cup of freedom, which the Great War had managed to preserve, while the tactics

35. Today many Hindus would like to believe that the partition of Bengal in 1905 was just a prelude to the partition of the subcontinent in the month of August 1947. But the partition of Bengal convinced the contemporaries like Bipin Chandra Pal and many other Bengalis of the futility of the moderate political tactics advocated by the Indian National Congress. The only road open to them was the one of merciless violence and organized terror against the colonial rule. More on this new type of patriotism see Bipin Chandra Pal, *Swadeshi and Swaraj* (The Rise of New Patriotism) (Calcutta: Yugayatri Press, 1954), pp. 17-20.
36. Prem R. Uprety, *Nepal: A Small Nation in the Vortex of International Conflicts. 1900-1950* (Kathmandu: Pugo Mi, 1984), p. 73.

taught by the Indian revolutionaries provided them the energy to live work and organize.

It was in the background of the liberal Western tradition that contrasted with arbitrary, repressive atmosphere that enveloped the Rana oligarchy the little known movement known as the *Prachanda* Gorkha was born. The timing was Shrawan 1988 (August 1931) and the place: Kathmandu. It was in the center of the nation's capital a movement that planned to uproot the Rana oligarchy with a heavy axe was born. But it was born in silence and the atmosphere was sullen and grave.

The Composition of the Organization

The members of the *Prachanda Gorkha* came from the middle class. The only exceptions were Umesh Bikram Shah and Laxman Raja, who were a part of the aristocratic fold. Caste-wise it was exclusively a Brahman-Chetri organization — two predominant classes in the social hierarchy. The chief spokesman of this organization was Khanda Man Singh, a veteran of World War I.[37] He had served the British Imperial forces during the Great War. But when the war came to a close he decided to quit the army and devote himself of peaceful avocations in life. Accordingly, he returned to his home country, a different situations awaited him. There the *Maharaja* Chandra Shumsher asked him to join the Nepali army so that the nation could benefit from his rich and varied experiences of the war. To make the bait more enticing the Premier offered him the rank of a captain, with the privilege to retain the salary he had enjoyed in the British army. The offer was tempting. Moreover, his sixth sense hinted him that it would be unwise to wave the wishes of the man, who was in absolute control over his life and property.[38] He, thus, joined the Nepali army with the hope that he could be of some use to his motherland.

37. The other members of the *Prachanda Gorkha* were: Khadga Man Singh Basnyat, Maina Bahadur, Umesh Bikram Shah, and Ranganath Sharma. See Ranganath Sharma, *Nepal ko Rajnaitik Bibechana* (An Analysis of Nepali Politics) (Ayodhya: Publisher N.K., 1950), p. 88.
38. See footnote No. 7, Chapter II.

His service in the Nepali army was dry and uneventful. However, an episode that occurred in the reign of *Maharaja* Bhim Shumsher did bring about a dramatic turn in his career. A faithful defender of the Rana oligarchy turned himself into a fiery rebel. The episode: one day during the hunting expedition of Nagarjun Khadga Man Singh pleaded with the Premier for a promotion and the subsquent increase in his salary. Premier Bhim Shumsher, being enraged at the exercise of such an open liberty by his subject humilated him with derogatory remarks. It was an usual practice of the Rana premiers to abuse any one, even their nearest and dearest. But Khadga Man Singh was no person to brook such an insult. His peculiar training and background compelled to arrive at two important decisions First, he quit the army job and, secondly, he pledged to rid his motherland from the despotic Rana oligarchy. National interest as well as the attitude for personal vengeance were the two overriding factors that shaped the feelings and emotions of the leader of the organizaion. To fulfil his ambitious mission he created an organization called *Prachanda Gorkha,* which did bring into its secret fold a few devoted fanatics.[39] He advocated the total destruction of the Rana oligarchy and thereby the political, economic and social structure that nourished it. To fulfil this aim he felt it necessary to turn every member-conspirator into a blind instrument of its leader; and accordingly, he advocated that everything that helped the destruction of the Rana oligarchy was moral and everything that hindered its attainment was immoral.[40]

Maina Bahadur, who belonged to the lower middle class, was another assertive member of the *Prachanda Gorkha.* His frequent visit India not only exposed him to the anti-colonial propaganda of the Indian National Congress; but also to the terrorist tactics devised by the Bengali militants after the partition

39. Interview with Khadga Man Singh Basnyat, May 5, 1983; also Chandra Bikram Budathoki, "History of Democratic Movement in Nepal, 1931-51", *op.cit.*, pp. 103-04; C.B. Budathoki, "Activities of the Prachanda Gorkha", *Voice of History,* Vol. II, 1976), pp. 27-28.
40. Interview with Khadga Man Singh Basnyat, May 5, 1983.

of Bengal in 1905.[41] He was convinced that the moderate agitation (both constitutional and non-violent type) of the Indian National Congress during the first quarter of this century was unsuited to Nepal. He rather looked upon the Indian terrorists as a perfect model efficacious to uproot the Rana autocracy in Nepal. His contribution in supplying the tactics and methodology to the organisation was, indeed, great.[42]

Another giant of the organization was Khadga Man Singh Basnyat. He belonged to the family of Abhiman Singh Basnyat, the powerful minister who had lost his life during the Kot Massacre staged by the first Rana Premier on September 15, 1846.[43] His father, a civil servant, in the Rana regime, had been sent behind the bars for eleven years for misappropriation of the state funds. These two episodes of injustices that struck his family helped greatly in moulding his anti-Rana sentiments. In addition, his association with the Indian revolutionaries of Bengal and Bihar like Bipin Chandra Pal, M.N. Roy, Kamal Nath Tiwari, and Kapil Deo converted him into a revolutionary conspirator, who was determined to end the Rana rule in Nepal even at the cost of his own life. The peculiar combination of members from the nobility, priestly class, and ex-military men gave the members of the *Prachanda Gorkha* an overwhelming confidence to form an anti-Rana organization. The most distinguishing feature common to all of them was their youth and the "new courage" emanating from it.

Objectives of the Prachanda Gorkha

It is difficult to pen down with an element of precision the detailed objectives of the *Prachanda Gorkha*, for, like all

41. Terrorist societies were organized in almost all the provinces of India after 1905, although they were the strongest in Bengal, Bombay and the Punjab. In Bengal alone the terrorist activity was responsible for killing 82, and wounding 121 persons between 1906 to 1917. See Sedition Committee, *Sedition Committee, 1918: Report* (Calcutta: Government of India, 1919), pp. 31-34.
42. Interview with Khadga Man Singh Basnyat, May 5, 1983.
43. Ludwing Stiller, *Letters from Kathmandu: The Kot Massacre* (Kathmandu: CNAS, 1981), pp. 282-320.

underground organizations it has left little records; and even the little it left has perished along with its members. The objectives of the organization can be broadly divided into two categories: the immediate and remote. The immediate objective of the *Prachanda Gorkha* was to establish a constitunal government in Nepal by a violent overthrow of the Rana oligarchy. However, its long term objectives are not clear. The name of the organization itself might offer to us some clues in this direction. The term *Prachanda* means a firy revolutionary while the expression *Gorkha* symbolizes all the Nepalis both at home and abroad. The remote objective of the organization was perhaps, to infuse a firy spirit in all Nepalis and strive for the prosperity of the whole country by providing them freedom and justice.

The methodology adopted by them was to use terror as a political instrument. They wanted to use terror as a means of self-defence as well as for forcing the basic transfer of power from the Rana oligarchy to the popular representatives of the people. The model for them was provided by the terrorists of the two provinces of British India: Bengal and the Punjab. They intended to blow the very bastion of the Rana by importing bombs from India.

A top secret meeting of the organization was held in Ashad 1988 (1931). It was attended by Laxman Raja, who was remotely related to Juddha Shumsher.[44] The plan was unfolded. The day chosen to blow up the Rana oligarchy was the annual ceremony day during which all the members of the ruling family came in their ceremonial carriage to offer their allegience to the *Maharaja*. As the discussion preceeded it was decided to uproot the entire family on that auspicious day. Thus, when the day came to an end there would be no one left to succeed the high office of the *Maharajaship*. But as the discussion was nearing its completion it was Laxman Raja who proposed an amendment, that the *Maharaja* should be killed with one bullet and wait for the succeeding *Maharaja* for reforms. But if he failed in his task he would be killed also. His objective was clear. He only wanted to use the organization to end the life of the then Premier so that

44. Laxman Raja was the brother of the son-in-law of Commander-in-Chief, Juddha Shumsher, whose relations with *Maharaja* Bhim Shumsher was not a happy one.

Juddha Shumsher could succeed, and stop. But the other members believed that the proposed assassination of the Premier would not end their problem; but rather lead to further reaction and repression. They recalled for themselves the period of extreme restrictive measures and Rusification of Alexander III of Russia, which followed the assassination of Alexander II on the noon of Sunday March 1, 1881.[45] They, thus were in favour of wiping out the entire house of the Ranas in one single bloody massacre. Thus, no one would be left to succeed to the post Premiership. However, the idea of the extinction of the entire house of the Ranas was an anathema to Laxman Raja. He, thus, marched straight to the Jawlakhel Durbar of Juddha Shumsher and unveald the dangerous plot.[46]

The result was by Shrawan 22, 1988 (August 1931) that all the members of the *Prachanda Gorkha* were arrested, until none of the members were left to attend the meetings. All of them were charged for the conspiracy of overthrowing the monarchy and the Rana Government. A speedy trial of the accused was held in the presence of the monarch. The accused, far from begging pardon, further enraged the *Maharaja* by asserting that they would have uprooted the oligarchial Rana rule in Nepal in the same manner the Russians had overthrown the Czarist regime from their fatherland. The reaction of the *Maharaja* was immediate and direct. He gave orders to whip them for hours and keep them in standing posture for four day without food or water. After the ordeal was over Umesh Bikram Shah was exiled to Palpa and Khanda Man Singh, Maina Bahadur, Khadga Man Singh Basnyat and Ranga Nath Sharma were sentenced for life imprisonment.[47*]

45. Sergi Pushkarev, *The Emergence of Modern Russia, 1801-1917* (New York: Holt, Rinehart and Winston, 1966), pp. 185-190.
46. Khadga Man Singh Basnyat, *Jail ma Bish Barsha* (Twenty Years in Jail) (Kathmandu: Gajanand 2040 (1983), pp. 67-86.
47. Ranga Nath Sharma, *Nepal ko Rajnaitik Bibechana, op.cit.*, p. 44; Balachandra Sharma, *Nepal ko Itihasik Rup Rekha, op.cit.*, p. 368, 402; Ramji Upadhyaya, *Nepal ko Itihas* (History of Nepal) (Banaras: Subba Hom Nath and Kedar Nath, 1950), p. 356.

* Bhim Shumsher had abolished the capital punishment otherwise all except Umesh Bikram Shah and Ranga Nath Sharma would have been executed.

The dungeon block, the nameless tomb that was assigned to them in the central jail was 10ft. long, 6 ft. in width and 5 ft. in height. The atmosphere was foul and the height of the cells hardly permitted them to stand erect. Moreover, they were not only clothed in rags, but an eighty pounds of iron ball hung to their necks and a thick chain circled their body from neck to the ankle. Their daily menu consisted of a small quantity of rotten corn. The Rana bureaucracy could not understand the subtle difference between political prisoners and other criminals. So the *Prachanda Gorkha* "agitators" were kept along with swindlers and first degree murderers.[48]

As time rolled on the Prachanda Gorkha members protested against the unedible grains supplied to them; and demanded that all prisoners should be supplied with rice rather than maize. Incidently, this was the first organized protest against the rules and regulations of the Nepali prison cells. As the protest gathered its momentum, the Rana bureaucracy thought it more prudent to concede to the demands of the prisoners. However, the rigors of the imprisonment were not relaxed. The result was that two stalwarts of the organization, Khanda Man Singh and Maina Bahadur, passed away as they were slowly consumed mentally by the psychological horrors of the prison atmosphere; and physically by the tuberculosis bacillus. After these two sad deaths were reported, the Ranas did released Ranga Nath Sharma, who had become half of his former self. He then silently left the Nepali scene to live in exile in India till February 1951.[49]

Prachanda Gorkha has been taken by some to be the first political organization created by the Nepali people to undo the Rana oligarchy.[50] But the fact whether it was a political organization or not will always be debated. Yet, out of the controversy one fact emerges very clear: in the *Prachanda Gorkha* we see the first organized attempt made by the Nepali people to

48. Interview with Khadga Man Singh Basnyat, May 5, 1983.
49. *Ibid.*, also Ramji Upadhyaya, *Nepal ko Itihas, op.cit.*, p. 351. His priestly origin might have been a significant factor that hastened his release. But this, at best, is only a controversal hypothesis.
50. For this view see *Awaz*, Chaitra 5, 2007 (March 1951), p. 1.

undo the Rana oligarchy. The attempt, however, failed at the initial stage even before the final program had been finalized. The plan of the "Group of five" to blow the entire bastion of the Rana autocracy by a single stroke of violence was extremely fanciful and highly speculative. In fact, they were impractical zealots, who in their quixotic dream of success grossly underestimated the strength of the enemy. They failed to realize that a true revolutionary must exclude from himself all shades of romantic illusions, sentimentality and even personal hatred or the impulse of revenge.

Solidarity among the revolutionaries is an important precondition for the success of a revolutionary cause. Thus, unity is the very center of a revolutionary organization. Revolutionary compatriots should scrutinize all the major issues jointly and resolve them unanimously. It is only in the execution of the jointly agreed program that each member can chose to be independent. Unfortunately the members of the *Prachanda Gorkha* could not only come to an unanimous conclusion but also failed to guard the organization from the infiltration of spies like Laxman Raja. Moreover, their inability to enlist popular support coupled with their failure to percieve the need for strict neutrality or even positive support of the British Government of India was the single most important factor that made their plan to uproot the Rana regime in Nepal a complete fiasco.

The planning of the massacre was marked by a great deal of disagreement, confusion and even self-deception on the part of some members. If it was personal vendetta against the Rana System that had brought the conspirators together, it was their patriotic sentiments that sustained their zeal and energy. However, it was the lack of planning and vision and the skill in running the organization that was responsible for its failure.

The repression of the *Prachanda Gorkha* had quite a few important consequences. The first was the removal from the political horizon of about a half a dozen men who could have been a very potential threat to the Rana oligarcy. Second was that it strengthened the rigid, bureaucratic apparatus of the Rana oligarchy both in terms of its line of command and arbitrary powers. Finally, the members of the *Prachanda Gorkha* were more effective as martyrs than as insurrectionaries. Though their historical contribution is ambiguous, yet, they were important source of inspiration to a more broad-based and relatively more highly publishized anti-Rana movement of the *Prajaparisad*.

Nepali Nagarik Adhikar Samiti

The seed of anti-Rana agitation sown by the *Prachanda Gorkha* began to sprout with fresh leaves and flowers as the decade of 1930s unfolded. It was in 1937 the *Nepali Nagarik Adhikar Samiti* was born inside the rented-room at Mahaboudha, Kathmandu by a group of 13 persons under the dynamic leadership of Shukra Raj Shastri. The arrival of Raja Lal Kalwar, the regional Arya Samajist leader of India, was very crucial to the founding of the organization. The *Samiti* elected the learned scholar Shukra Raj as its president, Kedar Man Shrestha "Byathit" as secretary and Shanker Prasad Sharma as the secretary of publicity. A key function of the publicity secretary was to go to India in search of support and cooperation; while the general secretary was to devote his energy to the organizational matters at home.

It must be rememberd that the Mahabir school, which was born in May 1936 at Khimhal tole, Kathmandu, to impart education on modern lines, served as a prelude to the formation of the *samati*. The leader of this educational movement was also Shukra Raj Shastri. As expected, the school served as a venue for anti-Rana agitation. Thus, the Ranas could not tolerate the operation of such a school right in front of their nose. So they ordered its closer and sentenced 28 of its teachers to long term imprisonment.

The working of the *Nepali Nagarik Adhikar Samiti* can be divided into two distinct phases; the Phase of Social Welfare and the Phase of the Enlightenment of the Masses.

Social Welfare Phase: Shiva Samiti

It was in Falgun 1994 (1938) the *Shiva Samiti* was born to help the countless number of pilgrims that came to the temple of Pasupati Nath during the *Shiva Ratri* festival from the different parts of Nepal and India. The mission of the sub-*samiti* was highly successful as they helped in providing food, shelter, and medical aid to the pilgrims. The Kathmanduites had never experienced the functioning of such an organization in the popular sector. The mission, though purely social, had political overtones. So the Ranas were highly alarmed by the capability of the Kathmandu dwellers to organize themselves to attain a specific goal. Though the *samiti* was an eye-sore to the Ranas, yet, they followed the policy of "wait-and see-ism" and took a deep breath of relief when the *Samiti* fell into oblivion when the *Shiva Ratri* festival week ended.

Enlightenment Phase: Religious Discourses

The principal aim of this phase was to arouse a new kind of awareness among the Nepali, who were in a deep slumber, through the medium of the recitation of the scriptures. Accordingly, Shukra Raj Shastri left for Banaras to search a suitable *pandit* who could disseminate pure Hindu canonical ideas among the masses. Finally, the *Samiti* entrusted this delicate task of Pandit Muralidhar Sharma. Thus, the daily recitation of the epics and the *puranas* became a common event in the *dabali* (squares) of *Asan* and Indra Chowk — the very hub of national life in Kathmandu. People flocked in huge numbers as the Banarasi Pandit Muralidhar Sharma delivered his analytical sermons on the sacred Hindu scriptures. These discourses extracted from the epics and the *puranas* though religious in content were not free from political overtones, especially when the learned interpretor contrasted the duties of the ideal ruler Ram with these of the Ranas. Such recitations, simple as they were from the present perspective, were revolutionary for the time when tongues were cut off and lips were burnt for the "slightest whisper of free thinking".[51] These discourses were so

51. Shukra Raj was helped in setting up this private school by his trusted colleagues like Chandra Man Maskey, Fate Bahadur Singh, Purna Bahadur M.A., Chiniya Lal, Ganga Lal Shrestha, Siddhi Charan Shrestha, Bakpati Raj Joshi, Tanka Bilas, Surya Bahadur, Kali Ram, Mahanta Lal, Kedar Nath Sharma, Raghu Nath Sharma and Ananda Ram. Interview with Kedar Man "Byathit", October 14, 1984; Balachandra Sharma, *Nepal ko Itihasik Rup Rekha, op.cit.*, p. 375.

popular that even General Baber Shumsher and other senior commanding generals attended the delightful, thought provoking sermons incognito.

If this was the activity of the *Nagarik Adhikar Samiti* in the public sector, then at the underground level its anti-Rana activities were significant. It was in 1938 Raja Lal Kalwar organized an anti Rana group in Kathmandu. The meeting was attended by Shukra Raj Shastri, Pandit Muralidhar and Shanker Prasad Sharma. The topic in the agenda was how to devise ways and means to arouse the people to revolt against the Rana oligarchy. Shanker Prasad, an agriculture graduate accordingly, decided not to accept a Government job, but rather, went to India. There he formed a students union at Allahabad and remained a political activist throughout the Rana period.[52]

A mass meeting was organized under the auspicious of the *Samiti* during which Shukra Raj Shastri gave a lecture on *Gita* and *Karma Yogo*. The place: Indra Chowk and the time was 3 p.m. on the month of Bhadra 1997 (1940). During the speech he attacked the bureaucracy for not faithfully implementing the reforms of the child marriage. However, Ganga Lal Shrestha a student of I.Sc. II year was more open in his criticism of the Government. The Ranas immediately struck by with their heavy iron cudgle. Both Shukra Raj and Ganga Lal were arrested.[53] However, in spite of the imprisonment of their leaders the members of the *Nagarik Adhikar Samiti* continued their work with unbated vigor and enthusiasm. But with the explosion of the *Prajaparisad* Movement and the subsequent reign of terror that followed the work of the *Samiti* came to a sudden and a violent end.

It was in the 1930s three notable social leaders, Nag Bhagawan Dass, Buddesh Lal and Udya Raj Lal attempted to spread political consciousness among the Nepali folks in the Eastern

52. Muralidhar Bhattari, *Nepal Kranti ma Mero Jail Jivan* (Kathmandu: Publisher N.K., 1953) p.3.
53. See *Secret Report*, Supplied by Commanding Colonel Ganga Bahadur on the persons associated with the *Janta* paper of Patan, p. 2, E. No. 6, *Poka* No. 11, File No. 14, *Na*.

Terai. They, while giving their usual commentaries on the epics, *smritis* and the *puranas*, often did not hesitate to stir up the people for an open revolt against the Rana *Raj*. Juddha Shumsher, the astute Premier, was quick to discover the methodologies adopted by them in provoking the people to rebel against the *Raj*. The axe of Rana autocracy , thus, fell heavily upon the triumvirate. Accordingly, their property was confiscated and they were exiled to India.[54]

THE PRAJAPARISAD MOVEMENT

Organization

The *Prajaparisad* was the first well organized political party in Nepal, which drew its members from several ethnic groups and castes. Almost all its members came from the middle class. It is an irony of history that by and large the *Parisad*[55] members came from families who, besides forming an integral part of the Rana bureaucracy, enjoyed high confidence of the Ranas.[56] The economy of this class was very pitiable, when compared to the aristocratic class. It was this class that took up the cudgle against the Rana regime. Three episodes served as the prelude to the inauguration of the *Parisad* movement in August 1938. The first was the melancholic atmosphere that filled the hearts of the Nepali elites when the property of Shanker Prasad Sharma, an agriculture graduate, was confiscated for having refused to join the State service on a meager salary of seventy five rupees a month. He then went into self-exile in the United Provinces of India. The second was the impact of the discussion between Mahatma Gandhi and the Nepali social leader Shukra Raj Shastri which stressed the urgent necessity of social and political reforms in Nepal; and finally the news of the forcible abduction of a few beautiful Nepali maidens to gratify the

54. See the diary of Chandra Kanta, Footnote No. 19 of Chapter III, p. 507-628; also interview with Laxmi Bahadur Raj Bhandari, a class fellow of Ganga Lal at Trichandra College, April 4, 1982.
55. Netra Bahadur Thapa, *A Short History of Nepal* (Kathmandu: Ratna Pustak Bhandar, 1962), p. 160.
56. *Parisad* is an abbreviation used for *Prajaparisad*.

amorous ways of living of the Ranas enraged the Nepali intelligentsia in the 1930s.[57]

Two distinguished Nepali patriots, Dharma Bhakta Mathema and Dasrath Chand, were instrumental to the formation of the organisation. Hectic activities leading towards the inception of the organization were seen as early as October 1937. It was under an oath of absolute secrecy that Dharma Bhakta Mathema communicated to his colleague, Chandra Man Dangol, the formation of an organization entitled *Prajaparisad* to uproot the Rana regime in Nepal. This message was subsequently communicated by the latter to Tanka Prasad Acharya in an environment of tight concealment. However, almost a year had lapsed from its inception to birth. So it was only in August 1938 the founders of the *Prajaparisad* gathered at the Oam Bahal residence of Dharma Bhakta and took off to the sacred grove of Gugeswari.[58] Here before *Gueswari Mata* they took a collective oath of being the founding fathers of an underground organization called the *Prajaparisad*. They knew fully well that by doing so they were walking under the shadow of gallows. The two leading contenders to the office of the president were: Dharma Bhakta Mathema and Dasrath Chand. But in Nepal as the priestly class was immuned from capital punishment it was thought to be more prudent to elect the office bearers of the organization from this class. Thus, Tanka Prasad Acharya and Ram Hari Sharma were elected president and secretary of the *Parisad* respectively. A small working committee of the organization consisting of Dharma Bhakta Mathema, Dasrath Chand, Jiv Raj Sharma including the president and the secretary

57. To be illustrative the grand father of Chuda Prasad, an influen-Parisad member, had enjoyed high confidence of *Maharaja* Chandra and his father was the Governor of Jaleshwar. Interview with Chuda Prasad, April 5, 1976.

58. D.R. Regmi, *A Century of Family Autocracy in Nepal* (Banaras: Nepal National Congress, 1958), p. 170; also the Diary of Chandra Kanta in Shukra Raj Shastri, *Madhava Raj Joshi ka Jivan Charitra, op. cit.*, p. 606. A letter from *Maharaja* Juddha Shumsher to G.L. Betham, May 17, 1940, E. No. 6, *Poka* No. 11, File No. 4 *Cha.* Also "Some Recorded Facts Against Shanker Prasad", E. No. 6, *Poka* No. 11, File No. A 14, *Gha,*. FMAN.

was also formed. The other influential members of the *Parisad* were Chuda Prasad Sharma, Pushker Nath Uprety and Chandra Man Dangol.

As the organization matured, the euphoria generated during its inauguration subsided; and the problems associated with the implementation of the ideals began to baffle them. The first problem that crept up in the *Parisad* was the question of the admission of new members. This problem took such a severe turn it split the *Parisad* into two distinct fragments. A minority group led by Jib Raj Sharma was totally against the idea of expanding the organization at such an initial stage. They feared not only the leakage of its secrets but believed that it would ultimately loose its underground character. However, Dharma Bhakta Mathema and Ram Hari Sharma, who had the majority support, insisted on the expansion of its membership if they were to carry out their mission in any meaningful degree. The differences between the two groups became so insurmountable that it resulted into the exit of Jib Raj and his supporters from the organization. Dharma Bhakta Mathema and Ram Hari Sharma were instrumental to giving a new life to the organization by enrolling new members.[59] The *Parisad* members forgot that solidarity among the founders was the very center of the revolutionary cause. The *Parisad* members failed to understand that a vital question like membership should have been resolved by them jointly and unanimously.

Objectives of the Parisad

The objectives of the *Parisad* are not been spelled out in any documents. In reality, no documents of the organization has survived to give a clear picture of its aims and goals. All the secret minutes and the proceedings of the organization were

59. The controversy over the actual place of birth of the organization has given rise to conflicting views. Many believe that the *Parisad* was born in the house of Dharma Bhakta Mathema at Oam Bahal in Kathmandu. Interviews with the *Parisad* members like Tanka Prasad Acharya, and Ram Hari Sharma, August 5, 1978. Others point out that it was born in India, somewhere at banaras. It then shifted to Patna and ultimately to Kathmandu. See D.R. Regmi, *A Century of Family Autocracy in Nepal, ibid.*, pp. 177, 237.

destroyed by the then regime. The search was so careful and complete that even the plasters of the walls and bricks of the house of Dharma Bhakta were removed in an effort to uncover any incriminating evidences against the *Parisad* members.[60] However, a few blurred set of objectives can be reconstructed from the interviews with the members of the *Parisad* and a few surviving pamphlets of the organization. The organization had two sets of objectives: broad and specific types. The broad objectives can further be sub-divided into social and political categories. In the social sphere, it aimed at establishing a society based upon the principles of "New Socialism" where each individual could develop his personality freely and fully based according to the dictum: "from each according to his ability to each according to his needs. "Thus, the emergence of a new society in Nepal would be free from exploitation, oppression, class distinction and class struggle.[61] While on the political front, its aim was to establish a constitutional government in Nepal, where every individual could enjoy to the fullest extent civil liberties and fundamental human rights.

The specific objectives were, however, of more varied in nature and can be listed as follows: The first was to devise the ways and means to dislodge the Rana oligarchy from the

60. If on the one hand Dharma Bhakta Mathema enriched the organization with a group of Newar members like Ganga Lal Shrestha, Ramji Joshi, Ganesh Man Shrestha and Sahu Hari Krishna, then Ram Hari Sharma added to the organization a list of Brahman-Chetri elites like Bhola Bahadur Pandey, Chakra Bahadur Khatri, Phadendra Raj Hamal, and Dhurba Nath Dwivedi. See Dharma Ratna Yemi, *Nepal ka Kura* (Samickchhatmak Itihas) (The Happenings in Nepal, A Critical History) (Kathmandu: Yemi Prakasan, 1957), p. 199.
61. See a pamphlet of the *Prajaparisad dated* Falgun 15,2007 (February 1951) pp. 1-2. It refers to the past objectives of the *Parisad*. To quote "This was what the *Prajaparisad* workers had dreamed for a decade in the Kathmandu dungeon and what the workers are working to turn into reality today". The socialist view of the *Parisad* was taken from the Gotha Program of Karl Marx, see T.B. Bottomore, *Karl Marx; Selected Writings in Sociology and Social Philosophy* (New York; McGraw-Hill Book Co., 1964). p. 258. Interview with Chuda Prasad Sharma, August 5, 1980.

political map of South Asia.The second included the provision of the economic minium to the people like fooding, housing and shelter; and finally it aimed to raise the living conditions of the peasant masses, who constitute the very backbone of Nepali economy.[62]

Methodology

At the initial stage, the *Parisad* members thought of exploiting the internal contradictions among the members of the Rana family as well as the strained relations between the monarch and the Premier to the best of their advantage. But it did not take long for the members of the *Parisad* to realise that no direct tangible results could be obtained by pursuing such a mystic path. They, thus, approached the problem in two fronts. First, they entered into a pamphlet-warfare so as to discredit the regime in the eyes of the people; and secondly, they made the underground preparations to blow up the bastion of the Rana oligarchy by forceful terrorist tactics. While leaving the Gandhian tradition of non-violence to their fellow revolutionaries of Banaras and Patna, they decided to carry the Nihilist torch lit by the Russian nineteenth century anarchists like Michael A. Bakunin and Sergei G. Nechaev. The Indian terrorist group known as the *Anushilan* party greatly influenced them.[63]

The working of the *Prajaparisad* on the political horizon can be divided into two phases: the phase of the Press and Pamphlet-Warfare and the Terrorist Phase of Violence.

Warfare Through the Press and the Pamphlet

The political reforms that England experienced in the nineteenth century established an almost unlimited freedom of

62. *Ibid.*
63. Perhaps the best expression of the Russian Nihilist doctrine in the nineteenth century is found in the advice to the conspirators by two devoted fanatics Michael A. Bakunin (1814-1876) and Sergei G. Nechaev (1847-1882) entitled *Katekhizis Revolutsionera* (The Catechism of Revolutionary). It was written in exile in Geneva on 1868. For extracts for the Catechism see Basil Bmytryshyan *Imperial Russia* : A *Source Book* (New York: Holt, Rinehart and Winston, Inc., 1967), pp. 241-247. Also a letter from G.L. Betham to *Maharaja* Juddha, Nov. 4, 1940, E. No. 6., Poka No. 11, File No. 4, *cha.* FMAN.

the press for the Englishmen. Accordingly, some Englishmen in India as well as the westernised Indian elites attempted to exercise the same kind of freedom in India. Among others the Indian press, in particular the vernacular press, became a convenient vehicle to attack the policies and programs of the British Government in India. As the decade of the 1930s unfolded, the Indian press was frequently used by the Nepali freedom fighters to attack the Rana regime in Nepal.

In the beginning the *Parisad* members even thought of starting their own newspaper or a weekly journal to voice their opinion before the mass. But they were quick to discover that this was only a wishful thinking for they neither had the finances nor the capability of escaping the strong censorship of the Rana government. It was, however, through the personal efforts of the Indian socialist leader Jaya Prakash Narayan that the *Parisad* members managed to get a column in the weekly journal of the *Janta* published by Ram Briksha Benipuri of Patna. The articles published in the socialist weekly for about three years at different intervals were highly critical of the Rana Government. The first article in the *Janta* appeared on June 20, 1938 and was followed by a series till 1940. The thematic structure of these articles were either a satire on the Rana Government or a personal attack on the Rana Premier often edging to the side of polemics.[64]

The writers of articles in the *Janta* remained anonymous. Many of the articles in the *Janta* were written by the *Parisad* member, Dasrath Chand, himself, a student in II year I.Sc. in Trichandra College.[65] Among others, one article in the *Janta* column announced in a mock-heroic style the marriage being solemnized between the Crown Prince Mahendra Bikram Shah and the grand daughter of Premier Juddha.[66] The Ranas were taken unaware, for, everything was a secret up to the time. Again the last article that appeared in 1940 revealed the plan of

64. D.R. Regmi, *A Century of Family Autocracy in Nepal, op.cit.*, pp. 174-75.
65. Bhim Bahadur Pandey,*Tes Bakhat ko Nepal* (The Then Nepal), Vol. I (Kathmandu: CNAS, 1982), p. 379.
66. Dharma Ratna Yemi, *Nepal Ka Kura, op. cit.*, p. 196.

the *Parisad* to launch a *Satyagraha* Movement.[67] This announcement was, however, only a hoax. It was only to test how the Ranas would react to the mild announcement. The publication of a series of virulent anti-Rana articles was a cause of great concern to Rana bureaucracy and the British leadership. The Government of India did proscribe three issues of the *Janta* and finally closed the paper under the Section 135-A of the Indian Penal Code. The British Government of India also raided the office of the *Janta* thrice in an effort to find any incriminating evidences against the writers of articles. But all these efforts to please the Ranas were fruitless.[68] The Government of Nepal had, however, banned the *Janta* paper in the kingdom of Nepal.

However, all the vigilence on the part of the Rana Government, and the tool of proscription used by the British Government of India under the Section 135-A of the Indian Penal Code was of little practical value for the anti-rana articles in the *Janta* came to the notice of the Government of India only a few hours after the publication. Thus, by that time the "mischief" had already been done. The proceedings under 108(b) of the Indian Criminal Procedure Code and those under 135-A of the Indian Penal Code were frequently protracted and sometimes brought about :

> The very results which they are designed to prevent,as they give wide publicity to articles in the paper or pamphlets which might in the ordinary case be read only a limited circle.[69]

67. Francis Tucker, *Gorkha: The Story of the Gurkhas of Nepal* (London: Constable and Co., 1957), p. 207.
68. D.R. Regmi, *A Century of Family Autocracy in Nepal, op. cit.*, p. 174.
69. Background see N.G. Barrier, *Banned Controversal Literature and Political Control in British India 1907-1947* (Columbia: University of Missouri, 1974) pp.3-15; also a letter from Punjab Government to the Government of India, Home (pol.), File No. 3375-S-H 1927, p.3; Correspondence between PG to GI October 3, 1927, Home (pol.) File No. 74/1928, p.3, NAI. If this was the state of the politics of proscription in the closing decade of 1920s it was more so during the close of 1930s.

The same can be said about the articles proscribed by the Government of India that appeared in the *Janta*. The anti-Rana issues of the *Janta* periodical were smuggled into Nepal in such large numbers that by April 1940 it became the talk of the town among the elites circle in Kathmandu. The common cry that came from the then Nepali youths of Kathmandu was: "Oh the real truth was there![70]

While the *Janta* periodical was creating an unprecedented stir among the Nepali youths in Nepal and India, the *Prajaparisad* had commenced a pamphlet warfare against the Rana aristocracy. The *Parisad* had by 1938 successfully smuggled into Nepal a mimeograph machine,[71] which became very handy in printing leaflets and pamphlets. The "people's committee" of the *Prajaparisad* was entrusted with the task of production and distribution of the pamphlets in both India and Nepal.[72] The committee distributed pamphlets three times from July to September 1940.[73]

The jovial, carnival atmosphere of gambling, music and laughter of the *Bhoto Jatra* formed a perfect backdrop for the inauguration of the pamphlet warfare in Nepal. The time was July 1940 and the place: the personal residential premise of Premier Juddha Shumsher at Jawakhlel. The first pamphlet was penned by Tanka Prasad Acharya himself while the others were written by Dasrath Chand.

The thematic structure of these pamphlets can be divided into four categories. The first type of pamphlet besides being a bitter attack on the Rana regime spoke of the risky nature of their mission in phrases like they were "treading on the edges

70. D.R. Regmi, *A Century of Family Autocracy in Nepal, op.cit.*, p. 174.
71. The mimeograph machine was purchase by Prokash Nath somewhere between December 1939 to January 1940 from Roneo Ltd., Dalhousie Square, Calcutta. See a letter from G.L. Betham to *Maharaja* Juddha Shumsher, March 1, 1941, E.No.6, *Poka* No. 11, File No. 14, *n.a.*
72. Francis Tucker *Gorkha: The Story of the Gurkhas of Nepal, op.cit.*, p. 207.
73. D. R. Regmi *A Century of Family Autocracy in Nepal, op.cit.*, p.178.

of the double edged sword" or "walking under the shadow of the gallows".[74] The second group of pamphlets consisted of specific instances of virulent attack on the Rana oligarchy. The third series of the pamphlets attacked those who had occupied leading positions in the Rana bureaucracy; while the last group of the pamphlets announced the launching of *Satyagraha* as a prelude to open violence.[75] These leaflets and pamphlets were posted in and outside Kathmandu Valley specially in the Terai regions. These pamphlets were posted at Singha Durbar, the Kathmandu Patan and Bhaktapur palace complexes. They were also scattered on the streets, plazas and *bahals* of Kathmandu and posted as bumper-stickers on the automobiles of the Rana family. Mukunda Nath after distributing anti-rana pamphlets in Kathmandu went to Patna and continued the work.[76]

The contents of the pamphlets read like wild fire beyond the hills and dales of the valley of Kathmandu. While it filled the Nepali youths with "new courage" and inspiration, the Ranas drooped in a pensive mood with fears and apprehensions. They struck back by announcing in the *Gorkhapatra* of July 26, 1940 a monetary reward to one who could give a clue to the mischief.' The *Naya Istihar* in part ran :

> The Police *Goshwara* (Department) has informed us that the mimeographed *parchas* (pamphlets or leaflets) have been either posted on the walls or left loosely at the crossroads. The contents of the *parchas* show that these propagandists have committed an act of treason against the nation and the monarch and have violated the military laws of the country. Anyone who is aware of such clandestine activities should report the matter in person to Shri 3 *Maharaja* at Singha Durbar. Such a person would not only be immuned from prosecution but will also be rewarded with a sum of rupees 5,000;

74. Dharma Ratna Yemi, *Nepal ka Kura, op.cit.*, p. 201.
75. Dharma Ratna Yemi, *ibid.*, p.178. D.R. Regmi, *A Century of Family Autocracy in Nepal, op.cit.*, p.178; Bhim Bahadur Pandey, *Tes Bakhat ko Nepal, op.cit.*, p. 379; Interview with Chuda Prasad Sharma, a Member *Prajaparisad*, May 4, 1978.
76. Shukra Raj Shastri, *Shri Madhab Raj Joshi ka Jivan Charitra, op.cit.*, p. 628; also a Note prepared by General Nara Shumshere, Director General of Police on Mukunda Prasad, E. No. 6. *Poka* No.11, File No. A 14, *Na*.

while those who withheld such information will be punished according to the laws of the realm.[77]

The Tactics of Violence

Violence is the last option left to a group of desperate people who rightly or wrongly feel that they have been denied justice and in a fit of emotion do not hesitate to resort to violence, either to right the wrong or just to attract national or even world attention. The *Prajāparisad* members were convinced that the Rana oligarchy in Nepal was rotten to the core and had to be replaced as soon as possible. But this could be accomplished only through violence. The leading members of the *Prajaparisad*, accordingly, made periodic visits to Burma and India to learn more about the structure, organization and methodology of the South Asian terrorist groups. The underground leaders of the subcontinent like Dr. Jagadish Chandra Ghosh and Chandra Shekhar Azad, who were living dangerously under the shadow of gallows, served as their model. The Nepali terrorist leader, Dasrath Chand, had brought with him ten to twenty bombs from India which were kept in concealment in the residence of Bal Bahadur Pandey;[78] while Dharma Bhakta Mathema had brought with him a large quantity of dynamite.[79]

In October 1940 the *Prajaparisad* made a determined bid to destroy the entire edifice of the Rana Oligarchy and establish a republican type of government. All the members of the Rana family were to be massacred on the *dipavali* day while they were offering their customary presents to the Monarch. Should the plot fail they would be taken to the private theater of the king to see the latest movie production from Bombay, where they

77. For more on the *New Istihar* see *Gorkhapatra* July 26, 1940 (Shrawan 11, 1997), p. 1. The Istihar was posted in all places of public importance in bold, black letters throughout the kingdom.
78. Dharma Bhakta Yemi, *Nepal ka Kura, op. cit.*, p. 197.
79. See "Supply of Dynamite to Dharma Bhakta Mathema", a letter from G.L. Betham to *Maharaja* Juddha, September 19, 1941, E. No. 6, *Poka* No. 11, File No A 14, *na*.

would be blown up with explosives manufactured by the Indian terrorists.[80]

The plot was, however, detected in time. Two factors served as the catalysts in the detection of the plot. First, the New *Istihar*, which offered a reward of 5,000 rupees in cash to a person who could unveal the plot had the desired effect. Allured by the tempting offer, two members of the *Parisad Kharidar* Ramji Joshi and Pandit Muralidhar Sharma unvealed the cloak of secrecy to the Rana Premier.[81] In their zeal to expand the organization Dharma Bhakta Mathema and Ram Hari Sharma were unable to prevent the entry of the spies into the organization. History showed that Jiv Raj and his associates who had preferred to leave the secret club rather than yield to the concept of expansion of the organization was right. Secondly, the bursting of the gunpowder in the ropeway during the long aerial journey via the Chandagiri pass lead to a vigorous inquiry into the plans of the *Parisad*.[82] Again the possibility of letter bombs being sent from India made the Ranas more suspicious.[82a]

It was a little before 4 a.m. on Kartik 2, 1997 (October 1940) that a regular troop of well armed police surrounded the Om Bahal headquarters of the *Parisad*. Here the police immediately arrested Dharma Bhakta Mathema and seized the mimeograph machine, some pamphlets and several thousand Indian currency notes. The other members of the *Parisad* were also kept under

80. *Political External Collection*, 21-26, Reg. No. 1632, 4866/1941. Also conversation between Prof. Jay Chand and S.P. Upadhyaya, E. No. 6, *Poka* No. 11, FMAN.
81. Ramji Joshi, the brother of Shukra Raj Shastri, operated as a confidental spy of Bahadur Shumsher within the *Parisad;* while Pandit Muralidhar Sharma had come under a close grip of General Nara Shumsher, the Director General of Police. See Dharma Ratna Yemi, *Nepal ka Kura, op.cit.*, p. 203; Balachandra Sharma *Nepal Ko Itihasik Rup Rekha, op.cit.*, p.404; Interview with Kedar Man Byathit, October 14, 1984; also with Ram Hari Sharma, July 14, 1980.
82. Francis Tucker, *Gorkha: The story of the Gurkhas of Nepal, op.cit.*, p. 209.
82a. This information was contained in an unnamed letter posted to the Maharaja from Bankipore, India on October 4, 1940, E. No. 6, *Poka* No. 11, File No. 4, *Cha*, FMAN.

custody during the clean sweep of the Nepali C.I.D. officers.[83] Thus, by Kartik 4, 1997 (October 1940) eighteen of the *Parisad* members had already been rounded up and kept in confinement inside Singha Durbar. In its search for the enemies, the Rana Government could not distinguish between the *Parisad* members, the school teachers, and social workers. Thus, a total of 300 persons were put behind the bars.[84]

Tanka Prasad, the President of the organization, was at the time at Banaras. His presence at Banaras was an eyesore to the Ranas. So the Governor of the *Goshwara* of Jaleshwar was asked to send an urgent, fake telegram to him in the name of his father with the content: "I am dying come immediately!" The fake message had the desired effect in dragging Tanka Prasad Acharya to the Indo-Nepal border of Jaleshwar where he was caught, handcuffed and chained. Thus, with iron balls hanging on his neck and leg-irons chaining his feet, he was given a *doco* ride to Kathmandu.[85] At Singha Durbar he weapt bitterly to see the fate of all his comrades. He then mustured up all his courage and boldly told the Premier "I am alone responsible for the whole affair; so please release all my friends who know nothing about it.[86] Then with eyes all violent, fierce, and full of fire he further went on to say "the Government is the heart of the nation; but when it is infected with germs and viruses surgery is the only remedy".[87] And as these words had barely escaped his lips General Nara Shumsher gave him such a buffet that he fell to the ground almost senseless. His plea to release his companions also faded away in the following roaring remarks of the Premier "How can I liberate you scoundrels? After all I have spent five *lackhs* to capture you folks!"[88] The official media, the *Gorkhapatra*, the Kartik 9, 1997 (October 1940) gave the following information to the people of Nepal.

83. Interview with Ram Hari Sharma July 2, 1986; also Bhim Bahadur Pandey, *Tes Bakhat ko Nepal*, Vol. II, p. 380-381.
84. Dharma Ratna Yemi, *Nepal ka Kura, op.cit.*, p. 206.
85. A *doco* is a basket made of bamboo that is used to carry men, goods, and artifacts across the mountain trails.
86. Interview Tanka Prasad Acharya, April 13, 1978.
87. *Ibid.*
88. *Ibid.*

> A treasonous group has been rounded up for being instrumental to the production and distribution of anti-national literature. Court proceedings are going on against them; and the ultimate outcome will be reported later.[89]

The court proceedings associated with the episode of 1940 was divided into three sections; *Narahity Parba Phat, Prajaparisad Parba Phat* and *Purano Phat*.[90] A tribunal was set up under the chairmanship of General Shanker Shumsher to look into and conduct the extraordinary trial of high treason.[91] The first victim of the Rana outrage was Ganga Lal Shrestha. He was removed from the bamboo cage and was greeted with a few powerful slaps on his face. He was followed by Chandra Man Dongol and Dharma Bhakta Mathema who were inflicted with 1,200 and 500 lashes respectively. The trial lasted a little over three months and finally the judgement was delivered against the conspirators (members of the *Prajaparisad* and the Propagandist of the *Janta* paper of Patna). But before the judgement was delivered the *Maharaja* held an unusual *Durbar* so as to receive some sort of legitimacy for his actions against the "traitors".[92] But none of the participants of the *Durbar* dared to lift their tongue. Their pin-drop silence only gave a tacit approval to the actions of the *Maharaja*. The *Maharaja*, however, charged the traitors for violence and sabotage in his short extempore address. The Premier made it a point to tell his courtiers that even Mahatma Gandhi had condemned their

89. *Gorkhapatra*, Kartik 9, 1997 (October 1940).
90. The *Narahity Parba Phat* looked into case of those individuals who apparently were in the payroll of the Royal Place. The *Prajaparisad Phat* analyzed cases associated with the members of the *Parisad;* while the *Purano Phat* dealt with the charges brought against Arya Samaj leaders and private school teachers. See Dharma R. Yemi *Nepal ka Kura, op. cit.*, 206-207.
91. The other members of the tribunal were: Col. Ganga Bahadur Basnyat, Col. Gamvir Jang Thapa, Khagendra Raj Guruju and Mir Subba Mahendra Bahadur, See Bhim Bahadur Pandey, *Tes Bahat ko Nepal*, Vol. II, *op. cit.*, 383.
92. Any one among them could have spoken on the side of justice. But none did for the stakes were too high.

actions and was totally disassociated with the *Prajaparisad* Movement in Nepal.[93]

The manner in which the trial was conducted was symbolic of the spirit of Rana judiciary. There was no public trial, no exchange of words between the prosecutor and the accused. It was simply a plain, unsentimental, unadorned and utilitarian march to the gallows. The regime was successful in destroying the bodies of many Nepali patriots; but the spirit of loyalty of the Nepali youths to the patriotic cause surged and swelled as the Republics of India and China did cast their shadows of liberty and secularism from across their borders. The first heavy axe to fall was on the head of Shukra Raj Shastri, who had been imprisoned for spreading the doctrine of the Arya Samaj in 1939. He was accused to be "the first *Guru Ghantal* who tried to disturb the peace and tranquility of the people of Nepal by circulating corrupt ideas and practices".[94] Altogether seven were awarded capital punishment[95] eleven were given life imprisonment, four were sentenced to eighteen years of imprisonment, six for twelve years imprisonment and seven of them for imprisonment varying from two months to six years. All the 28 teachers from the Mahabir School and Ram Chandra School were fined rupees ten and given a permanent vacation, while 57 against whom no *prima facie* evidence could be found were declared innocent and set free.[96]

93. D.R. Regmi, *A Century of Family Autocracy in Nepal, op.cit.*, p.189.
94. See the diary of Chandra Kanta, *op.cit.*, pp. 649-50.
95. Out of the seven who were given the capital punishment two of them (Tanka Prasad Acharya and Ramhari Sharma) being Brahmans were socially ostracized and their punishment was changed into life imprisonment. The *Maharaja* himself commuted the capital punishment of Subba Purana Narayan to 18 Years imprisonment. This left Ganga Lal Shrestha, Dasrath Chand, Dharma Bhakta Mathema and Shukra Raj Shastri to undergo the capital punishment. More on the judgment see the Note prepared by General Nara Shumsher, the Director General of Police, E. No.6, *Poka* No.1, File No. 14, *na*. Among those set free was a popular local physician, Jit Singh Malla.
96. *Ibid*.

The methods devised to impart capital punishment were most cruel and of hateful character. To some offenders the capital punishment was implemented by the firing squad. However, others were tied to the branches of trees and were hung by the neck till they were dead.[97] Space does not permit to depict the atmosphere associated with these cruel and inhuman modes of punishment, yet the martyrdom of Dharma Bhakta Mathema can be taken as illustrative of the cruelty. It was on Magh 12, 1997 (January 1941) at 9.45 p.m. a red limousine of General Nara Shumsher speeded towards the Central Jail to fulfil the secret mission of hanging the noted leader of *Prajaparisad*, Dharma Bhakta Mathema. He was taken out of the jail on the pretext of going to a temple for worship — curious irony for only dead corpses left the prison walls to commence their journey to the temple *ghats* for the purposes of the cremation. Then from the Central Jail the vehicle, with Dharma Bhakta Mathema, the hangman, a *pode*, Ram Babu Dhakal, General Nara Shumsher and his armed bodyguard, raced towards Basbari. It was, however, at 10 p.m. the automobile was stopped at Maharajgung by General Mohan Shumsher. Here he disuaded General Nara Shumsher from hanging the political prisoner so close to his residence.[98] Thus, the motor car changed its direction towards Shifale. Dharma Bhakta had by then became suspicious and even had the haunch that was going to be his last night. From time to time he questioned the General about the place where he was being taken. But silence was the only answer. But when he came to Shifale the drama had clearly unfolded. The rope hanging from the branch of a tree and a chair spoke themselves. Dharma Bhakta then told Nara Shumsher that he was being hanged by his own student.[99] However, General

97. The Ranas did not even prepare a gibbet for the purpose of hanging; but rather chose the inexpensive way of hanging the accused by tying them to the branches of trees. Two trees, one at Teku and the other at Shifale in Kathmandu still stand as the living withnesses to the unfortunate events.
98. The quivering voice of General Mohan Shumsher who feared from being haunted by the ghost of Dharma Bhakta compelled General Nara to make a last minute change in the schedule.
99. Dharma Bhakta had been a teacher of General Nara Shumsher in the sphere of physical training and exercises.

Nara with a heavy look but with a sprit a little daring replied "I am helpless, I am here only to fulfil the wishes of the Maharaja!" Finally, as the midnight struck 12 the curtain of the stage had fallen. A noble soul had breathed his last. Dharma Bhakta died instantly with a rope around his neck and an orange inside his pocket.[100] The fruit far from quenching his thirst to live served as a *sagun* (auspicious symbol) for his journey to eternity. Earlier, when the sentence was announced at Singha Durbar, Dharma Bhakta had uttered in a smiling voice "Now we are going to leave this world; and it is for those who are undergoing light punishment to fulfil our dreams".[101]

The dead bodies of the four martyrs were exhibited before the public for twenty four hours with posters stuck to their bodies, which warned the public against such activities in future. But the open display of the earthy remains of the martyrs had just the opposite effects. Kathmandu was in tears; and thousands flocked in order to bid farewell to those patriots who had died so that they might learn to live with honour and dignity that was denied to them. Many were silent, sullen and petrified; while others were angry and full of fire and were determined to rid the nation of the cruel, hateful and arbitrary regime. The then British Minister in Kathmandu could detect a strong feeling of the people against the Rana regime in general and Premier Juddha Shumsher in particular. This, he believed, was bound to explode with the advent of time.[102] The blood-soaked cloth that had wrapped the statue of Premier Juddha in the heart of the New Road can be taken as an index of the mood of the time.[103]

100. The information about the martyrdom of Dharma Bhakta was supplied to me by Ram Babu Dhakal, a close attendant of *Maharaja* Juddha who accompanied General Nara to report an eyewitness account of the whole event, September 10, 1982.
101. Interview Bhuvan Lal Pradhan, April 3, 1980.
102. See EC. 21-26, Reg. No. 1632/1941, IOL. For more on the Judgment of Betham see a telegram of Lord Linlithgow to Secretary of State, London, May 24, 1943, EC. 21-22, Reg. No. 2677/1943, IOL.
103. EC. 21-26, Neg. No. 1632/1941, IOL.

Thus, in utter dismay and confusion, the activities of the *Prajaparisad* came to an end. The fate of many of the *Parisad* members was no better than that of the members of the *Prachanda Gorkha*. Both the movements were born with high ideals but ended in a fiasco. Their historical contribution in removing the yoke of Rana oligarchy in Nepal is ambiguous. The direct and overt effect of their activity was that it generated reaction and repression from the rulers. The one momentous consequence was that it kept alive and handed over the zeal of a revolutionary tradition to the Nepali intelligentsia living in Nepal and India. It was this revolutionary tradition that enabled the Nepali Congress and other Nepali patriots to launch an armed struggle against the Ranas in 1950-51.

The Raktapat Kommittee (Bloodshed Organisation)

This was one of the many little known organizations that sprouted in Nepal with the sole objective to reduce the Rana oligarchy into ashes; and establish a republican government in Nepal. It operated from Kathmandu as well as Cwanpore and its permanent secretary was J.B. Malla. This small group of revolutionary activists had drunk deep from the cup of Russian revolutionary nihilism that appeared in the later half of nineteenth century. They were particularly influenced by the Russian revolutionary Jacobinism of Peter Zaichnevskii. To quote *Young Russia:*

> Soon, soon a day will come when we will unfurl the great banner of the future, the red banner and with a great shout: Long live the socialist and democratic Russian republic! we will march on the Winter Palace to destroy those who live there.....
> We shall give forth one shout: "to the axes" then...smash the imperial party.....smash them in squares, if those dirty swine dare to enter, smash them in their houses, in the narrow alleys of the city, on the broad streets of the capital in the countryside and the villages.[103a]

103a. Peter Zaichnevskii was a model Russian Nihilist-Jacobin activist, who organized a radical circle at the University of Moscow, printed illegal materials abroad and smuggled into Russia. His inflammatory *Young Russia* was the most radical and alarming document of the era. See Philip Pomper. *The Russian Revolutionary Intelligentsia, op.cit.*, pp. 88-96.

The inflammatory pamphlet No. 1 of the Bloodshed Committee is close to the very language, theme and sentiments of *Young Russia.* This is best illustrated by the following lines:

> Time is fast approaching when the high-souled members of our *Kommittee* will be flying its republican flag at Singha Durbar, Lalitpur Royal Complex and the Bhaktapur Palace Plaza and the streets of Kathmandu.....We can assassinate one day this disgrace to the Nepali family in such a way that even his bones will have perished. The Nepalis will be greatly relieved on the day in which we will have destroyed the leper.....then we can feed the vultures and jackals with his flesh.[104]

The secretary of the organization was confident that "the *kalantar mantra* (deliverance) will surely come in the opportune *Oam* hour".[105]

The blood thirsty nature of the pamphlet as well as the contacts of the revolutionary conspirators with the Bolshevik politburo and the *Kalong Samiti* of the Japan highly alarmed the Rana bureaucracy in Nepal. The pamphlet dated September 7, 1940 was already in possession of *Maharaja* Juddha by September 15. It was on the *Indra Jatra* festival the Premier acquainted the British Minister G.L. Betham with the English translation of the pamphlet.[106] After the Minister had rapidly skimmed over the pamphlet the Premier told with confidence that it was the work of one of Nepali anarchists living in India. He then went on to say that they must, be treated according to the fourth clause of the Treaty of Friendship of 1923.[107]

It was on the month of February 1942, the *Raktapat Kommittee* issued another radical leaflet entitled "Long Live the Republic

104. See the Pamphlet No. 1 of the *Rakta Pat Kommittee*, E. No. 6, *Poka* No. 11, File No. *cha,* 1997/1940, FMAN.
105. *Ibid.,* p. 3.
106. The Premier thought it to be prudent to delete the severe polemical attacks on himself.
107. The Article IV of the treaty of 1923 ran: "Each of the high contracting parties will use all such measures as it may deem practicable to prevent its territories for inimical purposes to the security of each other." See *Gorkhapatra,* Pouse 9, 1980 (December 21, 1923), p. 3. For the drafts, proposed and ammended version of the treaty see E. No. 1, *Poka* No. 1, FMAN.

of Nepal". Thus, for the first time the absolute need for inaugurating a republic in the very heart of the Himalayas was boldly expressed. The main reason for doing so as the pamphlet goes was that the then *Maharaja* Juddha Shumsher lacked the qualities of a noble ruler. While the *Maharaja* was a free booter of public funds, an impetuous despot, a gambler and a sex maniac his eldest son was half-witted, incompetent and an unbalanced drunkard. The rule of Juddha had, thus, become a burning hell to the people. People not only suffered for the want of food, clothing and medicare but also from humane laws. His arbitrary style of operation, which can be coined in one word namely "misrule" is the outcome of his total insanity. So the Rana oligarchy with the mad idiot (Joota Shumsher) at the helm of state affairs was very incongruous to the rapidly changing times. He should, thus, be beheaded like Charles I of England; and republic system of government should replace the hateful Rana regime. The members of the organization were confident that Japan would be very instrumental in helping Nepal in making the radical, swift transition from despotic oligarchy to the people's republic. The leaflet concluded in a very sentimental way the dire need for a republic :

> How long are we to bear this misrule? This insane *Maharaja* is not even afraid of *dharma* (religious precepts).....No! it is too idle to expect anything from a man who is always indulging with a prostitute, gambling, and filling his private coffer by starving the people. In fact, he after wasting many amorous years with a public prostitute, the Bharadri Nani of Lagan, has elevated her to the dignity of *Kanchi Maharani*. It is, thus, a disgrace to the nation to permit him to live any longer. So he should either be shot dead or banished immediately. Then we shall rejoice and chant the slogan 'Long Live the Republic of Nepal!'[108]

The *Kommittee* members had built high hopes and expected full support and cooperation from the Japanese government in their effort to establish a republic government in Nepal. Japan at the time was heading towards South and South-east Asia and

108. See the Revolutionary leaflet issued by the *Raktapat Kommitttee* in February 1942 entitled "Long Live the Republic of Nepal!", E. No. 6, *Poka* No. 11, File No A, 14 *Ga*, 1944, FMAN.

was being hailed as a liberator of her Asian brethren from the ugly yoke of Western imperialism. But the fall of Japan on August 9, 1945 came as a rude shock to shatter the Republican dream of the *Raktapat Kommittee* members. The turning of the tide of international events had a direct impact in blowing to pieces masterplan of the Republic edifice the *Kommittee* members had so carefully erected (at least in paper) for so many years.[109]

SOCIO-POLITICAL ORGANIZATIONS — ABROAD

The All India Gorkha League

The Gurkha soldiers who returned home after the Great War (1914-18) or those who had preferred to stay in India after active service abroad could not be the same in taste, opinion and intellect. The return of 200,000 Gurkha soldiers from the combat operations in the West, thus, served as a catalyst for the liberalization of the Nepali social order. It was the liberal atmosphere generated by the homecoming soldiers that pressurized *Maharaja* Chandra Shumsher to end two major social evils : the *sati* and the slavery system in the 1920's.[110] But the endless battle against the caste system was still there. In 1921 *Maharaja* Chandra receives a threatening letter from Ranu Damai of Darjeeling which boldly pointed out that in Nepal the blacksmiths, the *gandharvas* (musicians), tailors and cobblers are living as if "they have no king". He then further goes on to say "there is no taste (sic) to subject in the *Gorkha Raj*. You should therefore give up your *Raj*".[111]

109. For more on the fall of Japan in the World War II. See Prem R. Uprety, *Nepal : A Small Nation in the Vortex of International Conflicts, op.cit.*, pp. 232-36.
110. *Sati* was abolished on July 8, 1920 see Government of Nepal, *Jyanmara ko Muluki Ain* (Laws Relating to Murder) (Kathmandu: Naxal Bhagabati Press, 1927), pp. 50-52. The slaves were emancipated on April 13, 1925 see "Dasatwa Mochan" (Emancipation of Slaves) *Gorkhapatra*, August 20, 1926, p.3; Pioneer "The Nepalese Slaves Emancipated" August 29, 1926,p.8.; Indian Social Reformer, September 4, 1926; *The Times of India*, August 30, 1926, p. 1.
111. *Foreign Political Department* (External B), August 1921, Nos. 120-137, NAI.

The atmosphere generated by the Nepalis in North Western Bengal, gave necessary impetus for the inauguration of All India Gorkha League at Dehradun in the 1920s. Thakur Chand an ex-veteran of the Great War was instrumental to the founding of the League in 1921. During the first few years of its existence the League took a moderate line of action. It did not exhibit any political colour or in other words it was free from anti-Rana or anti-British outlook.[112] The League drew its members primarily from ex-servicemen living in India. Many of them had taken an active part in the Non-Cooperation Movement launched by the Indian National Congress under the leadership of Mahatma Gandhi for seven weeks from March to April 1919.[113] Thakur Chand himself was a strong Congress worker; but in 1922 he left the organization to devote his energies for the Gurkha cause. It was after this exit he was able to build the League into a dynamic political organization. The second annual conference of the League was a turning point in its history. The session of December 26/27, 1926 was well attended by many retired Gurkha soldiers; and many goodwill messages poured in from the regiments of the Gurkhas in the British army as well as the *Maharajas* of Sikkim, Jhalawar and Garhwal. Two of its resolutions were directly aimed at the Rana Government of Nepal. Both asked the Government of Nepal to reform itself and take the country on the path of modernization like Amir Amanullah of Afghanistan and the Dalai Lama of Tibet.[114] One particular resolution pertained to the detrimental impact of the restriction on foreign travels by Nepalis to receive higher education, medicare and even for the purposes of trade and commerce. This important resolution, which advocated self improvement through foreign travels in part ran:

112. Balachandra Sharma, *Nepal ko Itihasik Rup Rekha* (Banaras: Krishna Kumari, 1976), p. 401.
113. More on Non-Cooperation Movement or "Satyagraha in Action" see Joan V. Bondurant, *Conquest of Violence; The Gandhian Philosophy of Conflict* (Berkely: University of California Press; 1969) pp. 73-88; also M.K. Gandhi, *An Autobiography; The Story of My Experiments with Truth,* trans., Mahadev Desai (Ahmedabad; Navajivan Publication, 1972), pp. 336-340.
114. See E.C. 21-51, 861/1931, IOL.

> The League is of the opinion that the restrictions imposed on the freedom of the Gurkhas in connection with foreign travels for the purpose of education, discharge of duty, commerce and trade, medical treatment, as well as for the sake of change and travel in general is detrimental to the progress of the community and is merely a ramification of medieval, narrow-minded dogmatism.[115]

The resolution of the League, though social in its nature, did have political overtones for it was a direct blow to the policies of the Nepali Premier, which persistently aimed in keeping the Nepalis mute and dumb. To put it in a slightly different perspective, the League felt that the denial of exposer to the Nepalis to the outside world did compell them to live in their little tortoise-shell of traditional conservatism. The founding of the Gorkha League can, thus, be taken as a positive step towards the growth of political awakening of the Nepalis at home and abroad. The extent to which the Government of Nepal feared the contamination of Nepali society and polity by foreign exposer is perhaps nowhere better manifested than in the refusal of Nepal to participate in the International Convention on Slavery organized by the League of Nations in February 1926. The reasons given by the *Maharaja* for not attending the Convention, though odd and irritating, is at the same time interesting and amusing. In summary, his logic ran as follows:

> It is with no small satisfaction that my Government took these achievements (that is the abolition of slavery with compensation) and considers that under these circumstances there appears to be no necessity for Nepal for joining the conference of these nations among whom these hated institutions and abominable practises still linger.[116]

115. See the resolutions of the Gorkha League passed on the Third Anniversary of All India Gorkha League held at Dehra Dun on December 26/27, 1926, contained in a letter from editor of the *Gurkha Sansar* to Marichi Man, Private Secretrary to the *Maharaja*, June 4, 1928, E. No. 2, *Poka* No. 45, *Ka*.
116. See a letter from the British Minister H. Wilkinson to *Maharaja* Chandra February 10, 1926; also from *Maharaja* to Minister, February 10, 1926. Refer to *Poka* entitled "Membership in the United Nations", 1948, also *Tribune*, February 20, 1926, p. 6.

Thus, it was quite natural for the League to be very critical about the policies of the Nepali Premier.

In 1927 the League expanded its organizational structure by opening new branches at Dibrugarh and Assam. These were areas of strong concentration of the Gurkha ex-servicemen.[117] The League first brought out a paper entitled *The Himalaya Times* which was later changed into *Tarun Gorkha* and subsequently renamed *Gorkha Sansar*.

The All India Gorkha League, though basically a social organization, did not lag behind in laying out its political objectives. Among others, it demanded the representation of the Gurkhas in the round table conferences and criticized the Government of India for not taking part in the economic development of Nepal. In fact, the Government of India had forgotten that thousands of Nepalis had shed their blood for the safety and security of the British empire.[118] But apparently Thakur Chand Singh came under a strong influence of Premier Chandra Shumsher, which led to a setback in the activities of the League throughout the decade of 1930's. It again passed through its rejuvination phase in the 1940s. On this occasion it was Damber Singh Gurung who took the lead. If the World War I provided the necessary impetus for the birth of the League then it was the aftermath of the World War II that served as the perfect backdrop for its rejuvination. It was on February 1, 1943 three Gurkha youths came from Khurseong to Kalimpong to open a branch of this Gurkha Association there. A more ambitious course of action, namely to call a broadly represented Conference of the Gurkhas at Siliguri was decided upon by the Gurkha inhabitants of Kalimpong. Accordingly, the Gurkha delegates assembled in large numbers at Siliguri on March 7, 1943 to discuss the creation a representative forum which would go a long way in seeking the welfare of the Gurkhas.[119] The delegates

117. In the Assam district of pre-independent India the Gorkhalis constituted 7.1% of the local population, E.C. Reg. No. 3298/1930, IOL.
118. *India Foreign Political* (External Sec.), File No. 149/1933, IOL.
119. The Conference was attended by the delegates from Darjeeling, Khurseong, Kalimpong, Nepal and Tibet.

unanimously decided to open an association on all India basis under the convenorship of Rup Narayan Singh. A mammoth conference of the Gurkhas was held at Gurkha Nagar, Khurseong on May 13, 1945 during which the *Akhil Bharat Gorkha League* was born and Dambar Singh Gurung was elected its president.[120] The Reko cinema theater served as the venue for this meeting.

The slogan for this conference was "Freedom For All! Protect the legitimate rights of the Gurkhas in India!!"[121] The Conference decided to start an organ of its own to carry its views before the masses. So in January 1945 a periodical entitled the *Gurkha* was published under the editorship of Ranadhir Subba; and from November 2, 1947 it became an weekly periodical.[122] The resolutions passed by the All India Gorkha League on May 13,1945 besides asking for the recognition of the Gurkhas as a minority and its representation in the Constituent Assembly of India regretted that Nepal as a sovereign state had not been invited by the sponsoring powers to the San Francisco Conference where the United Nations was born.[123] As the decade of 1940s unfolded the dramatic turn of events in the sub-continent compelled the Gorkha League to devote its attention to the securing of the rights for the Gurkha citizens of India then being involved in the anti-Rana struggle. The center of anti-Rana agitation which began in Darjeeling, Dehradun and the surrounding areas in the 1920s had shifted to Banaras, Patna and Kathmandu by the 1940s as the *Prajaparisad* and the *Nepal Rastriya* Congress took this responsibility on their shoulders. However, the Gorkha League must be given the credit for having lit the candle of anti-Rana agitation in the 1920s. This

120. Damber Singh Gurung, "Akhil Bharat Gurkha League ko Janma" (The Birth of All India Gurkha League) in Ram Krishna Sharma (ed.) Jaya Gorkha: Gorkha League Smarika, 1948, p. 45.
121. See the Invitation Card issued by the *Gorkha League* on May 13, 1945, author's collection.
122. Tika Ram Sharma, "Gorkha ko Apno Itihas" (The Personal History of the Gorkha) in Ram Krishna Sharma, *Jaya Gorkha, op.cit.*, pp. 17-19.
123. Gorkha League, *Resolutions Passed at the Opening Session of the All India Gorkha League on 13th May, 1945* (Calcutta: Gorkha League, 1945), pp. 17-19.

torch of anti-Rana Movement was then successfully passed on to the members of the *Prajaparisad* and *Nepal Rastriya Congress* in the 1940s.

Nepali Rashtriya Congress

Two factors led to a period of lull in the political awakening of Nepal in the first half of the 1940. The first was the suppresion of the *Praja Parisad* movement in Nepal in 1940, which deprived the Nepalis of a political organization to ventilate their grievances against the System; and the second constituted the increasing cooperation between the British Government in India and the Rana's in Nepal both in the sphere of the supply of recruits and the Nepali contingent during World War II. In return for the unstinted cooperation during the World War II the British Government in India vigorously clamped down all the detectable anti-Rana agitations in India during the period.[124] However, the unfolding of events showed that the World War in the long run proved to be a blessing in disguise in accelerating the momentum and direction of political awakening in Nepal. If the Nepali elites were imbibed with the precepts of freedom and justice during the Second World War then the return of Gurkhas after their active participation in the Indian National Army or from the various theaters of war made them perfect recruits for the political movement against the Ranas in the late 1940's and during "The Armed Revolution" of 1900-50.[125] As the decade of 1940's was drawing to a close, the Nepalis living in India were greatly influenced by the sacrifices of the Azad Hind Fouz of

124. More on World War II and Nepali Cooperation see Prem R. Uprety, *Nepal: A Small Nation in the Vortex of International Conflicts, 1900-1950, op.cit.*, pp. 183-279.

125. The British Government had divided the Gurkha Prisoners of War into White Grey and Black in relation to the intensity they had imbibed the doctrine of the Indian National Army. The White category constituted those who were not affected by the propaganda of INA. The grey category constituted those who were molested while the Black were of the dangerous type, who were determined to uproot the British rule from India. See a letter from Minister G.A. Falconer to *Maharaja* Juddha, Dec. 8, 1945, E. No. 4, *Poka* No. 53, File No. 785, 2002/1945.

Subhas Chandra Bose and the *Azad Dasta* of Jaya Prakash Narayan.[126] Both the Indian organization encouraged the Nepali elites in India to form a strong successor of the *Prajaparisad*. The Nepali revolutionary sentiments were first expressed on October 1, 1946 when a few radical youths of Banaras gave birth to the Akhil Bharatiya Nepali Rastriya Congress.[127] A month later another radical organization named the Akhil Bharatiya Gorkha League sprouted on the street of Calcutta under the leadership of D.N. Pradhan and D.B. Pariyar.[128] But as early as 1946 the Nepali students studying at Banaras Hindu University formed an association called *Nepal Chhatra Sangh*, which may, indeed, be taken as a prelude to the evolution of a political organization that was to spearhead the movement which would ultimately overthrow the Rana oligarchy from Nepal.[129]

Then it became imperative to unite all the small anti-Rana groups operating in North India into one unified, monolithic structure with common ideals and objectives. To fulfil this difficult task a Conference of all the splinter groups was held in Calcutta to form the *Nepal Rastriya Congress* on January 26, 1947. The Khalsa High School of Bhavanipur, Calcutta, served as the venue of the Conference for the Government of India had

126. It was the *Azad Hind Fauz* that was determined to uproot colonial rule from India through an armed revolution, with the active support of Japan. More on the Azad Hind Fauz see R.C. Mazumdar *History of Freedom Movement in India*, Vol. III (Calcutta: K.L. Mukhopadyay, 1963), 900-35. The objective of the *Azad Dasta* was to launch a Gorilla warfare against the British from an island on the river Koshi named "Bakro ka Tappu" From Nepal. See Ram Briksha Benipuri, *Jaya Prakash Narayan* (Mazaffapur: Benipuri, 1957), p. 215.
127. See Balachandra Sharma, *Nepal ko Itihasik Rup Rekha, op.cit.*, p.407; also Ganesh Man Shrestha, *Satya Kay?* (Banaras: Nepali Congress, N.D. p. 10. The president of this organization was Devi Prasad Sapkota; while Balachandra Sharma Krishna Prasad Upadhyaya, and Gopal Prasad Bhattari were elected Vice-President, Secretary General and Secretaty of publicity respectively.
128. Grishma Bahadur Devkota, *Nepal ko Rajnaitik Darpan* (The Political Mirror of Nepal) (Kathmandu: Dhurba Prasad Devkota, 1971), p. 9.
129. Balchandra Sharma, *Nepal ko Itihasik Rup Rekha, op.cit.*, p. 407.

banned all public gatherings under Section 144 of the Indian Penal Code. The Conference was well attended by about fifty delegates, which included all age groups, both the sexes and all economic levels. They also represented different territories of Nepal as well as the pockets of Nepali concentration in India.[130] A notable delegate to the Conference was Ganesh Man Singh who had escaped from the Bhadragol prison of Kathmandu — thus leaving his term of rigorous life imprisonment far behind. The Conference opened with goodwill messages pouring forth from many distinguished Indian leaders like the then Congress President, Acharya J.B. Kripalani, Mrs. Vijaya Laxmi Pandit and Acharya Narendra Deva. Dr. Ram Manohar Lohiya was specially invited to inaugurate the Conference.

A careful scrutiny of the messages from the Indian leaders reveals two very pertinent streams of thoughts. The first hypothesis was that Nepal has always been a part of India; while the second that was very distinguishable was that the freedom and wellbeing of Nepal was only possible with the cooperation and full support of free India. The message of the Congress President in part ran:

> Nepal was always a part of India. Thus, Nepali's economic and political development is dependent upon free India. Hope that Nepal will follow the path of liberty and that while laying about its objectives will come to realize that the path of non-violence is far more useful and constructive than the path of violence.[131]

A similar forceful note rang in the message of the socialist leader Jaya Prakash Narayan. He clearly stated that "Nepal's progress and development is linked with that of India".[132]

130. From Nepal delegates came from Kathmandu, Nepalgang, Doti, Morang, Biratnagar, Taulihawa, Jaleshwar, Birgang Saptari, Mahotari, Dang and Dharan; while Nepalis living in India came from Darjeeling, Khurseong, Banaras, Almoda, Allahabad and Patna. See *Nepal Rastriya Congress ko Udghatan Samaroha (Bibaran), op.cit.*, p. 5.
131. Message of the then Congress President Acharya J.B. Kripalani to the inaugural ceremony on the *Nepal Rastriya Congress. Ibid.*, p. ii.
132. Message from Jaya Prakash Narayan at the inauguration, *ibid.*, p. 3.

The hypothesis of oneness of identical interest between India and Nepal was so picturesquely presented by the Indian leaders of national repute, that it had a hypnotic spell on all the Nepali delegates attending the Conference. This is perhaps nowhere better manifested than in the address of the Acting President of he Nepal Rastriya Congress, B.P. Koirala, which in part ran:

> Actually Nepal and India are not two countries. From racial, religious, and economic perspective and in all respects Nepal is a major organ of India. Today the political difference you find is basically the game of selfish diplomats and politicians.[133]

Even scholars like D.R. Regmi were fully convinced that it was not possible for Nepal to make the colossal transition from autocracy to democracy as long as India was in chains and servitude.[134] Thus, democratic government in Nepal was contingent on the exit of British rule from the subcontinent. So when India would be free then the Nepalis riding on the back of India would be able to rid their motherland from the evils of the Rana oligarchy. Accordingly, the first job of the Nepali revolutionaries was to lend their active support to the freedom movement of India so as to accelerate the pace of expulsion of the colonial rule from the soils of the subcontinent.[135]

Objectives of the Nepali Rastriya Congress

The objectives of the *Nepal Rastriya Congress* were of two types: general and specific. The general objective was to unite all the Nepali revolutionary elites both in India and Nepal so as to accelerate the process of development in Nepal. But the specific objectives were more clear and understandable. The first objective was to render all possible help to the struggle launched by the Indian National Congress against the British rule in India. The second was the establishment of responsible

133. Presidential Address at the inauguration of the Conference of B.P. Koirala, *ibid.*, p. 9.
134. See resolution brought by D.R. Regmi in the convention, *ibid.*, p. 6.
135. *Ibid.*

government in Nepal through peaceful means. The methodology adopted by the Congress to attain its goods ran quite contrary to the violent underground tactics of the *Prachanda Gorkha* and the *Prajaparisad*. The secret clubs, plots and counterplots, attempts at massacres and assassinations were replaced by the politics of the masses. This politics of the masses was to be conducted in a non-violent way.[136] The logic was to establish a responsible government one had to go to the people; and without the cooperation of the people a free democratic society was not possible. The inauguration of the slogan "go to the people" was a peculiar response to a variety of frustrations both logistic and psychological. It involved in the rejection of the tactics of violence that had been preached by the previous political organizations.

The conference passed several important resolutions. These resolutions indicate that the founding fathers of the Nepali Rastriya Congress were under the spell of the achievements of the *Prajaparisad* and the struggle for *Swaraj* launched by the Indian National Congress. The first resolution stated that it was not possible to establish a democratic administrative system in Nepal as long as the British empire lingered in South Asia. Accordingly it asked all the Nepali brothers and sisters to render all the help as far as possible in the war of liberation of the Indians against the colonial regime. Secondly, the conference not only dedicated itself to the martyrs at the outset but also went ahead to put on record its deep appreciation of the sufferings and sacrifices of the *Parisad* members, who did not even hesitate to give up their precious lives for the greater cause of their motherland — the freedom of their Nation. This resolution ended with these inspiring words:

136. To Gandhi "non-violence in its dynamic condition means conscious suffering. It does not mean meek submission to the will of the evil doer, but it mean the pitting of one's whole soul against the will of the tyrant. Working under this law of our being, it is possible for a single individual to defy the whole might of an unjust empire......." See M.K. Gandhi, *Young India*, January 19, 1921, p. 5.

We hope that one day we will be able to celebrate Nepal, *Rajbandi Divas* as a national festival.[137]

The fourth resolution made it clear that in the view of the changing situation the secret terrorist tactics of the *Prajaparisad* was to be replaced by the people's movement in Nepal. The *Nepal Rastriya Congress* hoped that the *Parisad* members would wholeheartedly support the newly born organization. In an effort to maintain the continuity with the *Parisad* movement, Tanka Prasad Acharya, the president of the *Prajaparisad,* was made the president of the new organization. It was by electing Tanka Prasad Acharya as its president that architects of the *Nepali Rastriya Congress* hoped for a complete merger of the two organizations. Another resolution was devoted to international affairs. It prayed for the liberation of Indo-China from the imperial masters.[138]

The final work of the Congress was to elect its office bearers and choose Banaras as the headquarters of the organization. However, the unity among the different factions of the *Rastriya Congress* proved to be shortlived. Three factors were primarily responsible for the withering of this unity resulting into a formal split of the organization within a year of its birth. First, the composition of the diverse elements within the Congress opened fresh avenues of conflict within the party superstructure. Secondly, the intimate association of a powerful section of the Congress members with the Socialist Party of India introduced a new element of fear among some members of the Congress. This fear, which was their constant companion even during the inauguration of the *Rastriya Congress,* convinced them that an organization that was so dear to them would soon lose its

137. *Ibid.*, p. 6.
138. *Ibid.*, p. 8. The office bearers of the organization were: Tanka Prasad Acharya (President), B.P. Koirala (Acting President), Balachandra Sharma (Secretary), Krishna Prasad Bhattari (Organizing secretary), Dilli Raman Regmi (Chairman of the Publication Division) and Devarat Pariyar, Dharma Narayan Pradhan, Gopal Prasad Upadhyaya, Lakha Chhering Sherpa and Rudra Prasad Giri were to assist D.R. Regmi in the publicity work.

identity and become a wing of the Socialist Party of India.[139] Finally, leadership conflict has always been a persistent and, indeed, an endemic problem in Nepali party politics. No major political party in Nepal has escaped some or more or less disruptive form of leadership conflict; and the *Nepali Rastriya Congress* was no exception. The factional model looks to factors of personal ambition and struggle for personal position of power. Accordingly the personal rivalry between D.R. Regmi (a holder of Ph.D. degree and a budding historian) and B.P. Koirala (a lawyer and a short story writer) for the position of leadership within the party was the most critical factor in explaining the causes of the inner party conflict within the *Rastriya* Congress. Culminating into a formal split of the organization towards the close of 1947. In short, the personalization of the conflict, which is in conformity with the traditional cultural stylistic norms was the most important element that led to the tragic division of the party.

The arrest of B.P. Koirala at Biratnagar on March 1947 during the nation wide strike in support of the demands of the mill workers brought a leadership crisis in the National Congress. When B.P. Koirala was in jail in Kathmandu, D.R. Regmi become the president of the Nepali Rastriya Congress.[140] The

139. B.P. Koirala himself was a staunch active member of the India Socialist Party. This fear was not unfounded for the socialist leader Dr. Rammanohar Lohia was specially invited to inaugurate the opening session of the *Nepali Rastriya Congress.* Besides B.P. Koirala and his associates worked in close cooperation with and even permitted the Indian Socialist leaders to attend the meetings of *Rastriya Congress.* See Dharma Ratna Yemi, *Nepal Ko Kura, op.cit.*, p. 237; also Prem Bahadur Kansakar, "Satya Yo?", in Grishma Bahadur Devkota, *Nepal Ko Rajnaitik Darpan* (The Mirror of Nepali Politics) (Kathmandu: Dhurba Bahadur Devkota, 1979), pp. 13-15. Kansakar even labels B.P. Koirala as an "agent" of India, p. 13.

140. According to one source when B.P. Koirala was in jail it was decided to give the temporary post of presidentship to M.P. Koirala but it was Ganesh Man Singh, who did not like the post to fall with the same family proposed the name of D.R. Regmi. See Dharma Ratna Yemi, *Nepal Ko Kura, op.cit.*, pp. 246-47; also, Agni Prasad Sharma, *Akhil Nepal Rastriya Mahasabha ko Dwi Mukhi Congrsss haruma Chetawani* (The Warning to the two faced Congress by Akhil Nepal Rastriya Mahasabha) (Kathmandu : *Akhil Nepal Rastriya Mahasabha,* 1951), p. 1.

personal ego and the craze for power took D.R. Regmi one step further than his predecessor. He strongly felt that in the exigencies of the time it was no longer useful or even desirable to act on the behalf of the imprisoned *Parishad* leader Tanka Prasad; so he declared himself to be the full-fledged president of the *Nepali Rastriya Congress.* The release of B.P. Koirala brought a headlong conflict within the party. The situation turned into crisis when B.P. Koirala declared himself to have taken over the charge of presidentship from D.R. Regmi. The Congress, thus, divided itself into Regmi and Koirala Groups.[141]

However, it was the declaration of the Constitution for Nepal to be effective from April 1, 1948 which gave the impetus for the general meeting of the Rastriya Congress at Banaras on January 2, 1948. The Conference, though called to study the reforms contained in the new constitution, was significant in the sense that it strengthened the position of the Koirala group.[142] This meeting reiterated its full confidence in Tanka Prasad Acharya as its president and authorized B.P. Koirala to discharge the functions of the president as long as the former was in prison. In addition, Balachandra Sharma, and Narendra Prasad Regmi were elected as the General Secretary and the treasurer of the organization respectively. Regmi showed his dissatisfaction with the working of the Congress. This led Koirala group to hold a special meeting of the Congress at Biratnagar and expelled D.R. Regmi for a period of three years from the Congress. The Regmi group also retaliated and called a Nepal National Political Conference in February 1948.[143] The Conference expelled B.P. Koirala from Nepal Rastriya Congress for a period of two years. It also advocated the establishment of a democratic

141. The statement of B.P. Koirala after his release roused serious doubts namely,"Mohan Shumsher is a king who is bent upon reforms "roused the suspicion in the minds of some leaders of the Congress that he had become the agent of the Ranas. See Dharma Ratna Yemi, *Nepal Ko Kura, op.cit.*, p. 267; Chandra Bikram Budathoki, "History of Democratic Movement in Nepal (1931-1951) (Ph.D. Thesis, Patna University, 1974), p. 170.

142. *Ibid.*

143. Yugbani, January 21, 1948, p. 1.

government in Nepal by adhering to the Gandhian principles of non-violence; and withheld its support to the constitutional reforms in Nepal as having falled far behind in establishing a responsible government for Nepal.[144] The counter resolution passed by the Regmi group showed that the struggle for leadership within the Congress did clearly split the party into two fragments. Both the factions blamed each other for the split. Thus, up to April 1950, two organizations with identical names functioned in India. The Indian leaders of the Socialist party continued to lend its support to the Koirala faction.[145] The active interest taken by the leaders of India in the affairs of Nepal compelled some Nepali leaders not only to doubt their genuineness; but made them apprehensive of the fact Nepal "would soon be transferred into the arena of Indian party politics".[146]

The year 1948 saw a new element entering into the political horizon of Nepal. The C class Ranas and their loyal courtiers, with their vast wealth accumulated through business in India gave birth to a political organization called Nepal Democratic Congress on August 15, 1948.[147] The party convened its first meeting on December 24, 1948 during which Mahen Bikram Shah was elected its president and Surya Prasad Upadhyaya its secretary. To give publicity to its views and programs it started the official organ, the *Nepal Pukar*. Its first issue was published

144. Ramji Upadhyaya, *Nepal ko Itihas Arthat Digdarsan* (History of Nepal and Its Analysis) (Banaras: Gopal Press, 1950), p. 392.
145. A resolution passed by the socialist Party on March 6, 1949 in short ran: "the conference sends its greetings to Shri Bishweshwar Prasad Koirala, president Nepal National Congress, Shri Dharmo Narayan Pradhan, Shri Tanka Prasad Upadhyaya, Tilak Raj and Mahendra Narayan Nidhi and over six hundred brave souls of Nepal who are languishing in different prisons of the country and are under fetters or subjected to other types of barbarous treatment". See Ram Manohar Lohiya, *India, China and Northern Frontiers and Hyderabad* (Hyderabad: Navahind Publication, 1963), pp. 167-108.
146. D.R. Regmi, *Wither Nepal, op.cit.,* p. 47.
147. The leaders of this movement were Subarna Shumsher and Mahabir Shumsher.

on October 6, 1948.[148] The entry of the Rana nobility into the democratic movement of Nepal brought a train load of docile faithful servants of the Ranas into the main stream of national politics. This was a cause of much concern to many leaders of national repute. This fear and apprehension is perhaps nowhere better expressed than in this sentimental note of a contemporary leader. To quote:

> It is very unpleasant spectacle to see erstwhile courtiers of the Ranas, relations and faithful servants of theirs masquaerading in the roll of patriots engaged in playing a nasty game which has polluted the newly emerging structure of our national democratic movement.[149]

The manifesto of the party declared that its first and foremost objective was to extinguish the flame of Rana autocracy in Nepal and replace it by a constituent assembly consisting of delegates elected on the basis of direct universal adult franchise. Its methodology, however deviated from the path of non-violence followed by the Nepali National Congress. On the contrary, it chose a more radical method of "armed revolution" to fulfil its objectives.[150] The most important session held by the Nepal Democratic Congress was its fourth session, which concluded on January 2, 1949. The session was significant in a number of ways. First, it boldly urged for the formation of an interim government representing the popular parties in Nepal. This "popular government" would then shoulder the grave responsibility of holding elections on the basis of adult franchise to the sovereign constituent assembly, which would draft a constitution for the country. Secondly, it appealed to the United Nations to reject the admission sought by the Ranas to include Nepal into the world body unless they were prepared to set up a democratic government in Nepal. Lastly, it placed on record the fact that political freedom was meaningless unless it was closely accompanied by economic freedom to the starving

148. Grishma Bahadur Devkota, *Nepal ko Rajnaitik Darpan, op.cit.*, p. 20-21.
149. D.R. Regmi, *Wither Nepal, op. cit.*, p. 48.
150. Balachandra Sharma, *Nepal ko Itihasik Rup Rekha., op.cit.*, pp. 412-13.

millions. These resolutions passed by the Congress are indicative of the fact that the Nepali opposition leaders had by the time reached a stage of maturity and had a clear vision of the future path and momentum of politics in Nepal.[151]

However, with the dawn of 1950 many Nepali leaders sincerely felt that the anti-rana movement in India could not make any headway without a resonable bond of unity among the different splinter groups. Thus, as early as March 18,1950 the working committees of the Koirala led *Nepal Rastriya Congress* and the Napal Democratic Congress decided on the issue of the merger in the interest of unity among the progressive forces in Nepal so that with the combined efforts "democracy may be installed at the earliest date.[152] The presidents of both these organizations expressed their continued interest in the merger in these forceful words:

> Both the organizations have decided that the country should be prepared for a fight to the finish against an autocracy that has no parallel in ruthlessness. [153]

The official merger between the two foremost political organizations operating from India against the Rana regime occurred on April 9, 1950.* The result of this historic union was the birth of a new organization called the Nepali Congress. The

151. *The Hindu*, January 3, 1949, p. 6.
152. The joint statement was issued by Matrika Prasad Koirala, President Nepal National Congress and Mahendra Bikram Shah, President Nepal Democratic Congress, *The Hindu*, March 19, 1950, p. 9.
153. *Ibid.*

* The reason that had prevented an eary merger was the difference that developed between the two organizations on the structure of the center. The constitution of the Nepal Democratic Congress had given all powers to a central executive consisting of three of five members but the Nepal National Congress wanted the president to be all powerful. However, the joint conference of both the parties helped to cut the ice as all authority was given to the president. See the statement by Ganesh Man Singh before a special tribunal at Singha Durbar, Poush 5, 2007 V.S. (December 195, E. No. 6, *Poka* No. 11, FMAN.

day was to be remembered. The five hundred delegates that had assembled took a pledge to dedicate themselves to the historic mission of uprooting the Rana *Raj*. The president of the new organization, Matrika Prasad Koirala addressing the huge gathering "asked the people of Nepal to remain united and launch a movement for people's freedom".[154] As the Congress was in session messages of greetings an congratulations poured forth from the Indian National Congress and the Socialist leaders. The president of the Indian National Congress, Dr. Pattabhi Sitaramayya, besides expressing his sentiments of support to the Nepali Congress pointed out that "the Nepali people needed sympathy and moral support cooperation of the democratic forces of the world in a struggle to emancipate themselves and establish a popular rule".[155] Thus, with the combination of the popular element with the material resources of the Nepali plutocrats the Nepali Congress built in itself a firm base for struggle against the Rana oligarchy.

154. Matrika Prasad Koirala was elected the President of the new organization and Mahendra Bikram Shah and Subarna Shumsher its General Secretary and Treasurer respectively. See *The Hindu*, April 10, 1950, p. 4.
155. *Ibid.*

4

INSTITUTIONALIZATION OF OPPOSITIONAL POLITICS, 1941-1950 AND THE RANA RESPONSE

You are wrestling with the enemies of the Human Race, not for yourself merely, for you may not see the full Day of Liberty, but for the Child hanging at the Breast.

Instructions of the London Corresponding Society to its travelling delegates, 1796.[1]

The suppression of the *Prajaparisad* movement brought a temporary lull in the growth of oppositional politics in Nepal. The setback was both physical and psychological. The Nepali revolutionary patriots were deprived not merely of a political platform from which they could voice their grievances against the obsolete Rana autocracy; but in the defeat many lost their courage and confidence and some, perhaps, even their convictions. Above all, their romantic vision of overthrowing the sturdy Rana oligarchy with a few sticks of dynamites and several other explosives faded into oblivion leaving a strong political vacuum behind. The international situation, namely

1. Instructions of the London Corresponding Society to its travelling delegates, 1796. See E.P. Thompson, *The Making of the English Working Class* (New York: Alfred A. Knope, Inc., and Random House, Inc., 1963), p. 16.

the outbreak of the World War II, did help in more than one way to strengthen the iron grip of the Rana oligarchy. The Anglo-Nepali alliance became stronger than ever before, for, if on one hand the British were sorely in need of the Gurkha recruits, then on the other Rana were also in dire need of the cooperation of the British Government of India to curb the anti-Rana activities carried from the Indian soil.

The city of Darjeeling in the North-West of Bengal served as the venue for several anti-Rana meetings of the Nepalis in India as the decade of the 1940s unfolded. The first meeting was organized within the Dhir Dham temple complex[2] in September 1941, a little before the *Puja* holidays. It is an irony of history that a temple built by the Rana Premier himself served as the venue for anti-Rana activities within a few years span of time since its construction. It was equally frustrating to the Ranas that members of the temple trusteeship became the most vehement critics of the Rana rule in Nepal.[3] The meeting, though sponsored by the president and secretary of the temple trusteeship committee, yet, the agenda for discussion had nothing to do with the administration of the temple. The objective of the gathering far from being religious was wholly political or to be more specific it was anti-Rana in nature, style and content. The members who attended the meeting came from different ethnic groups, caste and classes, yet, the Brahmans predominated. The names one comes across in this meeting like that of D.R. Regmi, Krishna Prasad Koirala and B.P. Koirala were to figure very prominently in Nepali national politics in the succeeding years

2. The name of the temple Dhir Dham is spelt differently in the official records of the GI for example Dheerdam, Dhir Dum, Dheerdum, and Dhir Dum.
3. The leading members of the Temple Trusteeship Committee were: Rai Sáhab Hari Prasad Pradhan (President), Dharani Dhar Sharma (Secretary). The other members were: Surya Bikram Gyawali, Sardar Bahadur Hansa Jit Diwan (retired Deputy Superintendent of Police), Major *Subedar* Ganesh Bahadur and N.K. Upadhyaya. See deposition in Nepali May 29, 1943, by N.K. Upadhyaya, E. No. 6, *Poka* No. 1, File No. A, 14, *Kha,* 1945. FMAN.

and decades.[4] It was Pandit Dharanidhar Sharma who at the outset set the tone for the meeting by asserting that there was no point in talking about reforms in Nepal without driving the Ranas out of the country.[5]

A follow-up meeting was immediately held at the residence of Santabir Lama in Sukhiya Pokhari.[6] It was during this meeting that the triumvirate Agni Prasad Sharma, Dharanidhar Koirala and Surya Bikram Gyawali jointly introduced the idea of opening a school inside Nepal, which was to serve as the headquarters for all anti-Rana organizers. The resolution was unanimously adopted. They further hoped to raise through voluntary contribution a sum of 100,000 rupees for the purpose. But if the scheme failed Santabir Lama was even prepared to loot the treasury of Nepal Government at Dharan and thereby collect the one *lakha* of rupees that was so indispensable for the noble cause. The money would then be used to run the school as well as to purchase arms. The arms would ultimately be used to drive the British and the Ranas from power; and the timing was during the Japanese invasion of South Asia. B.P. Koirala and his cousin Dharanidhar Sharma left for Nepal to arrange an anti-Rana meeting at Kathmandu in October 1941.[7]

4. The other members who attended the first meeting of 1941 were: Santabir Lama, Agni Prasad Sharma, Gajadhar Pandey (Bhattari), Hari Prasad Pradhan, Shanker Prasad Sharma, Agni Prasad Sharma (Kharel), Surya Bikram Gyawali, Dr. S.P. Pradhan, Nima Lama, Shri Prasad Sharma (Kharel), Bishnu Prasad Sharma (Kharel) and Tharoo externee Subba of Nepal. It was this group that attended the follow up meeting also. *Ibid.*
5. See the abstract of the first meeting in E.No. 6, *Poka* No. 11, File No. A 14 *Kha,* 1945; also "A Note on Anti-Rana Agitation" in the same file.
6. Santabir Lama was born in Dhodray, Nepal. He had escaped from a Nepali prison, where he had been detained, apparently, accused for a murder sometime during 1927-28. He then came to Sukhiya Pokhari and started a successful private business and finally became the citizen of the British empire in 1933-34. See English trans. of deposition E. No. 6, *Poka* No. 11, File No. A, 14, *Kha,* 1945, FMAN.
7. See "The Grounds of Detention of Nepalese Subjects", *ibid.*

A third meeting was probably held in June 1942 in the house of Dharanidhar Sharma, a teacher at the Government High School in Darjeeling.[8] The overall results of all these secret meetings was the formations of the underground organization called *Akhil Nepal Barga Mahasabha* with branches at Banaras, Dehra Dun and Darjeeling where Dilli Raman Regmi, Agni Prasad Sharma and Santabir Lama were respectively placed in charge. Krishna Prasad Koirala and his son B.P. Koirala were assigned to help Santabir Lama in his delicate and dangerous mission, particularly in 13 Myiung and the 17 Thoom of the Limbuan country where they had considerable influence.

The primary aim of the organization was to overthrow the Rana Government of Nepal by even resorting to violence if necessary. Santabir Lama volunteered to be the permanent president of the organization. D.R. Regmi, Agni Prasad Sharma and Dharanidhar Koirala were entrusted with the task of organization; while Krishna Prasad Koirala and B.P. Koirala were to help Santabir Lama prepare a secret scheme to outset the Rana oligarchy from Nepal. Accordingly it was decided to open the branches of the *Akhil Nepal Barga Mahasabha* in as many districts and villages as possible. A Centre of operation was to be established in Nepal; while in India places like Banaras, Darjeeling and Dehra Dun would be used as the nucleus for planning and promoting the organization. The success of the organization, however, rested on the cooperation and active support of the Nepali hill folks of Eastern Nepal — the Rias, Limbus and the Kirats. Thus, a school named Udyog Prakash was to be opened at the *bazar* of Thirteen Thum Maglung, which would go a long way in imparting political consciousness among the inhabitants of the area.[9]

The objectives of the school fell into two categories: overt and covert types. The overt objectives were as follows:

8. See the English trans. of deposition by Krishna Bahadur Subba, May 25, 1945, *ibid*.
9. The idea of opening a school as a center for political training and operation was suggested by *Pandit* Dharanidhar Sharma. See the Letter No. F 791-X/1940, External Affairs Department from GI to the GN, July 1, 1941. IOL. See also the Work Plan of the *Akhil Nepal Barga Mahasabha* as narrated by its founding member, Agni Prasad Sharma. See E. No. 6, *Poka* No. 11, File No. A 14, *Kha*, 1945.

(*i*) To produce scholars well grounded in the *Vedic Samhitas, Smritis* and *Shastras*. The aim was to create an intelligentsia which was not only physically strong but also mentally innovative so that they could uphold the glorious tradition of the Aryan culture.

(*ii*) To educate the Brahmans in the *mimamsa* philosophy* and its related disciplines as well as in the ritualistic traditions of the *karma kanda.* The other castes were to be taught sciences like etymology, astrology, economics, agriculture, animal husbandry, political science, management and literature.

(*iii*) To infuse in the students the virtues of moral piety, patriotism, gentleness, deligence and dexterity so that they could develop a sound body and mind.

(*iv*) To provide education, food, clothing and shelter to orphans so that they could be self-reliant and useful members of the society.

(*v*) To turn the school into a center for conducting examinations on the above subjects.

(*vi*) To develop a cader of talented students who could fill the bureaucracy of the government and lead the country on the path of development.

(*vii*) The rules and regulations of the institution would also be announced in the curriculum.[10]

The covert objectives of the *Barga Mahasabhite's* school were the use of the tactics of propaganda as well as violence to achieve their end. The first was to incite the Nepali masses,

* The *mimamsa* philosophy believes in the absolute authority of the *Vedas,* which are eternal and self-existing. Our mission in life according to it was to perform what the *Vedas* commands us to do. More on the *mimamsa* philosophy see Ainslie T. Embree (ed.), *The Hindu Tradition* (New York: Random House, 1966), pp. 180-90; Charles A. More, S. Radha Krishna (ed.), *A Source Book in Indian Philosophy* (Princeton: Princeton University Press, 1970), pp. 424-452.

10. See "An Appeal" printed in the name of Jotirbind Pandit Shri Prasad Sharma in Hitaishi Printing Works, Banaras and handed over to GI by Narendra Keshari Sharma, E. No. 6, *Poka* No. 11, File No. A 14, *Gha.*

through the press and platform, to rise and revolt against the Rana oligarchy. Thus, books and pamphlets and political tracts were to be published and distributed in various parts of India and Nepal. This would pave the way to the sending of the secret armed *jathas* (groups) of the Rias, Limbus and Kirats to Kathmandu. When the *Barga Mahasabhites* had made their position sufficiently strong in Kathmandu and its suburbs, on the appointed day the attack would be made. The day would coincide with the momentous event of the Japanese invasion of India, and the overthrow of Western imperialism from South Asia.[11] To make such a comprehensive master plan a success, money and arms were indispensable. Two sources for the collection of money were to be tapped. One would be the voluntary contributions of the Nepalis living in Nepal and India, and their sympathisers. The other was the raiding of the national treasury of the Nepal Government by its revolutionary comrades. By and large these comrades would come from the Nepali hills of the Eastern Nepal. As regards the collection of arms two prominent members of the organization, Santabir Lama and Agni Prasad Sharma, were in close contact with the powerful Bengali terrorist organization called the *Anushilan Samiti*, whose headquarters were in Dacca. A highly placed member of the *Samiti* had promised to provide the Nepal *Barga Mahasabhites* with arms worth 10,000 rupees. The money plundered from the Nepali treasury would be used liberally to purchase arms from the Indian underground organizations.[12] Once the Ranas were ousted from power and authority "all would be beheaded without exception".[13] This highly ambitious "militant work plan" was approved unanimously by the full meeting of the organization held in June 1942.[14]

The Propaganda Phase

This phase constituted an outburst of literary activities in the form of books, leaflets, pamphlets, and political tracts

11. Work Plan of the *Akhil Nepal Barga Mahasabha, op.cit.*, footnote no. 9.
12. *Ibid.*
13. *Ibid.*
14. *Ibid.*

which were not only critical of the Rana regime but were often virulent in tone style and content. The *Akhil Barga Mahasabha* had entrusted D.R. Regmi and Agni Prasad Sharma for the production of a series of anti-Rana literature. The first anti-Rana tract that appeared in this series was an article entitled "Deterrent Repression in Nepal" by Nara Dev Shastri. It appeared in the Hindi weekly *Sachitra Durbar* published from Delhi on August 6,1942. Another article, with a slightly different version, appeared in the name of the same writer in the *Pratap*, a daily newspaper from Cwanpore, on August 8, 1943.[15] Likewise, D.R. Regmi write an article on the Newars of Kathmandu in the *Modern Review of Calcutta* in August 1942. The Government of India looked upon the article on the Newars as an attempt to incite a revolting spirit of the Newars by telling them that they are the original inhabitants and the rulers of Kathmandu Valley.[16] He also wrote a monograph entitled *An Appeal to the Congress* (of India) with the objective of winning the support of the Indian National Congress for its anti-Rana struggle.[17]

It was, however, in September 1942 Agni Prasad Sharma came out with a virulent leaflet entitled "The Seven Star Kings of Nepal". It was printed in the Sulaiman Press at Banaras. The thematic content of the tract was the narration of a few instances of the dreadful high-handed suppression of the people by the Rana Prime Ministers since 1846. The tone of the leaflet that the Ranas have not only left the people mute and dumb but also

15. Though the article appeared in the name of Nara Deva Shastri, a Congress organizer of Dehra Dun, yet, the records of the GI indicates that it was written at the instigation of D.R. Regmi and was assisted by Mukunda Nath Sharma. See the copies of document handed over by the GI to GN entitled, "Anti-Rana Agitation", E. No. 6, *Poka* No. 11, File No. A 14, *Gha,* 1940, FMAN.
16. *Ibid.* Also a Note handed by the GI to GN called "Grounds of Detention", of those involved in anti-Rana agitation in India. It is contained in a report of the Intelligence Bureau of the Home Department, May 5, 1943, E. No. 6, *Poka* No. 11, File No. A 14, *Ga.*
17. For *An Appeal to the Congress* by D.R. Regmi see the Note of the Director of Intelligence Bureau of India, *ibid.*

had deprived the monarchs of the use of their wisdom and scruples is of much interest and curiosity. It then poses a very sincere question and attempts to answer it.

> How long will the jackal (premier) covering with a shroud of a tiger's skin pull on.... A day will come when these selfish deamons will be destroyed. When the people of Nepal join together then they will be able to root out the selfish abominable creatures from Nepal. In the present moment the poor Nepali subjects have been oppressed and sucked so much that only their bones remain. The result is that we are doomed. Thus, the destroyer of the people, the corrupt system of hereditary Premiership must be destroyed. This is the objective of the appeal and it is for this and this reason alone we have created the *Akhil Nepal Barga Mahasabha.*[18]

The leaflet ended with the expression of a firm conviction that the *Mahasavites* were determined to establish a parliamentary system based upon the Westminister model. This they took it as an act of faith.

The propaganda phase reached its climax with the completion of the manuscript entitled "Jagriti" by the learned scholar Agni Prasad Sharma. The writer had given the manuscript to the prominent leaders of the Indian National Congress like Pandit Jawahar Lal Nehru and Purushottam Das Tandon for comments and criticisms. Both showed much interest in the manuscript and the latter even suggested that the title of the work should be "Jagriti", which the writer gladly accepted. The "book" was revolutionary in thematic approach and subject matter. It was not only extremely critical of the Rana regime but ran on communistic line as far as the mechanism of the seizure of political power and the mode of production, distribution and exchange was concerned. In short, the "book" outlined the future constitution for the democratic state of Nepal.[19]

18. See the English Trans. of a leaflet entitled *The Search for the Seven Star Kings of Nepal*, E. No. 6, *Poka* No. 11, File No. A 14, *Gha.*
19. English trans. of a deposition by Narendra Keshari Sharma; also Grounds of Detention of the Nepali Subjects in India, May 25, 1944. A note prepared by the Intelligence Bureau, Home (dept.), GI; Also Copies presume given by the GI to GN; E. No. 6, *Poka* No. 11, 14, *Gha*, FMAN.

The Militant Phase and the Japanese Connection

The ultimate objective of the *Akhil Nepal Barga Mahasabha* was to organize a militant group of revolutionary commandos of its own who would infiltrate into the nation's capital and blow the entire bastion of the Rana oligarchy into fragments. The attack would be launched with the full support of the Japanese army, after it had liberated India from the clutches of the English rule. Thus, it was quite natural for the Nepali *Barga Mahasabhites* to anxiously wait for the day when the British empire would be erased from the map of the subcontinent. So the entry of Japan towards the close of the 1941, as an Axis power in the World War II, brought a new dimension to the conflict.[20] The opening of the Eastern Theater of the war if it brought signs of gloom and despair in the faces of the Allies then it saw in an inversely proportionate scale the rise of new hopes and aspirations in the hearts of the South Asians who were struggling to relieve themselves from the rule of despotic and arbitrary governments.

Two militant organizations the *Barga Mahasabha* and *Azad Hind Fauz* began to pine their hopes upon the Japanese connection for the liberation of South Asia from cruel and irresponsible governments. It was therefore quite natural for the British Government in India to express its deep concern over any kind of possible Japanese influence over Nepal. Two examples may be taken as illustrative of this fact. First, the information that eighteen Japanese and some pro-Nippon Mongols had moved into Nepal from Tibet as early as September 1941 in connection with Pro-Axis activities was a cause of much concern to the British Bureaucracy in the subcontinent.[21] Secondly, the Bri-

20. Prem R. Uprety, *Nepal: A Small Nation in the Vortex of International Conflicts, 1900-1950* (Kathmandu: Pugo Mi, 1984), pp. 214-220.
21. The Japanese had conducted their operations across the mighty Himalayas with utmost secrecy. The result was either the Nepali representative in Lhasa or the Government of Nepal could locate the Japanese presence in Northern Nepal. See a letter from *Maharaja* Juddha Shumsher to British Minister G.L. Betham May 28, 1942; also a letter of September 29,1942. See also the file entitled "The Coming of the Eighteen Japanese and Some Mongols to Nepal", E. No. 2, *Poka* No. 77, File No. 553 of 1943, FMAN.

Government expressed its alarm over a plan of the Education Department of Nepal to send a batch of Nepali students for higher technical training in Japan.[22] The plan, though formulated long before the Second Sino-Japanese war of 1937, yet, it ran into a snag due to the climate of the time. The assurance given by the Government of Nepal did help to mitigate doubts and fears from the British mind. An extract from a letter of the Nepali Premier of August 1940 in short ran:

> There is no question of sending any Nepalese students to Japan so long the Sino-Japanese war lasts or while the relationship between Japan and Britain remained strained.[23]

The militant phase of the *Barga Mahasabhites* aimed at coup d'etat in Nepal through the Gurkha regiments and the deserters in the War. The central thrust of this coup was hinged upon the success of the Japanese military units in Eastern India. The task of the *Barga Mahasabhites* was, thus, to discourage the Gurkha regiments in the British army and those of the Nepali contingent of the state army from fighting with the Japanese; and also to prevent the flow of recruits into the Gurkha regiments. Two prominent Nepali leaders Krishna Prasad Koirala and Surya Prasad Upadhyaya were entrusted with this work. A little later another Nepali revolutionary Shanker Prasad Sharma, an

22. The GI came to know of the plan of the Education Department of the GN through a group of students studying Japanese language in Calcutta as a prerequisite course prior to their departure. An anti-Rana group led by D.R. Regmi at Banaras was trying to convince the GI that at a time when the relations between Japan and Britain were at its lowest ebb the GN is sending a batch of students to study in Japan. The conclusion was that the foreign policy of the Ranas was pro-Japanese. See a letter from G.L. Betham to *Maharaja* Juddha August 22, 1940, E. No. 6, *Poka* No. 11, File No. A 14, *Ga;* a letter from Krishna Shumsher to General Mohan Shumsher, April 4, 1942, *ibid.*, File No. A, *Kha,* 1945. For the role of D.R. Regmi in this issue see a letter from Krishna Shumsher to Mohan Shumsher October 10, 1942, *ibid.*
23. See a letter from Nepali Premier Juddha to British Minister G.L. Betham August 25, 1940, "The Register of the Copies of Letters Sent by the *Maharaja* to the British Minister from May 7, 1940 to March 27, 1942, FMAN.

agriculture graduate from India, also joined the team. Their agents, thus, began their work in the Gurkha recruiting centers at Gorakhpur, Raxaul, Dehra Dun and Lucknow and in the field of operation in Assam such as Dimapur, Imphal and Manipur. Surya Prasad had successfully converted to his cause some of the Gurkha commandos and the parachutists operating on the Assam-Burma frontier. He even sent a Gurkha envoy, known as the Robin Hood among the British soldiers, to learn from the Japanese commando Mariyama* the precise timing of the Japanese invasion of India. The result of the mission of the *Barga Mahasabhites* was that more and more Gurkhas left the British army and joined the Japanese side in the eastern theater of the war.

To facilitate its program of operation the *Barga Mahasabha* had to keep a lid of tight secrecy over the minutest details of its activities. So it devised the following code phrase: *Pasupati Nath ki jai* for ordinary talks and *Guheswari Mai ki jai* for most secret talks. In addition, to communicate message from the Assam-Burma frontier to the headquarter at Banaras a cipher of code in Hindi was prepared. The title of the code was Srong-tsen Gampo,** a Tibetan king who had Nepali connections in the seventh century A.D.[24]

The records on the techniques evolved by the organization to train the commandos for an effective operations against the Rana oligarchy are scant. However, from the imperial records

* Mari Yama could speak Hindi very fluently and was important in connection with the Japanese operations in the Indo-Burma frontier.

** The code was to be scanned on the top horizontal column each *matra* and consonant to be put at the head of the verticle column. *Ansuvara* and the sign of halant was to be treated as *matra*. Below the code word in the verticle columns the whole alphabet was be scanned, consonants under consonants and *matras* under *matras* in the usual alphabetical order. Each letter in the chart was represented by a syllible to be made up of the consonants vertically arranged on the side of the chart.

24. See the statement of Professor Jai Chand Vidya Lankar, who was detained as security prisoner in Lahore contained in letter from G.A. Falconer the British Minister, to *Maharaja* Juddha, June 10, 1944, E.No. 6, *Poka* No. 11, File No. A 14, *Ga*, FMAN.

one gathers that this training consisted of two phases. The first phase consisted of the constructions of the *akaharas* (gymnasia) for the training of Nepalis youths in sword fencing, *lathi* (stave manoeuvrings) and other skills designed to enhance physical capability. Accordingly, Ayodhya Prasad Singh, a staunch *Barga Mahasabhite,* established a gymnasium in Tansen, Palpa to train the Nepali youth in physical culture and martial arts. In this serious task he was helped by his colleagues like Dayanand Sharma, *Kharidar* Krishna Bahadur and the Mani Brothers.[25] Again, the three Indian teachers in Dhankuta were also paving the way for the training of the commandos by spreading the revolutionary gospel of Subhas Chandra Bose.[26] The second phase was that of the training of the Nepali commandos in India by of the members of the *Anushulian Samiti.*[27]

The sudden and swift reverses of the British army in Assam and Imphal and the bombing of the port of calcutta by the Japanese airforce had brought the masterplan of the *Akhil Nepal Barga Mahasabha* very near to success. The euphoria during the initial phase of the victory by the Japanese is documented by a letter from the activist of the *Azad Hind Fauz* J.R. Bhatarjee of September 1943. The important letter in part ran:

> Be careful! you (Premier Juddha Shumsher) will not live long. We are gradually taking India from the British and as soon as it is ours we will attack Nepal. Do not think that your unsurpassable mountains will help you — we are employing and handsomely paying you own ex-sepoys to conduct the attack as they know the lie of the land. Victory will be ours!!! What can you do with an army of thousands to our millions? Your days of unparalleled luxury will soon be at an end.[28]

25. The Mani brothers were: Padma Mani and Ratna Mani.
26. The three Indian teachers were: Sanak Mohan Das (Headmaster, M.A.BL.), Nripendra Kumar Day Sirkar (B.A.) and Prafulla Kumar (B.Sc.). See a letter from G.A. Falconer, British Minister to General Bahadur Shumsher, May 17, 1944; also a letter entitled "The Three Bengali Teachers", from *Maharaja* Juddha to G.A. Falconer, May 25, 1944, E.No. 6, *Poka* No. 11, File No. A 14, *Ga,* FMAN.
27. *Ibid.*
28. A letter from J. Bhattacharjee, to *Maharaja* Juddha Shumsher, September 18, 1943, E. No. 4, *Poka* No. 94, FMAN.

But when success was almost at hand Japan had to withdraw from the Indo-Burmese theater of the war to contain the increasing Allied pressure in the Pacific. Thus, the unfortunate turning of the tide for Japan adversely affected the scheme prepared by South Asian revolutionaries for the liberation of the subcontinent. Then the surrender of Japan to the Allied forces on August 1945 turned the dreams of the *Akhil Nepal Barga Mahasabhites* and the *Azad Hind Fauz* into an illusion. Thus two South Asian institutions that rose to life during the conducive atmosphere generated by the World War II died a natural death when the war bugles ceased to play their historic notes.

Anti-Rana Agitation in India and the British Response

The policy of the British Government in India towards the Ranas of Nepal was one of cooperation and goodwill. The Ranas in return championed the British cause as their own and tried their best to maintain a steady flow of recruits to the British army. Friends in peace, the English and the Ranas were allies in war. However, the dawn of anti-Rana agitation in India brought an increasing strain in the relationship between the two governments. The then Nepali bureaucracy wanted the Government of India to extradite all the anti-Rana conspirators whether they were British subjects of Nepali origin or those Nepalis domiciled in India.[29] But the British Government could not fulfil all the wishes of an incensed oligarchy for the political life in India was regulated by the freedom of press and parliamentary institutions to a fair degree. Thus, while keeping the Nepali Premier in good humour the British Government also exercised a degree of restraint and moderation; and at times dilute its inability to act through lipservice.

Once the flames of the *Prajaparisad* movement were extinguished at home the Ranas attempted to stamp out its sparks abroad. Accordingly, the *Hakim Subba* of the *Jangi Kot* (Magistrate) dispatched a list of over 23 separate requisition orders to the Government of India for the surrender of the

29. See the abstract translation of a conversation between *Maharaja* Juddha and Minister G.L. Betham, September 15, 1940, E.No. 2, *Poka* No. 560, File No. 421, *Kha*, 1997/1940, FMAN.

accused, who were involved in a conspiracy to overthrow the Government of Nepal, or in other words those who were using the territory of a friendly country for purposes inimical to the security of the Government of Nepal. There were certain elements of commonality in all the requisition papers: the name of the accused, their parentage, the possible whereabouts, the evidence of nationality, and the charges as well as evidences. The purpose was clear: no one even remotely connected with the anti-Rana agitation in India escaped from the list. The three Kharel brothers* were the first three victims of, what one might call the Nepali *lettres de cachet*, operating outside the Nepali frontier. The distinguished Kharel brothers were followed by other towering figures in Nepali oppositional politics like Dilli Raman Regmi, Surya Prasad Upadhyaya and Santa Bir Lama.[30]

The Government of India by and large cooperated with the Rana Government for two reasons. First, as the World War II was in full swing the Government of India thought it prudent to follow a policy that would not alienate a faithful, valuable, and a staunch ally like Nepal. Secondly, as the anti-Rana agitators had strong connections with the absconders of the Indian Socialist Party it was in conformity with the British interest to make a thorough search of the anti-Rana strongholds. The British Government devised a number of methods of clamping down anti-Rana agitation in India. First of all it appointed a special officer in the Alien's Branch of the Police to maintain a constant watch over subsersive activities directed towards Nepal.[31] Second, as early as November 1940 the Government of India issued an important instruction to the provincial governments, which had borders with Nepal (United

* The Kharel brothers were: Agni Prasad Kharel (Sharma), Bishnu Prasad Kharel (Sharma), Shree Prasad Kharel (Sharma). All of them played the leading role during the early phase of the anti-Rana agitation in India and Nepal.

30. See requisitions of the surrender of the accused persons from the *Hakim Subba, Sadar Jangi Kot*, Kathmandu, entitled "Anti-Rana Movement", December 24, 1940; also a letter from G.L. Betham to *Maharaja* Juddha, December 24, 1940, E.No. 6, *Poka* No. 11, File No. *Cha*, FMAN.

31. See a letter from G.L. Betham to *Maharaja* Judda, June 22, 1942, E. No. 6, *Poka* No. 11, File No. A 14, *Ga*, FMAN.

Provinces, Bihar and Bengal) to conduct an active search of the whereabouts and the hideouts of the anti-Rana conspirators, whether, British or Nepali subjects, mentioned in the list given by the Government of Nepal on November 14, 1940. Accordingly, special and immediate instructions were issued by the provincial governments of U.P. and Bihar to arrest *Subba* Adhi Bhakta Mathema, Batuk Raj, Bhet Narayan, Shanker Prasad Sharma and Mukunda Nath Sharma.[32] Likewise, the Government of Bengal, upon the command of the Center, ordered the arrest of Santabir Lama, who was at the time taken to be the arch-conspirator against the Ranas.[33]

The searches conducted by the provincial governments in India were rewarded with some success. The Government of Bengal made a through search on seven individuals and the result can be summarized as follows. *Subba* Adhi Bhakta was arrested and detained in jail. Thakur Nath Rimal, who was detained by the police in Bengal disclosed a letter from the southern anti-Rana Commander in Nepal asking him to join him immediately. Santabir Lama was also put behind the bars in Darjeeling, so was Bhet Narayan but as the latter was suffering from an advanced case of tuberculosis, he was sent to a sanitorium. The premises of D.B. Pradhan and *Subba* Man Kazi were also searched but nothing incriminating was found against them. The Government of Bihar also launched a full scale search of the residences of B.P. Koirala, Raj Lal Kalwar and Gopal Singh Nepali but nothing incriminating could be discovered.[34] The governments of the United Provinces and Bombay also made their investigations but no arrests were made.[35]

32. Adhi Bhakta was the father of Dharma Bhakta Mathema. He and his other friends were accused of possessing anti-Rana pamphlets and being closely associated with the *Prajaparisad* Movement.
33. A letter from G.L. Betham to *Maharaja* Juddha, Dec. 24, 1940. See File entitled "Anti-Rana Movement", File No. 1, *Cha, ibid.*
34. The other residences that were searched were that of Odhashore Prasad Singh, Mahabir Prasad, Debendra Prasad and Laxmi Bilas Upadhyaya.
35. See a letter from G.L. Betham to *Maharaja* Juddha containing the summary of the results of the searches made in India by the Provincial Governments, Feb. 17, 1941, E. No. 6, *Poka* No. 11, *Cha,* 1997/1940.

By 1943 repressive measures against Nepali nationals as well as the British subjects of Nepali origin in India became severe. As a result Krishna Prasad Koirala and his son B.P. Koirala were arrested at Patna on November 29, 1942.[36] At one time the Government of India even thought of handing over B.P. Koirala as a detenu; but later changed its mind for his Nepali identity could not be fully established. Thus, he was imprisoned for a little over two years and released only on January 6, 1945 when the War was virtually coming to a close. Though released, the movement of B.P. Koirala was restricted to the city of Patna in Bihar. The indiscriminate arrests of Nepalis in India was a topic of much concern in the Indian press and parliament. The comments of the press was supplemented by questions raised in the Central Legislature of India regarding the arrests of Nepali nationals like Surya Prasad Upadhyaya and others. But the Government of India evaded the whole issue by saying that the case was subjudice.[37] But as the public opinion in India ran high in favour of the Nepali freedom fighters in India, the British bureaucracy released all those detained in anti-Rana conspiracy; but restricted their movements within the city of their residence. The action taken by the Government of India against the British subjects of Nepali origin and those whose Nepali identity could not be established was limited.[38]

There were occasions when the Government of India permitted the Nepali secret service agents to trace anti-Rana

36. See the papers forwarded by the External Affairs Dept. of the GI in a despatch from G.L. Betham to *Maharaja* Juddha, May 10, 1943, File No. A 14, *Gha, ibid.*
37. See questions raised in the Central Legislature of India on Surya Prasad Upadhyaya and others. A letter from G.A. Falconer to *Maharaja* Juddha, Nov. 11, File No. A 14, *Ga, ibid.*
38. The restriction orders of GI of Jan. 1945, thus, released B.P. Koirala, Santabir Lama, Rajeshwari Prasad, S.B. Gyawali and Dharanidhar Sharma, who were under detention from periods varying from ten months to two years. See "Statement of Actions Taken by the Government of India Against persons involved in Anti-Rana Cases", See a letter from G.A. Falconer to *Maharaja* Juddh, File No. A, *Kha, ibid.*

agitators in India. An agreement reached between the two governments as early as November 1941 permitted Nepali officers to trace two most wanted Nepali conspirators — Mukunda Nath Sharma and Shanker Prasad Sharma. However, the Government of India imposed two restrictions that very much restricted their operations. First, they had to work in close cooperation with the special branch of police of the province in which they were operating. Secondly, if they succeeded in tracing the suspects they were required to telegraph to the External Affairs Department direct or through the Government of India. It was only after the fulfilment of this process the Government of India would issue instructions to the Provincial governments to effect their arrest.[39] As an index to continued cooperation between the governments by July 1942 two Nepali secret agents *Subba* Prem Bahadur Thapa and Ditha Lok Bahadur Chetri were working in close collaboration with the J.P. and I.P. Deputy Commissioners of Police in Calcutta. They had taken with them a letter of introduction to E.E.S. Fairweather, the Commissioner of Police in Calcutta from the British Minister in Nepal. The letter made it clear they were on a mission to trace two dangerous suspects in India—Mukunda Nath Sharma and Shanker Prasad Sharma.[40]

The British in an effort to please the Ranas during the exigencies of the war period even went to the extent of intercepting many letters from the Nepali individuals and handing them over to the Nepal Government. To institutionalize this process, the Government of India decided to introduce a limited censorship of mail passing to and fro from Nepal via Raxaul, Farbisgang, and Nautanwa post offices.* Some of these letters were in code languages, thus, it becomes very difficult if not impossible to deciphere the real message. An extract from a letter intercepted

39. A letter from G.L. Betham to *Maharaja* Juddha, Nov. 25, 1941, E. 6, *Poka* No. 11, File No. A 14, *Na*, FMAN.
40. See a copy letter of introduction by the Minister Geoffery Betham to the Secret Agents of Nepal, July 5, 1942, File No. 14, *Gha, ibid.*

* See a letter from G.L. Betham to *Bada Kazi*, Nov. 30, 1942, *Basta* No. 79, FMAN.

by the Government of the United Provinces on June 11, 1941 may be taken as illustrative.

> My letter might have been miscarried otherwise I would have replied to it. A few days before I left Lucknow you had told me to get a fish from Madras. Now the fish must be with you, and you had promised to get that fish up to Raxaul for me. I have not heard about those fishes.... What about that.. If you are willing to arrange I will send my man to Raxaul.[41]

However, there were many occasions when the letters intercepted by the British Government and handed over to the *Maharaja* had a direct baring on the activities of the Nepali freedom fighters in their self-imposed exile in India. A letter from Banaras by Kul Nath Lohhani to Dilli Raman Joshi (Regmi) in Naya Tola, Bankipore, Patna can be taken as a perfect example. An excerpt ran:

> I have the pleasure in imparting to you the following piece of news, which will be the cause of no little relief to you. This is the Jn., and a few others (above a dozen and a half) have been set free unconditionally I was informed of it ten days ago. There is no other news except that things are coming back to normal and the apprehensions have definitely abated. Meanwhile H. keeps guarded reserve on all topics. I have not yet saught his advise on future course of action. He does not volunteer any. I have been asked by V to resume the work, which I had to leave this time last year.[42]

41. This is an extract form the letter from Col. Khagendra Bikram Bahadur Rana, Oam Bahal, Kathmandu to Dr. A.P. Singh. Nepali colonel had gone to Lucknow on March 1, 1941. The fish in the letter is a code language. Dr. Ayodhya Prasad Singh was a man of extreme views, a staunch member of Manbendra Nath Roy's Radical Democratic People's Party. File No. 14, *na, ibid.* See also letter confiscated by the British Minister at Kathmandu dated April 22, 1940, from Ram Chandra Vas, Professor, Trichandra College to his Communist friend in Karachi. Register of Secret Letters sent by the *Maharaja* to the British Minister, May 7, 1940 to March 27, 1942.
42. A letter from Kul Nath Lohani, Banaras to D.R. Regmi (Joshi), Bankipore, Patna, Jan 22, 1941. It was intercepted by the GI and handed over to GN, E.No. 6, *Poka* No. 11, File No. 14, *Na,* FMAN.

The Government of India also never hesitated to pass important information concerning anti-Rana activities in Kathmandu Valley itself. Thus, as for example on June 14, 1941 the Government of India passed an important message that referred to an widespread anti-Rana agitation in Kathmandu. To be more specific, the agitators were using a Buddhist stupa situated eight miles from Kathmandu as a headquarter of their activities. It also referred to the sister of Shukra Raj Shastri who was instigating anti-Rana feelings among the women folks of Nepal.[43]

But in spite of all these positive gestures the Government of India made it abundantly clear that the anti-Rana agitators were very unlikely to be repatriated as undesirable aliens unless concrete evidences furnished by the Government of Nepal proved that they had violated the Defence of India Act; and that they were not British subjects. The British Minister to Nepal made this point specifically clear in these carefully chosen words:

> I need hardly emphasize that the Government of India's desire to help Your Highness' Government. I feel confident that Your Highness will appreciate the difficulties that we must inevitably face unless we are armed with substantial proof to meet the public opinion and criticisms in the legislature — particularly at a time present.[44]

The Government of India had by 1945 handed over the three of the requisitioned anti-Rana agitators to the Government of Nepal, namely, the Kharel brothers.[45] But refused to surrender the others either on the ground of their ill health or because of the lack of sufficient evidences for their extradition. The efforts of the Ranas to get the extradition of anti-Rana revolutionaries like Mukunda Nath Sharma, B.P. Koirala, Shanker Prasad Sharma, D.R. Regmi, Dharanidhar Koirala, S.P. Upadhyaya,

43. See Confidential letter from G.L. Betham to *Maharaja* Juddha, June 14, 1941, File No. A 14, *na, ibid.*
44. A letter from G.L. Betham to *Maharaja* Juddha, Jan. 26, 1942, *ibid.*
45. The Kharel Brothers were: Agni Prasad Kharel (Sharma), Bishnu Prasad Kharel (Sharma) and Shri Prasad Kharel (Sharma).

and Surya Bikram Gyawali were frustrated.[46] Thus, there was a point to which the British could go to detect the anti-Rana elements, then could go no more. This ambiguous behaviour of their British friends, the Ranas, never fully understood. They could not see difference between a country that was ruled by law and the one where laws emanated from the lips of the Premier.

Post-War Developments and Oppositional Politics

When man awoke from the nightmare of World War II Europe no longer was the master of world's destiny. Slowy and reluctanty France and England came to realize that there were only two superpowers in the world and they were not one of them. For the people of Asia and Africa a new wave of decolonization was already afoot. They either had gained independence or were on its threashold. One thing was sure: they were "out of control" of the Europeans and were seeking their legitimate place in this sunny planet.[47] As India was counting her days of servitude coming to an end, the Nepalis at home and abroad had become more determined than ever before to uproot the Rana regime in Nepal. But with India's liberation in August 1947 the anti-Rana movement in Nepal received an added momentum. The climate of the time is, perhaps, no where better expressed than in these stirring remarks of a contemporary popular leader, D.R. Regmi:

> With India liberated and heading towards socialist democracy, how can Nepal remain in the grip of family rule? Autocracy would be a misfit and die a natural death in due course and no empire could save it.[48]

As India was on the eve of her independence, her sister Nepal was preparing herself for her first *satyagraha* movement.

46. See a letter from G.A. Falconer to *Maharaja* Juddha Dec. 21, 1944, File No. A 14, *Ga, ibid.*
47. For more on the post-war climate of opinions and trends see Ronald N. Stromberg, *European Intellectual History Since 1789* (New York: Merdith Co., 1968), pp. 273-247.
48. D.R. Regmi, *Nepal* (Banaras: Nepal National Congress, 1948), p. 26.

Satyagraha in fact involves the techniques of non-cooperation as a force to effect change in the heart of the evildoer through the instrument of self-suffering. Her model was Mahatma Gandhi who had launched five relatively successful *satyagraha* campaigns in India: and came to be regarded by the posterity as the author of her independence.[49]

The Satyagraha Movement

The genesis of the *satyagraha* movement in Nepal goes back to the passing of the "Company Kanun" (The Industrial Act),[50] which led to the evolution of an industrial complex in Biratnagar in 1936. Thus, the inevitable historic struggle between the factory workers and the mill owners was set in motion. To use the Marxian terminology the Nepali factory workers sold themselves in piecemeal like a commodity, and, thus, exposed themselves to all the vicissitudes of competition and all the fluctuations of the market. The result was that they became not only an hourly and daily slave of the machine but also of the Rana factory owners and the Rana state oligarchy. Thus, in the absence of trade unions, and factory legislations to protect the conditions of the workers, the condition of the workers in the Biratnagar industrial complex steadily declined. There was no protection of the women and children labourers from long hours of work with heavy machines. What the Rana factory owners had accomplished was to transform the wives and the children of the workers into "articles of commerce and the instruments of labour".[51] Thus, a class struggle between the greedy factory owners and the starving factory workers began.

49. For more on *satyagraha* as a socio-political action see Joan V. Bondurant, *The Conquest of Violence : The Gandhian Philosophy of Conflict* (Berkely: University of California Press, 1969), pp. 36-102; also Norman Brown, *The United States and India and Pakistan* (Cambridge: Harvard University Press, 1967), p. 89.
50. More on the *Company Kanun* see Bhim Bahadur Pandey, *Tes Bakhat ko Nepal* (The Then Nepal) (Kathmandu: CNAS, 1981), pp. 401-406.
51. For this analogy see Karl Marx and Friendrick Engles, "Manifesto of Communist Party", in Louis S., Feuer (ed.), *Marx and Engles: Basic Writings on Political Philosophy* (New York: Doubleday & Co., 1959), pp. 1-41.

The leader of this new of class consciousness in the Biratnagar factory complex was one of its worker; Man Mohan Adhikari, who was also a member of the communist party of India.[52] The struggle against the Rana factory owners began to take shape in the form of strikes and *satyagraha.* It was in March 1947 Man Mohan Adhikari was able to launch a strike in the textile and jute mills of Biratnagar for an indefinite period.[53] The mobilization of 10,000 workers for a common cause was a very impressive show of strength against the mill owners, who were the Nepali ruling elites. Thus, for the first time we see the emergence of the working class who came to feel an identy of interest among themselves as against their rulers and employers. This class did not emerge like the sun or the moon at a fixed date; but was a product of historical evolution that grew along with the capitalistic mode of production in Nepal.[54] The tradition government of Nepal was taken aghast by the rise of "a new power" in the streets of Biratnagar that apparently leapt out of the chimneys of the factories. Not knowing how to handle the new kind of political foment that consisted of mass meetings and demonstrations the *Bada Hakim* (Governor) of Morang could think of no better alternative than to attend their meetings in an effort to persuade them to resume their factory duties. But these honest of efforts of persuasions on the part of the Governor failed to show any impact. The striking workers, however, through their leader Man Mohan Adhikari, insisted on an adequate living wages and improved working conditions before they could return to work.[55]

52. The Communist Party in Nepal came into existence only on September 15, 1949. See *The Manifesto of the Communist Party in Nepal,* September 15, 1949. Author's collection.
53. D.R. Regmi, *A Century of Family Autocracy in Nepal* (Banaras: Nepal National Congress, 1950), p. 195.
54. More on the capitalistic mode of production see Karl Marx, *Capital: A Critique of Political Economy,* Vol. I (Moscow: Progress Publishers, 1977) Chapter I.
55. Man Mohan Adhikari was able to wield a tremendous influence among the workers for he was one among them and, thus, understood their feelings and aspirations, the motives and manifestations of their character.

The successful operation of the strike for about a week had a far reaching impact at all levels of the Nepali society. On the political front, the Nepali Rastriya Congress, which was then only two months old decided to take up the cause of the striking workers as their own. Accordingly, the working president of the Congress as well as the members of the executive arrived at Biratnagar on March 9, 1947.[56] Their first work was to issue an appeal to the Government of Nepal to be sympathetic to the demands of the workers who were on strike. But their appeal was only a cry in the wilderness in the jungles of Morang. The Government of Nepal, far from striving at an amicable political solution decided to crush the voice of the striking workers by their bayonets. Thus, on March 25, 1947 the army fired at a huge procession of workers who were simply shouting for an adequate living, killing three women and wounding many others.[57] This was followed by utter confusion and a mass arrest including that of Man Mohan Adhikari, B.P. Koirala, the members of the congress executive and other striking workers. The *Nepali Rastriya Congress*, with full concurrence with Man Mohan Adhikari issued a strongly worded ultimatum to the Government of Nepal, which asked for immediate release of all those arrested in connection with the strike and the fulfilment of the demands of the workers. Failure to do so would bring the government face to face with the *satyagraha* or the non-cooperation movement. An analysis of the ultimatum shows that it did provide the basis for a face-saving for the government and the mill owners as well as an useful and constructive solution to the problems of the striking workers. In other words it tried to bring a modus vivendi between the two antagonistic classes that came into being with the advent of industrial revolution in Nepal.[58]

56. Devendra Raj Upadhyaya, *A Glimpse of Nepal Under Rana Tyranny* (Calcutta: Nepal National Congress, 1948), p. 6; D.R. Regmi, *A Century of Family Rule in Nepal, op. cit.*, p. 195.
57. Devendra Raj Upadhyaya, *A Glimpse of Nepal Under Rana Tyranny, ibid,* p. 6.
58. *Ibid.*

The Satyagraha in Action

The *Satyagraha* is a technique of political action, which strives to bring about changes within a conflict situation. It in fact consists of adherence to stated truth by non-violent behaviour, which includes self-suffering. The whole thrust of *satyagraha* action is to bring about change by converting the mind of the evil-doer to morality, reason and justice. Since the Government of Nepal closed all avenues of negotiations the oppositional politics in Nepal took a sharp revolutionary turn in the direction of the *satyagraha* movement for the attainment of civil liberties in Nepal. The fulfilment of the demands of the workers was pushed to the periphery as the movement to root out the political culture of the Rana oligarchy was on its making. The operation of the *satyagraha* was carefully selected at five different points: Biratnagar, Illam, Birgang, Janakpur and Kathmandu. The help rendered by the Indian Socialist leader, Ram Manohar Lohiya, was extremely valuable not only during the early stages of the planning but also during the implementation phase as well as equipping the *satyagrahis* with the new moral courage and tools of injunctions. The tools of injunctions laid for the *satyagrahis* were: non-violence, no molestation of the "blacklegs", no dependence upon alms, but self-support through other labour and no surrender, however, long the strike was.[59] The *satyagraha,* which lasted from April to September 1947, scored an unprecedented success all over the country. The most affected area of the *satyagraha* movement was the capital city itself — Kathmandu. The *satyagrahis,* consisting of the young boys and girls, led a procession of 30,000 people in down town Kathmandu. This show of unprecedented strength had the desired effect. Thus, the official and semi-official organizations like the Electricity Department, the Department of Mint and the Nepal Bank and Bir Hospital also joined the striking workers of Biratnagar, for better pay and amenities.[60] *The Hindu,* a daily newspaper from Madras reported :

59. Joan V. Bondurant, *Conquest of Violence: The Gandhian Philosophy of Conflict, op.cit.,* pp. 38-39.
60. *The Hindu,* September 29, 1947, p. 6; also Chandra Bikram Budathoki, History of Democratic Movement in Nepal, 1931-51" (Ph. D. Thesis, Patna University, 1974), pp. 158-60. For a sketch of the movement see also *Yugbani,* April 1, 1948, No. 10, Year 1, p. 26.

> The road and the streets of Kathmandu are deserted and the people have become panicy. The normal civic life has been paralyzed... and the liberal minded Premier is contemplating resignation.[61]

The Government retaliated by mass arrests including the arrest of leaders like Man Mohan Adhikari and B.P. Koirala. Both were taken under a heavy escort to Kathmandu and the journey took a month. As arrests continued, thousands of innocent men and women found themselves breathing in the foul atmosphere of the prisons.[62] The Government also prohibited mass meetings and processions in Kathmandu; but it spread like wild fire to other twin cities of Bhaktapur and Lalitpur. In Kathmandu firey youths like Puspa Lal, Tanka Bilas, Amir Bahadur and five girls defied the prohibitory order and shouted anti-Rana slogans. But some of their slogans were pro-Padma, which gave an opportunity to the rightist faction among the Ranas to speculate on Premier Padma's involvement in the *satyagraha.*[63] But this was only a wishful thinking. The *istihar* that was printed in the *Gorkhapatra* of Baishak 24, 2004 (May 1947) makes the position of the Premier amply clear, it he accused the satyagrahis as being:

> A handful of lawbreakers, who by imitating the tactics of political parties of other countries had indulged in making derogatory speeches from different political platforms and had incited the people to act against the king, country, and the system.[64]

Birganj constituted another important locale of the *satyagraha* campaign. Two distinguished *satyagrahis* were the radical poet Juddha Prasad Mishra and Gopal Prasad Bhattari, a prominent Congress member.[65] They and their colleagues were arrested for organizing a procession in the city and taking an active part

61. *The Hindu,* September 29, 1947, p. 6.
62. See the statement by D.B. Periyar, the secretary of Calcutta branch of Nepal National Congress. *The Hindu,* September 29, 1947, p. 6.
63. D.R. Regmi, *A Century of Family Autocracy in Nepal, op. cit.,* p. 176.
64. *Istihar* in the *Gorkhapatra,* Baishak 24, 2004 (May 1947), p. 1.
65. The other *styagrahis* were: Thakur Kumar Prithvi and Ram Krishna Karki.

in the distribution of anti-Rana pamphlets.[66] The *Bada Hakim* (Governor) of Birganj, thus, imposed a round the clock curfew in the city of Birganj; and armed troops were seen marching in trucks. The border of Birganj with Raxaul of India was also armed with pickets of the regular Gurkha soldiers of the State Army. Thus, all those who entered Nepal from India were thoroughly searched; and the provincial government of Bihar had in cooperation with the Rana Government promulgated the section 144 of the Indian Penal Code, which banned all meetings and processions in sympathy with the *Nepal Rastriya Congress* for fifteen days.[67]

The *satyagraha* did have positive effects. Above all the Rana Government under Premier Padma Shumsher panicked; and promised to introduce reforms in Nepal within twelve days. The part played by Pandit Jawaharlal Nehru was very instrumental in bringing about an acceptable compromise between the Rana Government and the *Nepal Rastriya Congress.* The result was that the acting president of the *Nepal National Congress* suspended the *satyagraha* movement in Nepal. But since reforms did not come in twelve days the *satyagraha* movement lingered on.[68] The constitutional reforms promised by Premier Padma came only on January 26, 1948.[69] But as the reforms made no change in the prorogative of the Premier or the hereditary rights of the Ranas, the reforms proved to be merely a hoax or an eye-wash. So the country had to prepare for a new wave of struggle.

The *satyagraha* movement launched by the political opposition in Nepal did score a meaningful victory. It brought a totalitarian government of the Ranas on the path of reforms. It also gave to the people a sense of their latent power and made them realize that even a mighty despot was a "paper tiger" and had to yield

66. See "Nepal ka Dainiya Jail-Jivan" (The Miserable Prison-Life in the Nepali Prisons), *Sansar,* November 27, 1947, p. 8.
67. *The Hindu,* June 4, 1947, p. 4.
68. Devendra Raj Upadhyaya, *A Glimpse of Nepal Under Rana Tyranny, op.cit.,* p. 7; Balachandra Sharma, *Nepal ko Itihasik Rup Rekha* (An Outline of the History of Nepal) (Banaras: Krishna Kumari, 1976), p. 413.
69. More on the reforms see *Gorkhapatra,* January 27, 1948, p. 1.

to the popular will of the people. However, events moved in the direction little anticipated by the Nepali revolutionaries. The limited reforms announced by the government were an anathema for the rightist faction of the Ranas led by the *Mukhtiyar*, Mohan Shumsher. Thus as the intra-family feud intensified *Maharaja* Padma Shumsher, who was crowned on November 30, 1946 decided to relenquish his office and live as a reculse in Rachi where the Bihar Government had alloted 25 acres of land to raise a building.[70] The new Premier *Maharaja* Mohan Shumsher shelved the reforms of his predecessor and decided to rule Nepal with an iron fist like his father.[71] Though the *Nepali Rastriya Congress* rejected the reforms as inadequate to meet the legitimate aspirations of the people for a popular government, yet, a group of determined youths in Kathmandu Valley decided to use the institutional framework provided by the reforms of 1948 to establish "the rule of the people". Thus, they organized themselves into a party called *Prajapanchyat*.

The Prajapanchyat Party

The quiet exit of Premier Padma from the political horizon of Nepal sounded a death knell for the future politics of reforms in Nepal. So a moderate section of middle class in Kathmandu Valley organized themselves under the banner of the *Prajapanchyat* Party. The chief architects of this new political organization were: Dharma Ratna Yemi, Tripubar Singh, Gopal Prasad Rimal and Vijaya Bahadur Malla.[72] The youths of Kathmandu Valley enrolled in thousands,[73] which was an index to the rise in

70. *The Hindu*, January 28, 1948, p. 5.
71. For more on the accession of Premier Mohan see Statesman May 1, 1948; also an article entitled "Nepal's New Prime Minister His Highness *Maharaja* Mohan Shumsher Jang Bahadur Rana", *Amritbazar Patrika*, May 1, 1948; a Communique issued by Nepali Consulate General in Calcutta on April 30, 1948, E.No. 8, *Poka* No. 3, Fiie No. 907, *Kha*.
72. The other members of the organization were: Surya Bahadur "Peba" (Bhaktapur) Kesheb Bhaju and Bishnu Bhakta (Patan), Joshi Das Amatya and Nara Bahadur (Kathmandu).
73. It enlisted 900 volunteers from Bhaktapur, 700 from Patan and 700 from Kathmandu. See Dharma Ratna Yemi, *Nepal Ka Kura*, *op.cit.*, p. 259.

popularity of the organization. B.P. Koirala, being puzzled and confused by the rapid increase in popularity of the *Prajapanchyat Party,* attempted to explain the new phenomenon to the sweep of communist wave in Kathmandu Valley. This he thought to be very dangerous to the country and the royal family.[74] But as the *Prajapanchyatists* scored significant success in their oppositions against the Rana rule B.P. Koirala was compelled to soften his attitude and even asserted that the party of the *Prajapanchyat* was a foram of the Congress. One of his trusted colleague Ganesh Man Singh saw no difference between the *Prajapanchyat* and the Congress when he said that *satyagraha* movement launched by the former was in fact the work of the Congress.[75]

It was on the day of *Vijaya Dasami* Kartik 2005 (October 1948) the Prajapanchyat was inaugurated by Hira Devi.[76] The newly born organization outlined three objectives in its struggle against the despotic government. The first objective was to establish a government by law, which was to be in accordance with the *Baidhanik Kanun* as announced by the Rana Premier himself. Second, while agitating for the rule of law, they would not deviate from the provisions set forth by the constitution itself. Finally, its immediate objective was to establish a responsible government.[77] While defining its objectives, it also made it clear that the new party had nothing to do with the *Nepali Rastriya Congress.*[78]

Thus, eight years after the suppression of the *Prajaparisad* movement a political organization was born in Nepal, whose line of tactics and operation was far more moderate than its historic predecessor. It is true that in October 1940 a group of moderate intellectuals like Kamaksha Devi, Pushpa Lal Shrestha, and Prem Bahadur Kansakar did organize themselves into a "*Prajatantra Sangh* so as to continue the work of the *Prajaparisad.* But this organization could not make any headway due to the

74. *Ibid.*
75. *Ibid.*, 259-61.
76. Hira Devi was the wife of Dharma Ratna Yemi. The inaugural meeting was chaired by Tripubar Singh.
77. D.R. Regmi, *A Century of Family Autocracy in Nepal; op.cit.*, p. 227.
78. D.R. Regmi, *A Century of Family Autocracy in Nepal, op.cit.*, p. 222.

political climate of the time. The *Prajapanchyat Party,* thus, decided to go to the people and use mass-participation as a means to agitate against the Rana Government. An important decision taken by the party was to launch a *satyagraha* campaign in Nepal. B.P. Koirala, who was at the time in Kathmandu, attempted to dissuade the new party from launching the movement, for, the Congress was preparing to commence an armed struggle against the Ranas. But his advice went unheeded. So action committees were set up in the three cities of the Kathmandu Valley as well as other parts of the country. Dharm Ratna Yemi was despatched to Raxaul in India to open an office to facilitate the *satyagraha* campaign.[79] By the beginning of December 1948 the *satyagraha* movement was in full swing.

The noted *satyagrahi,* Vijaya Bahadur Malla, delivered a speech before a mass of 500 people. Speeches from the pulpits were novelties of the time so in spite of prohibitory orders people flocked in thousands to listen to their leaders. The notification of the police prohibited them but the constitution gave the freedom of expression. The then Rana Government was therefore operating under such contradictions. The feelings in Kathmandu, thus, ran very high, and the atmosphere was tense.[80] Repression of the Government soon followed. Over two hundred persons were arrested in Kathmandu Valley for taking part in the *satyagraha* campaign. The objective of the *satyagraha* was to establish civil liberties in Nepal.[81] But the movement was nipped at its budding stage, as the Rana Government was able to put its principal leaders behind the bars. The failure of the *Prajapanchyat* made two things clear. First, the Rana oligarchy inspite of its rhetoric on reforms was in no mood for a peaceful transfer of power to the people. Secondly, it convinced the Nepali revolutionaries that an anti-Rana movement could not be launched from within.

79. Dharma Ratna Yemi, *Nepal Ka Kura, op.cit.,* p. 260.
80. D.R. Regmi, *A Century of Family Autocracy in Nepal, op.cit.,* p. 223.
81. *The Hindu,* December 13, 1948, p. 4.

5

THE DYNAMICS OF "THE REVOLUTION" : 1950-1951

> The revolutionary is a doomed man. He has no interest, no affairs, no feelings, no habits, no property, not even a name. Everything in him is wholly absorbed by a single exclusive interest, a single thought, a single passion — the revolution.... He is an implacable enemy of this world and if he continues to inhabit it, it is only to destroy it more effectively.
>
> **M.A. Bakunin, S.G. Nechaev[1]**

Few words have been subjected to more conflicting interpretations than the term revolution. The reason being that it carries different meaning in different context. It is sometimes used to denote the overthrow of a regime that is outdated, rotten and corrupt. At times the expression revolution implies cultural, intellectual and industrial changes of far reaching consequences. Perhaps, the greatest revolution that ever took place in the history of mankind was his departure from his

1. Basil Dmytryshyan (ed.), "Catechism of a Revolutionary "(History of Nachaev Affair" in Imperial Russia: A Source Book, 1700-1917) (New York: Holt, Rinehart and Winston, 1967), p. 241.

primate state of being to his enlightened manhood.[2] In Nepal "the revolution" of 1950-51 resulted in the overthrow of a political culture that had guided the destiny of a government and society for a little over a century.

Revolutions are rare in history specially when compared with wars, natural calamities and economic depressions. There is also a tendency among historians to give the label of a revolution to minor historical events like the Indian Sepoy Mutiny of 1857 and the battle of Plassey of 1757.[3] However, a Marxist would even look down upon the French Revolution as a bourgeois revolution for as Lenin argues "without a revolutionary theory there can be no revolutionary movement".[4] While viewed in the light of the Russian or the French Revolution one could very easily remove the lebel of revolution from events that occurred in Nepal in the period between 1950-51. A characteristic feature of any revolution is that it makes a distinct departure from the past. A revolution, thus, occurs when all efforts to preserve the existing order fails and forces of disequilibrium in the society triumph over the forces of equilibrium. It is at this point that a nation steps into the shoes of a revolution.[5] It is true that the Nepali revolution was not a turning point in modern civilization but it was nevertheless a

2. The crossing of the "rubbicon" from the "animal" state to "human" state of existence is a riddle to many minds. To some it is the kindling of the fire, to other it is the emergence of man as a tool maker and to some it is the development of the speech area in the brain that brought this revolution. See, Miles Burkitt, *The Old Stone Age: A Study in Palaeolitic Times* (Calcutta: Rupa & Co.,1963). pp. 3-5.
3. Philip Woodruff sees the battle of Plassey as the revolution in Bengal while to V.D. Savarkar the "Mutiny" of 1857 was India's first revolution against the British. See Philip Woodruff, *The Men Who Ruled India: The Founders* (New York: Schocken Books, 1964), pp.93-103; Savarkar, Vinaya Damodar, Barrister, *The Indian War of Independence of 1857, by an Indian Nationalist* (London : Publisher N.K., 1909), pp. 451, vii.
4. Progress Publishers, VI. Lenin: Selected Works, Vol. II (Moscow: Progress Publishers, 1975), pp.155-166.
5. More on the nature of the revolution see Crane Brinton. *The Anatomy of Revolution* (New York: Prentice-Hall, Inc., 1952).

"revolution" in a very limited sense that it brought a change of one government by another.[6]

If we are to believe in the doctrine of historicism* all things that are born are subject to death and decay, so all powerful empires and absolute governments must one day come to an end. Likewise the Rana regime in Nepal went through a phase of metamorphosis from birth to old age and finally became extinct. Now the question that naturally arises is : when did the Rana regime show signs of decline? It is difficult to pinpoint at the period in which the Rana oligarchy began to show cracks in its regime.

One could convincingly argue that the Rana regime began to show signs of decline during the rule of its founder—*Maharaja* Jang Bahadur. Some would like to attribute the fall of the Rana regime in Nepal to the repressive policies of Premier Juddha Shumsher; while others would even detect the signs of the decline of the Rana regime in Nepal in the days of the powerful Premier Chandra, when the Rana regime had attained its full adolescence. As the Chinese proverb goes "the moon begins to wane when it is the fullest". Similarly the Rana regime began to show some cracks on its monolith during the life of Premier Chandra. It was in the first quarter of twentieth century we witness two significant changes in the political culture of Nepal, namely, the growth of a revolutionary intelligentsia and the institutionalization of criticisms against Rana autocracy.

6. In the eyes of a Jesuit educator F.W. Rawding the revolution of 1950-51 was a movement "to establish the Shah Dynasty in place of usurper Rana oligarchy", see F.W. Rawding, Thirty Five Years of Jesuit Education in Nepal : 1951-1986 in *St. Xavier's Godavari, 1951-1986 :Anniversary Souvenir*, 35 April 1986, p. 39. A scholar like D.R. Regmi looks upon the events of 1950-51 as the replacement of Ranacracy with the "king's autocratic rule with a shadow of democracy". See D.R. Regmi, *Wither Nepal* (Kathmandu: Publisher N.K., 1952), p. 104.

* The belief that history can unlock the present, past and future is known as historicism, or in other words future is determined by the nature of past events. See Lewis S. Feuer (ed.), *Marx and Engles: Basic Writings on Politics and Philosophy* (New York: Doubleday & Co., 1959), pp.47-67.

Another important question that perplexes our fancy is the question : was the "revolution" of 1950-51 mostly a series of blunders or a long postponed necessities. One could argue after Edmund Burke the Nepali revolutionaries of 1950-51 were neophytes, incompetent and dangerous neophytes, who were moving from the arena known precepts to the unknown. They were trying to escape from the established customs and beliefs into the boiling cauldron of anarchy and brutality.[7] A contemporary observer remarks:

> The old order had collapsed. The new one had not been established. Beset with immense difficulties, the Rana-Congress coalition could find solution to none. It could either restore or establish anything. It gave to the Nepalese neither order nor liberty....The new rulers had no conception of government, how to administer, how to plan and how to progress.[8]

The new rulers may have been neophytes or impractical zealots but they were heirs to a new tradition of freedom in all forms—freedom from arbitrary power, freedom of speech, freedom to realize one's talent, freedom of aesthetic response and the freedom of an individual to choose his own destiny in the world. They were quite different from their Rana colleagues who were heirs to an outmoded system bent on "upholding a blood thirsty regime of oppression".[9] It is difficult to see how the Ranas, who had shut themselves in a shell of traditional conservatism, could embrace the sweeping changes that were altering the face of the world in the second half of the twentieth century. Once the "revolution" of 1950-51 picked up its momentum, it began to express in the idioms and language of the twentieth century democracy: "power of the masses", "popular representation", "constituent assembly" and "fundamental human rights". The Ranas could not accommodate themselves with this new mode of thinking. Thus, Mohan

7. Edmund Burke, Reflections on the French Revolution, Works (4th ed.) (Boston: Little Brown & Co., 1871), pp. 276-348.
8. Francis Tucker, *Gorkha: The Story of the Gurkhas of Nepal*, (London: Constable and Co., 1957), pp. 263-64.
9. Tony Hagen, *Nepal: The Kingdom in the Himalayas* (New Delhi: Oxford and IBH Publishers, 1980), p. 91.

Shumsher, when he resigned under the force of circumstances painfully declared that his days were over and could not stand on the way of progressive forces that were destined to lead the country to a bright future.[10]

The Origins of "the Revolution" of 1950-51

Though the sowing of the seeds of the revolution of 1950-51 can be traced to the foment of the Nepali intelligentsia in the first quarter of this century, yet, the flowering of this revolutionary tradition took place throughout the decades of 1930s and 1940s. The immediate setting was, however, provided by the birth of the Nepali Congress on April 9, 1950. Two revolutionary, but opposing line of actions were charted by the newly born organization. Although, its covert program was to launch "an armed revolution" in Nepal, yet, overtly it continued to give lipservice to the non-violent and democratic nature of the struggle. It was the limited utility of the tool of the *satyagraha* in bringing the Ranas to their heels that compelled the Nepali Congress to rely more and more on its military strategies. However, the period between October, 1948 to April, 1950 was a period of utter confusion in choosing the methods of operations among the Nepali opposition leaders in India. This confusion was partly due to the acute division among the Nepali political leaders but it was primarily due to the lack of sheer vision in the leadership.

However, the Nepali Congress continued to develop its strategy of "revolution", though with less vigor and enthusiasm than in the *satyagraha* period. Accordingly, on October 12, 1948, B.P. Koirala, the working president of the Nepali National Congress, went on a secret mission to Kathmandu to strengthen the network of the Congress organization. In this mission, the Congress leader was helped by two of his trusted aids: Krishna Prasad Upadhyaya and Kedar Man Byathit. A month later B.P. Koirala was arrested and kept in chains under strict surveillance in the residence of the Premier himself. But as the plight of the political prisoners in Nepal did not differ from that of first degree murders, B.P. Koirala decided to go on hunger strike for

10. *The Hindu*, November 17,1951, p. 4.

the better living conditions of the political detinues in Nepal.[11] Then as the hunger strike gained its maturity the fast, deteriorating health of the Congress leader began to draw an increasing attention of the World Press. This mounting international public opinion prompted the Indian Premier Jawaharlal Nehru to negotiate his release from the Nepali jail.[12]

The Government of Nepal, however, took this occasion to issue a press note, which declared illegal all the activities of the "self-styled" Nepali National Congress, throughout the country of Nepal. Among other, it specifically accused the Congresites for sowing the seeds of hatred among the civil servants, the military and among different sections of the Nepali community.[13] A Note of the Department of Foreign Affairs further added that the number of Congressmen arrested in the year 1949 were 107.[14] The Nepali Congress also reacted to the repressive measures of the government in two ways: first, by accelerating the campaign of the *satyagraha* into the remote hilly regions of the West and secondly, by infiltrating revolutionary commandos in different parts of the country.

By March 1950, the plans for launching a mass *satyagraha* movement was already afoot. As the middle of May approached, the Nepali Congress successfully launched the *satyagraha* movement in the western hills. The Ranas were determined to teach the *satyagrahis* a lesson, thus, instructed the *Bada Hakims* (district governors) "to deal severely with the Nepali Congress leaders".[15] Many of the governors followed the instructions from the center literally. In Western Nepal, military contingents were posted at different points where the *satyagraha* movement was in full swing. It was at Sanja and Nawakot the *satyagraha* movement was on full swing. The result was that the military

11. See the statement by Balachandra Sharma, General Secretary, Nepal National Congress, *The Hindu*, January 4, 1949, p. 6.
12. Balachandra Sharma, *Nepal ko Itihasik Rup Rekha* (An Outline of the History of Nepal) (Banaras: Krishna Kumari, 1976), p. 394.
13. *The Statesman*, April 18, 1948, p. 5.
14. See the file entitled "Nepali Congress Arrested in the year 2005/1949" E.No.2, *Poka* No. 79, File No. 363,2005/1949, FMAN.
15. *The Hindu*, July 2, 1950, p. 7.

resorted to firing. This brutal episode left four casualties behind: two died subsequently including a woman and two were severely wounded. The *satyagrahis* did pay a heavy price but they were successful in moulding the psychology of the local populace in Western Nepal to such an extent that most of them refused to pay taxes to the government. The demonstration of the peasants in the remote areas like Palahi and Palpa is also indicative of the effectiveness of the *satyagraha* campaigns. Though the Government of Nepal had arrested the local leaders and outlawed forty-five important Congress workers, yet, B.P. Koirala, who visited the areas incognito found "the morale of the people very high and they were putting up a brave resistance to the repressive and terrorist tactics of the government".[16]

As the living conditions in the different jails of Nepal continued to be unbearable many political prisoners went on hunger strikes. But the Rana Government stood deaf ear to these vehement voices of protests. The result was a detenu, Krishna Prasad Sharma, who had gone in hunger strike since July 24 passes away peacefully inside the Malangwa jail on August 15, 1950.* Earlier, as the health of the political detinues steadily declined, the president of the Nepali National Congress, Matrika Prasad Koirala, appealed to the Government of India to use its influence over the Rana Government "to stress upon the human approach to the problem of the political prisoners in Nepal".[17]

The penetration of its armed commandos in different parts of the country was a part of its comprehensive strategy package of the Nepali Congress. A part of the package program was unveiled by the Nepali Congress in its declaration that was printed in thousands both in Hindi and Nepali. The gist of the declaration was to establish a responsible government in Nepal "through an armed revolution".[18] As a part of the Congress

16. *Ibid.*
  * See *The Hindu*, "Detenu Dies in Nepal Jail", August 17, 1950, p. 3.
17. Statement of M.P. Koirala, August 9, 1950. See *The Hindu*, July 11, 1950, p. 4.
18. For the declaration of the leaflet in Nepali see the collections of the author.

program of the infiltration of the commandos within Nepal, the most delicate and dangerous mission was assigned to Ganesh Man Singh.[19] He was the leader of a three member team* that was deputed to fulfil the commando mission in the capital city. By October 1950 Ganesh Man Singh and his colleagues had already crossed the Indo-Nepal border via Thori. They had with them one complete wireless kit, a mimeograph machine, one stein gun, two revolvers and strips of T.N.T., and a few boxes containing ammunitions.[20] However, at Thori a contingent of the border security guards under the command of C.P. Purush Dhakal was able to capture Ganesh Man Singh and his two other colleagues. The governor of Birganj lost no time in declaring Ganesh Man Singh and his colleagues as "dangerous bandits" and immediately despatched them to Kathmandu. But as Ganesh Man Singh and his friends were crossing the Chanda Giri Pass, a rumour was in the air in Kathmandu that a mob was ready to set free the Congress Leader and his colleagues. Thus, the Ranas made it sure that a busload of armed contingent escorted the Congress neophytes.[21]

19. Ganesh Man Singh was born a rebell. During his boyhood, when he was a *nausinda*, a clerk in the Rana bureaucracy, Ganesh Man was imprisoned for sketching a catoon of Premier Juddha Shumsher on the reverse (head upside down). The message was clear, namely Juddha was undergoing that kind of punishment for the atrocities he had committed against his people. Interview with Upendra Purush Dhakal, the Private Secretary of Premier Mohan. September 18, 1965, Kathmandu.

* The three membered team consisted of Ganesh Man Singh, Sunder Raj Chalisey and another Congress worker.

20. See the statement by Ganesh Man Singh before a special tribunal on the month of December 1950. The members of the Tribunal were: Brigadier Colonel Jhulendra Bikram Rana (Chairman), Sardar Som Prasad Upadhyaya, Sardar Bupa Dhoj Karki, Mir Subba Mahendra Bahadur Mahat and Subba Min Bahadur Thapa. See E. No 6, *Poka* No 11, File No. A 14, *Chha*.

21. Interview with Chetra Pratayendra Purush Dhakal, who was not only instrumental in the capture of Ganesh Man Singh and his colleagues but as the inspector of police accompanied the political captives from Thori to Singha Durbar. Interview with C.P. Purush Dhakal, November 8, 1984, Kathmandu.

As early as the beginning of October, 1950 the Rana Government was fully aware of the penetration of the armed commandos inside Nepal whose objective was to create anarchic conditions by killings, loot and sabotage.[22] The Government of Nepal, thus, lost no time in communicating to the Government of India the export by the Nepali Congress of terrorist commandos from India as a part of their overall conspiracy to overthrow the Rana oligarchy from Nepal. A letter from the Government of Nepal to the Indian Charged' Affaires further spoke of the entry of one group of conspirators whose aim was to "attempt to take the life of His Highness *Maharaja*, His leading members of the government; and in blowing up of government offices including the treasury, Thimi Arms and Ammunition Department and other important strategic buildings".[23] The gist of the letter was to remind the Government of India that it was high time that it stamped down with a heavy foot the terrorist groups who were operating from the Indian soil to blow the bastion of the Rana oligarchy. The reply given by the Indian Charged' Affaires of October 7, 1950, however, challenged the "conspiracy hypothesis" so carefully formulated by the Government of Nepal on the ground that it was almost exclusively based upon forced extractions of the statements given by the Congress detinues. The forceful letter in part ran:

> The Government of India will not hesitate to deal with persons committing acts of terrorism, but all actions of the Government of India has to be according to the laws of the land otherwise they will be challenged in the law courts and the Government of India will be placed in an embarrassing position.... The Government of India sincerely hopes that the Government of Nepal will appreciate their difficulty and will not regard their inability to take immediate

22. See statement given by Krishna Bahadur alias Kali Driver before the Special Tribunal, Aswin 11, 12, 2007 (October 1950); Statement by Sunder Raj Chalisey before the Special Tribunal Aswin 11-23 (October 1950); also a letter from Bijaya Shumsher, Director General Foreign Affairs, to Dr. S. Gupta, Charge D' Affaires, October 3, 1950. E. No 6. *Poka* No. 11, File No. A 14, *Chha*, 1945.
23. Two letter from Bijaya Shumsher to S. Gupta, October 3, 5, 1950, *ibid*.

> actions without adequate evidences as denoting any lack of concern on their part of the alleged conspiracy.[24]

The message imparted by the letter was clear and simple: the Ranas had to rely on its own news in dealing with the anti-Rana conspiracy; and the help they could except from the Government of India in this regard was at best the very minimum. As the "conspiracy cloud" continued to hover over the minds of the Ranas, the Nepali Congress thought it prudent to clarify its official view point in this matter. Thus, its statement of September 30, 1950 made it clear that the Nepali Congress was against all acts of individual terrorism for it would only isolate them from the people in their struggle of liberating their country from the Rana oligarchy. The Nepali Congress, however, in a few carefully chosen words did not hesitate to rule out the conspiracy tactics that could be underway by other groups of freedom-fighters. To quote:

> The policy of the Nepali Congress has always been a non-violent struggle for democracy. But we cannot expect all Nepalese fighting for democracy to share our views alongside with us. So if some of them are found carrying weapons and take recourse to armed combats, we are not to be blamed.[25]

The Drama of "The Revolution": The Curtain Falls Quickly

The very idea of "armed struggle" of the Nepali Congress was incompatible with the vision of Pandit Jawaharlal Nehru. He was convinced that any violent upheaval in Nepal would only pave the way for the communist take-over of the Himalaya region. As the year 1950 unfolded, Nehru became increasingly aware of the fact that "Tibet was a lost cause" so political developments in Nepal had to be carefully watched, influenced and even controlled.[26] It was national interest and national

24. A letter from S. Gupta to Bijaya Shumsher , October 7, 1950, *ibid.*
25. Joint Statement by Subarna Shumsher and Hiranya Shumsher in Calcutta, September 30, 1950, *Search Light*, October 2, 1950, p. 4.
26. More on the Chinese build up in Tibet see the statement by the Nepali consulate, Calcutta, March 27, 1950, E. No. 2, *Poka* No. 11, File No. A 1, *Chha*, FMAN.

security that compelled Nehru to become an advocate of peace and stability in the Himalayan region. Accordingly, India entered into the Treaty of "Peace and Friendship" with Nepal, which was signed in Kathmandu on July 31, 1950 and was subsequently ratified by the two governments.[27] The treaty gave ample room for Indian countermanoeuvres in case of Chinese moves in Nepal.

However, the Socialist Party in India decided to lend full support to the Nepali Congress in its final "armed struggle" against the Ranas. But the concept of "armed struggle" brought the Nepali Congress face to face with a series of intricate problems: how to organize an army of revolutionary commandos? How to acquire the weapons and how to transfer them to the sites of insurrection? The picture of the "armed struggle" was more or less drawn into the vortex of reality when Bhola Chatterji an Indian Socialist militant revolutionary took up the cause of Nepal as his own. His visit to Nepali Congress camp at Biratnagar in July 1950 filled him with hopes as well, as despair. If the sight of a small contingent of "liberation army", consisting of ex-military and ex-police men roused in him some hopes, yet, as the contingent was virtually unarmed he was in despair.[28] He was, however, encouraged by the fact that the nucleus of a

27. Article 2 of the Treaty of "Peace and Friendship" of 1950 made it mandatory for both the governments "to inform each other of any serious friction or misunderstanding with any neighbouring state likely to cause any breech of faith in the friendly relation subsisting between the two governments". For a full text of the treaty see *The Hindu*, July 31, 1950, pp. 48. However, the letters of exchange that accompanied the treaty — that was kept a top secret till 1959 — took the mandate still further by requiring both the governments to "consult with each other and devise effective countermeasures" in case of foreign aggression". See Jawaharlal Nehru, *India's Foreign Policy: Selected Speeches* 1946—April 1961 (New Delhi: Ministry of Information, 1961), p. 374.
28. The contingent had with them only a few automatic pistols, three or four revolvers, a dozen of stein guns and a number of outdated Lee-Enfield rifles that were introduced by the British in the Indian army in the 1850's. See Bhola Chaterji, *A Study in Recent Nepalese Politics* (Calcutta: The World Free Press, 1967), pp. 30.

revolutionary army was there. As the supply of arms could not be got from New Delhi, Bhola Chatterji decided to use the India socialist connection with the Burmese Socialist Government to procure arms for the Nepali "revolution". He, thus, took with him two letters of introduction from Jaya Prakash Narayan and flew to Rangoon to meet the Burmese Minister of Defence and the Minister of Religious Affairs. The Burmese gesture was positive. It was on October 31, 1950, Burma gave its consent to deliver its first consignment of arms to the Nepali Congress. Accordingly, a chartered Decota of Himalayan Aviation landed in Burma, and sealed boxes were loaded in the aircraft. The whole operation was completed within thirty minutes. The Decota then made a safe landing in the Bhita airport of Bihar — a site abandoned for aviation since the close of World War II.[29]

Once the arms arrived a comprehensive plan for an "armed struggle" had to be drafted at length. A steady flow of recruits for the "revolutionary army" had to be sought and careful attention had to be given to their indoctrination. The consensus on "armed revolution" arrived at the conference of Nepali Congress on September 26-27, 1950 at Bairganiya, India, had to be meticulously worked out.[30] It was finally decided that the armed struggle was to be launched simultaneously in three different sectors: the hilly region was entrusted to G.B. Yakthumba, Ram Prasad Rai, Hapa Gurung and Narad Muni Thrung; the eastern terai was under the command of Koirala and Giri brothers, and Mahendra Narayan Nidhi; while the western terai under the charge of Dr. K. I. Singh, Mahendra Bikram Singh, Balachandra Sharma, Tek Bahadur Panthi and Ram Baran Sharma.[31] The revolt was originally scheduled for August, then for September; but had to be postponed due to the difficulty in obtaining arms.

29. *Ibid,*. pp. 81-95.
30. For more on Bairganiya resolution see Balachandra Sharma, *Nepal Ko Itihasik Rup Rekha, op.cit.*, p. 415.
31. Dharma Ratna Yemi, *Nepal ka Kura (Samischhatmak Itihas* (The Happenings of Nepal: A Critical History) (Kathmandu: Yemi Prakashan, 1957), p. 280.

As the first week of November 1950 approached, the Nepali Congress had completed the plans for "armed struggle"; and the liberation army was only waiting for orders to strike at the opportune hour. It was at this critical juncture another silent, yet, an interesting development was taking place in the Narahity Royal Palace of Kathmandu. King Tribhuvan, taking advantage of the gathering storm of anti-Rana movement in and outside Nepal, had been increasing defying the authority of the Ranas. The conflict between the Premier and the King became so intense that at one stage it was reported that Premier Mohan made an unsuccessful attempt to force King Tribhuvan to abdicate in favour of the Crown Prince. But as pressure continued to mount, King Tribhuvan felt that his life in the nation's capital was not safe, so plans for the exit from Kathmandu were afoot. Two options were available to him. One was to go to Palpa in Western Nepal. A meticulous scheme associated with the Royal flight for Palpa was prepared in advance. Accordingly, it is said that Rudra Shumsher had come to Kathmandu as a *sadhu* (holy person) to materialize the secret scheme.[32] But as the difficulties associated with the scheme were so many that it had to be abandoned on technical grounds. Another secret, yet, a feasible move that was underway was to seek asylum in the Indian Embassy at Kathmandu and then leave the country. The Bengali Physician Shusil Chand Halder as well as the Swiss nurse Erika Leuchtag played an important role in the negotiations between the King and the Indian Ambassador. It is difficult to understand why Pandit Nehru, who had a few months ago had concluded a Treaty of "Peace and Friendship" with the Rana oligarchy should decide to champion the cause of King Tribhuvan. Two important considerations apparently motivated the Prime

32. The author was able to obtain this information from a very reliable source: and see for himself the picture of Rudra Shumsher dressed as a Hindu *sadhu*. King Tribhuvan was so grateful to Rudra Shumsher that he awarded him with the title of Field Marshal. The sons of Rudra were made governors of the Western provinces; and four being political sufferers each son was rewarded a forest worth 10,000 rupees each. See *Rastriya Congress Bulletins* No. 29, Bhadra 6, 2008 (August 1951), p.4; also Rastriya Congress Bulletin No. 58, Jesth 10, 2009 (May 1952), p. 4.

Minister of India to alter his stand. First, the sixth sense of Pandit Nehru convinced him that weaker Tribhuvan served as a better protector of India's national interest in the Himalayan region; and second, the exit of Rana oligarchy in Nepal would also remove the last bastion of British influence in South Asia, which was to India's advantage.

It was on the sixth of November 1950, King Tribhuvan, on a plea to go for a picnic at the Nagarjun Grove, loaded over half a dozen steel trunks with valuables, and left the Royal Palace with the members of the Royal family. The Royal family drove straight to Sital Niwas, the then chancery as well as the residence of the Indian Envoy. As soon as the Royal fleet of automobiles entered the Embassy of India, the main gate was closed. It was late in the afternoon that the All India Radio flashed the news that the King of Nepal had sought asylum in the Indian Embassy. Two concrete evidences are available to us to indicate how the Indian Ambassador in Kathmandu beautifully engineered this episode. First, the Indian Military Attache was at the gate with keys in his hand to lock the gate as soon as the last car of the Royal fleet entered the Embassy compound. Secondly, in the conversation between the Indian Ambassador C.P.N. Singh and Premier Nehru that was heard in the Nepali Radio sets at Kathmandu, Nehru praised the Envoy for his successful achievement. The Ambassador then triumphantly replied "Panditjee! ap bachterahia aise kam bahut karunge" or in other words "Panditjee! you will only have to live, I shall do more such things for you".[33]

33. More on the flight of King Tribhuvan see Daman Shumsher, *Nepal: Rule and Misrule* (New Delhi: Rajesh Publications, 1978), pp.110-11, Erika Leuchtag, "Erika and the King of Nepal", *Reader's Digest*, March 1957, pp. 26-27, D.R. Regmi, *Wither Nepal* (Kathmandu: Publisher, N.K., 1952), p. 108. When Premier Mohan was furnished by the Indian Embassy the list of the members of the Royal Family who had sought asylum there he to his surprise discovered that two princes, the second and third sons of the Crown Prince were not included in the list. A vigorous search was, thus, promptly conducted and the two princes on aged three and the other one were in the basement of the Royal palace. Their mother had died a few months ago. See *The Hindu*, December 1, 1950, p. 1.

The flight of the monarch to the Indian Embassy at a time when the nationalist revolt against the Ranas was at its threshold took the breath out of the Ranas, at least momentarily. The Rana oligarchy panicked and in a mood of desperation could think of no better plan than to convene. The Council of Elders and place Prince Jnanendra, the grandson of Tribhuvan, on the vacant throne. The baby monarch was hastily crowned on November 8 in the *Nasal Chowk* of Hanuman Dhoka Palace; and coins of different denominations were struck speedily to record the historic event to the future posterity.[34] But the coronation of Prince Jnanendra brought more problems than those it attempted to solve. *The Modern Review* has perhaps best highlighted the gravity of the problem in this picturesque way:

> Today in Nepal a tussle has ensued between two worthy descendants of illustrious Prithvi Narayan Shah and the Great Jang Bahadur — Maharaja Tribhuvan Vir Bikram Shah and Maharaja Mohan Shumsher Jang Bahadur Rana...; a baby king is again on the throne *Vive la Justice.*[35]

But the most important problem faced by the Rana oligarchy was the search for international legitimacy for its rash political adventure. Two types of diplomatic manoeuvres were clearly visible in the efforts made by the Government of Nepal to seek recognition of the new king. First, the Foreign Department of

34. Once the new king was installed Premier Mohan permitted King Tribhuvan and the Royal family to leave Kathmandu for new Delhi on November 11 on two Dacota aircraft of the Indian Air Force. Historical precedents also served to strengthen the conviction of the Premier that he could sleep with better comfort with the deposed King living in exile in India than in his own country. He certainly very well remembered how his august ancestor Jang Bahadur had engineered the abdication of King Rajendra in favour of the Crown Prince Surendra. Again the abdication of Maharaja Deva Shumsher and Maharaja Padma Shumsher were also fresh in his mind. But time was changing fast; and Mohan failed to realize that the same bag of tricks could not work for all generations, Press Note of Nepali Embassy, New Delhi, Nov. 11, 1950, E. No. 6, *Poka* No. 3, File No. 447.
35. Shiva Narayan Sen, "Nepal A Historical Sketch", *The Modern Review,* December 1950, p. 478.

Nepal informed the Nepali consulates in Lhasa and Rangoon to acquaint the respective governments with the extraordinary political developments in Nepal. The telegram in part ran:

> The Government of Nepal regrets to announce that H.M. Maharajadhiraja Tribhuvan Vir Bikram Shah Deva left his throne vacant by suddenly leaving the palace in the morning of November 6, 1950 accompanied by his family.... and going to foreign Embassy in Kathmandu, according to him to seek asylum there....that according to the laws, usages and the constitution of Nepal Maharajadhiraja Tribhuvan and the said members of the Royal Family had by their action forfeiled their right to throne. Accordingly, the second son H.R.H. the Crown Prince, who was born in 1947 was proclaimed and enthroned as King Jnanendra Vir Bikram Shah Deva on November 7 in Kathmandu amidst the proclamation of the people.[36]

Second, diplomatic moves were set in motion to seek recognition from the Governments of the United States and Great Britain, and the *Maharajas* of India. The British Government was initially prepared to recognize the new ruler and the United States would have most probably followed the suit had Nepal not sent a mission to negotiate with New Delhi. The response from the *Maharajas* of India was also not very encouraging though *Maharaja* Singh, the Governor of Bombay made a conditional statement in December 1950, "we should recognize the *'de facto'* Government of Nepal provided that it is stable".[37] Pakistan, with whom Nepal did not have diplomatic relations, was the only country that denounced the actions of the Government of India in the political crisis of Nepal. The

36. The contents of both the telegrams were identical. See telegram No. 17-1105 from Bijaya Shumsher, Director General of Foreign Affairs, to Major Nayan Bahadur, Lhasa, Nov. 8, 1950; also from Bijaya Shumsher to the Nepali Consul, Rangoon, Nov. 8, 1950; also a Press communique issued by the Department of Publicity, Kathmandu entitled "A New King Gynendra" on Nov. 7, 1950; See also File No. 447 of 2007/1950 entitled "Nepali Kangress ko Hamala Bare Jahere" (Report on the Congress Invasion, E.No. 6, *Poka* No. 3.
37. Statement by Maharaja Singh, the Governor of Bombay, *Free Press Bulletin*, December 14, 1950, p. 1.

Pakistan Radio went on the air to tell her people as well as the world that "the Ambassador of India had kidnapped the King of Nepal".[38] However, the All India Radio broadcast of November 9 had bluntly pointed out that the coronation of King Jnanendra was totally unacceptable to the Government of India; and regretted very much for the Government of Nepal had not given any attention to the advice of the Government of India.[39] The response of the Government of India became more clear when Pandit Nehru and his cabinet colleagues greeted King Tribhuvan when he landed at New Delhi on November 11. He was given all the honours that was due to a head of state.[40]

Even before the King flew to New Delhi the Nepali National Revolutionaries had already launched an "armed struggle" against the Rana oligarchy. The beginning of the struggle was marked by the dropping of leaflets by an unidentified aircraft in Kathmandu Valley and neighbouring areas. The leaflets in short pointed out that the armed struggle against the Rana Government was on. But the people were asked not to panic but lend every ounce of their cooperation to the revolutionary cause.[41] Then at midnight of November 10 the liberation army attacked Birganj.

38. See the Pakistan Radio broadcast on the morning of November 8, 1950 preserved in the Foreign Ministry of Kathmandu, E. No. 6, *Poka* No. 2.
39. For more on the broadcast see the file entitled "Nepali Kangress ko Hamala Bare" (The file relating to the invasion of the Nepali Congress), E. No. 6, *Poka* No. 3.
40. *The Statesman,* November 12, 1950, p. 1. Conversation between *Maharaja* and the Indian Envoy, Nov. 12 , 1950, 11 a.m. *ibid.* Premier Mohan told.*
    Mohan told the British envoy that "It was improper to accord the ex-king at his arrival the reception due to the Head of State at a time when the question of recognition was still under examination". He was sad that Panditjee had not respected his feelings; while he had respected the sentiments of Panditjee in arranging to send ex-king and his family. See E. No. 6, *Poka,* No. 3.
41. See a pamphlet in the possession of the author. On Sunday of November 12, an aircraft market VTCZO flew from India and dropped leaflets in Sisa Garhi, Dhankuta and Biratnagar, *op.cit.,* Footnote No. 39.

The Birganj Operations

Birganj, the gateway to the nation's capital, occupied the most strategic position among all the border towns of Nepal. Thus, the Nepali Congress High Command made the Birganj offensive the cornertone of a comprehensive strategic Kathmandu operations. It was Thir Bam Malla, the abliest commander of the revolutionary army, who masterminded the operation both in its planning and the execution phase. The plan in summary consisted of the capture of Birganj in a lightening raid at the zero hour of midnight. The methodology was the use of gorilla tactical warfare, that is, the surprise attack of the enemy under the cover of darkness and absolute secrecy. Once Birganj was liberated, the revolutionary army would dress themselves in the uniform of the state troops and attack Chisapani Gari, the last stronghold of the Ranas, before entering Kathmandu. Then with the cumulative strength of manpower, arms and ammunitions the Revolutionary army would march to Thankot and lay a seize of Kathmandu Valley, the last bastion of the Rana oligarchy.[42] It was on November 10-11 at the midnight hour, 200 armed volunteers of the Liberation Army crossed the Indo-Nepal border at the point of Raxaul and attacked Birganj from two directions. The leader was of course Thir Bam Malla assisted by his colleague Tez Bahadur Amatya. They had with themselves very limited supply of arms; a few hand grenades, four stein guns, four rifles, three revolvers and a large quantity of firecrackers, which helped to produce all the sound and fury.[43]

Birganj, however, fell with little effort during the surprise midnight attack. The Liberation Army, thus, laid hold on of the keys to the Kotes or the Bell's of Arms. But to their dismay the State army was poorly equipped. A bren-gun, two and three

42. Interview with the Guard Commander in the Liberation Army during the Birganj operations, Dharma Raj Dhakal, on November 10/11, 1950. He had also served as a Nayak (Sepoy) in the Nepali contingent during the World War II in the jungles of Burma Assam and Manipur.
43. Interview with Dharma Raj Dhakal, September 12, 1980; also Dharma Ratna Yemi, *Nepal ka Kura, op.cit.,* p. 296.

inches motars and a small quantity of rifles were all that was found. The revolutionaries then headed towards the treasury and seized 18 trucks of Mahendra Malli coins, 150 silver bricks and seven sealed boxes of currency notes.[44] The Governor of Birganj and his senior colleagues were also captured and were taken to Raxaul across the Indo-Nepal border.[45] An emergency administration was then established by the Nepali Congress to consolidate its position, under Tez Bahadur Amatya. However, the Birganj operation did have a price. Thir Bam Malla, who had engineered the whole episode, was killed by three pistol shots while he was addressing the civilian population to remain calm. In addition, several other commandos of the Liberation Army suffered serious injuries.[46]

The ease and swiftness with which Birganj fell spoke very well of the organization, commitment and military muscles of the national revolutionaries forces of the Nepali Congress. It made heroes out of Congress revolutionaries. The result was: the dramatic fall of Birganj received a worldwide publicity and hit the international headlines. The initial success gave confidence to the Congress volunteers; and a wave of anti-Rana movement hit the remotest corners of the country. Paradoxically, the fall of Birganj came as a rude shock to the Ranas at the most inopportune hour, when all its energies were diverted towards resolving the political crisis that was created at the wake of King Tribhuvan's flight to the Indian Embassy. The loss of the most strategic border town exposed the inefficient bureaucracy, the military bankruptcy and the poor communication networks of the Rana regime. Above all, the loss of Birganj showed how little the

44. It was the guard commander, Dharma Bahadur Dhakal, who handed over the above items to G.B. Yakthumba, which was subsequently taken to India to serve the revolutionary cause.
45. However, on Nov. 12 the Governor was released from captivity due to the efforts of GI. See a note prepared by the foreign Department, Kathmandu, entitled " Recent Events in Nepal", Nov. 12, 1950, E. No. 2, *Poka* No. 3, Press Communique issued by Nepali Embassy, New Delhi, Nov. 12, 1950, E. No. 6, *Poka* No. 3.
46. Interview with Dharma Bahadur Dhakal, September 12, 1982; also a message sent by S.K. Ghosh to the correspondent of PTI, Nov. 14, 1950, E. No. 6, *Poka* No. 3.

regime was anchored in the hearts of the people or in other words it deprived the Ranas of the moral authority to rule and administer the country.

The Ranas, however, quickly recovered from the shock. Reinforcements were, thus, immediately rushed from Kathmandu under the command of General Brahma Shumsher and Ekraj Shumsher. But by November 12, the liberation army with the help of four trucks of rifles moved north and occupied Kaliya, Simara and Amlekhgang.[47] Now a stage for confrontation was set between the state troops and the liberation army. Fierce fightings were reported from Amlekhgang, Simara and Kaliya. The revolutionary army was heavily outnumbered both in firepower and numerical strength. The result was Birganj was retaken by the state troops by 2 p.m. of November 20, 1950.[48] Altogether, 36 revolutionary comrades of the revolutionary army were killed, eleven were wounded and 84 of them were taken as prisoners.[49] Most of the casualties in the conflict occurred at Parawanipur. The state forces also captured a large quantity of arms and ammunitions and three wireless kits.[50]

So, by November 21, the Rana administration in Birganj was restored. Telephone communication between Kathmandu and Birganj was restored and the Nepal Government Railway operating between Birganj and Raxaul took up its normal

47. A note prepared by the Foreign Department of Nepal entitled "Recent Events in Nepal", Nov. 12, 1950; also news released by the Nepali Embassy, New Delhi, Nov. 16, 1950; also the broadcasts of All India Radio and Radio Saigon of Nov. 16, 1950; 6:15 a.m. and 6:30 a.m. respectively. These broadcasts were elected and compiled from the Foreign Department, Nepal by Kula Dharma Ratna Tuladhar. See E. No. 6, *Poka* No. 2.
48. See Communique of the Nepal Government No. 12, No. 20, 1950, 7 a.m. E. No. 6, *Poka* No. 3.
49. See communique of the Nepal Government No. 13 of Nov. 21, 1950, 7 p.m. and Communique No. 14 of Nov. 23, 1950, 7 p.m., E. No. 6, *Poka* No. 3.
50. The arms and ammunitions captured by the state troops from the national forces were; 133 rifles with 27,816 rounds of ammunitions, 26 rifles bayonets, three pistols, one stein-gun, tow powder packets and forty four *khukuris* (with and without scabbards). See the Communique of Nepal Government No. 14, *ibid.*

operations. Thus, the nine day old emergency administration of the revolutionaries ended. To use the expression of the epicurean poet Omar Khayyam it came like water and like wind it went.[51] The state government realizing the vital importance of Birganj to the survival of Kathmandu shifted four of its cannons from the fort of Chisapani to the border town.[52]

Biratnagar Offences

Biratnagar was the second target of attack of the Liberation Army. A preliminary attack on Biratnagar was launched by the revolutionary commandos on November 11; but it was repulsed by the state troops.[53] However, sporadic fightings continued in Biratnagar and Rangaeli. The Government did bring reinforcements to Biratnagar as fighting prolonged. Biratnagar was again attacked by 500 Congress Volunteers (mostly ex-Gurkha servicemen) on December 18, 1950. The seize of the industrial town including the Governor's residence lasted for a little over two weeks. An improvised tank built from a tractor worked wonders as it smashed the walls of the Governor's residence and the yelling volunteers burst into the courtyard. As the encounter was on progress, one of the sons of the Governor fell wounded and another fled with some Government sepoys. The Governor and the senior state officers sought refuge on the upper story. However, after two hours of serious fighting the Governor, Uttam Bikram Rana surrendered the industrial town to the revolutionary volunteers.[54] Once the Governor had surrendered, the state armory and the treasury fell to the Congress Volunteers, which proved to be extremely valuable during the entire eastern offences. Once Biratnagar fell a "Victory Parade" was organized by the 500 volunteers.

51. Edward Fitzgerald (trans.), *Rubaiyat of Omar Khayyam* (Delhi: Jaico Publishing House, 1981), p. 56.
52. For more on the transfer of cannons see to Birganj from Chisapani see the Letter No. 5 dated Magh 5, 2007 (January 1951). Book No. 291, MAN.
53. A report by S.K. Ghosh No. 15, 1950 to PTI Correspondent of India, E. No. 6, *Poka* No. 3, FMAN.
54. More on the Biratnagar encounter see *The Hindu*, December 25, 1950, p. 6.

When the parade was over B.P. Koirala, the Nepali Congress leader, unfurled the Congress flag with red and white stripes with four stars in the center, instead of the crimson red, before the Governor's residence, amidst acclamation of 15,000 audience. He then in a short extempore speech thanked the Congress Volunteers for their gallant sacrifices for democracy and exhorted them "to be ready for further trials and tribulations as the victory in Biratnagar marked only the beginning of the end".[55] The firey speech of the Congress leader in part ran:

> Weshall not rest and relax. We will continue our war for democracy relentlessly until we unfurl our flag on top of Singha Durbar (the Maharaja's residence) in Kathmandu.[56]

Biratnagar then served as the headquarter of the provisional Government of the Nepali Congress. But even before the city completely fell to the revolutionaries the Congress had set up a radio station of their own, which went on the air on the 40 meter band in Nepali and Hindi from 14.00 to 14.15 hours and 19.45 to 20.00 hours.[57] The administration of Biratnagar was then placed under the military Governor Kasheb Prasad Koirala.

The Revolutionary Army in Operation: The Eastern Sector

It was on December 10, 1950 a contingent of the Nepali Congress troops led by G.P. Rai took control of the Dharan Bazar. The subinspector of Dharan as well as other loyal Rana

55. *Ibid.*
56. *Ibid.* The Congress attatchment for their red and white flag was so strong that during the Rana-Congress coalition Government the Congress ministers continued to fly the Congress flag in their cars and residences till November 17, 1951. See *The Hindu*, November 18, 1951, p. 6.
57. The news broadcaster of the Prajatantra Radio of the Nepali Congress was S.N. Bahadur. The radio not only gave the news of the progress of the revolution but also appealed to the Nepali people at large for cash and kind for the continuation of the revolution until absolute victory was achieved. More on the *Prajatantra* Radio see the file entitled "The Congress Radio", E. No. 6, *Poka* No. 3, File No. 447, FMAN; also Narapati Sharma Pokharel. *Dhankuta ko Itihas* (*Naya Purano*) The History of Dhankuta: New and Old, (Lalitpur: Ram Prasad Pokharel, 1982). p. 29.

officers were then arrested and despatched to Biratnagar. A small section of the Liberation Army, however, continued to push ahead and advanced towards the Tamor Ghat 10 miles north of Dharan.[58] The Rana Established hearing the news of the speedy arrival of the Congress troops destroyed the bridge on the *Mul Ghat* of the Tamor river. But despite these obstacles, the revolutionary Commandos continued their drive ahead and subsequently overran Dhankuta by December 15. A provisional Government was set up, which lasted for four months.[59] Earlier, even before the fall of Dharan the Congress Commandos had conquered Bhojpur. This was a significant victory for a large quantity of arms and ammunitions came under their possession. Thus, with the newly acquired 1200 rifles with 40,000 round of ammunitions, two cannons and a large quantity of explosives one thousand Congress Volunteers were despatched for the conquest of Okhaldhunga. So before the close of December 1950 Khotan, Taplegung, Chainpur and Tera Thum were taken away from the Rana administration.[60] The conquest of Tera Thum was important for it lay on the route to the Hati pass, which was the main commercial route between Tibet and Nepal and then to India.

As the momentum of the "Revolution" rolled on, the Lahan Bazar situated 125 miles east of Kathmandu fell to the revolutionaries. It was on the dawn of November 28, 1950 a group of fifty armed commandos made a descent from the hills of Udaypur to the foothills of the Himalayas. The group was led by Krishna Prasad Upadhyaya, a militant youth of 24, who was a graduate of Banaras Hindu University.[61] This was immediately followed by the capture of an important military post of the Nepal Government Khapa.[62] Before the month of November

58. Voice of the *Prajatantra* Radio, Broadcast on December 21, 1950, *ibid.*, Narapati Sharma Pokharel, *Dhankuta ko Itihas, op. cit.*, p. 29-34.
59. Bhojpur fell on December 9, 1950, see the Radio Broadcast December 10, 1950, *Ibid.*, also *The Hindu*, December 31, 1950, p. 1.
60. *Ibid.*
61. *The Hindu*, December 1, 1950, p. 4.
62. *The Hindu*, December 22, p. 6.

came to a close Malangwa, the headquarter of Sarlahi district came under the full control of the volunteers. The "revolution" then pushed itself to the banks of the Mechi river. Jhapa, which was located 35 miles east of Biratnagar fell to the *Mukti Sena* on January 14, 1951. The seize of Jhapa was as difficult as that of Biratnagar, and it lasted for a month. The same crude tank that was used in Biratnagar worked wonders here also. It broke the compound wall of the fortified residence of "the subdivisional magistrate" of Jhapa,thus, compelling him to make a total surrender. A small contingent of state troops (seventy five in number) laid down their arms as the four star banner fluttered in the soft breeze of the Mechi river.[63]

Revolutionary Army in Operation: The Western Sector

It was at dawn of November 15, 1950 the Liberation Army of 100 to 150 strong and 200 in the support line attacked Bhairawa, the headquarter of the Butwal district. They used smoke screens and automatic weapons in the conflict. But the state troops were able to repulse the attack and according to a press communique issued by the Government succeeded in killing three of the commandos, including the commander. Thus, by noon of November 15 the battle was almost over and Captain D.B. Rai made arrangements with the state troops for a cease-fire.[64]

Perhaps the most interesting episode of the revolutionary movement was the fall of Tansen, the headquarter of the Palpa province. This province in Western Nepal was second in importance to Kathmandu as far as strategic and political importance was concerned. The fall of this province from the Ranas was a result of a successful *coup d'etat* organized by the former Commander-in-chief of Nepal, General Rudra Shumsher. General Rudra had been ousted from the Governorship of Palpa in the middle of November because of his pro-Congress sympathies. Thus, the Congress in collaboration with General

63. *The Hindu*, January 16, 1951, p. 5; also the Voice of the *Prajatantra* Radio, January 15, 1951, *op.cit.*
64. Press Communique of GN 3 and 4, Nov. 15, 1950, 10 a.m. and 1 p.m. respectively, E. No. 6 *Poka* No. 3.

Rudra was able to gain complete control of Palpa province by the first week of January, 1951. General Kshatra Bikram Rana, the Commander of the military installations at Tansen also joined revolutionaries.[65] This was followed by the fall of Butwal, the most important commercial town in Western Nepal on January 7, 1951.[66] A little earlier, by December, 1950 the two important districts of Western Nepal, Kailali and Kanchanpur fell to the Congress Commandos with relative ease and swiftness; and the Governor *Subba* Mahikar Deva Narayan Singh of both the provinces fell dead with nine gunshot wounds.[67]

As the year 1950 came to a close, the Nepali Liberation Army was in control of remote areas like Okhaldhunga, and Ilam in the east, Mahottwari and Saptari in the South and Chitwan in the Center. More than half of Nepal was, thus, under the control of the Nepali Congress and was subsequently being administered by the provisional governments established by them. But to be more specific more than 30,000 square miles out of the total area of 56,000 square miles was under to direct control of the Liberation Army.[68]

The Volatile Political Climate of Kathmandu

As the year 1950 drew to its closing weeks, the Nepali Congress announced its tactical military strategy, which was labeled as "princer move" against Kathmandu or to be more specific the assault on Kathmandu was to be directed from the eastern and the western sector and would finally converge at a point before the attack of the Kathmandu city. The spokesman for the Nepali Congress then in a soft, yet, a firm voice went on to say "God willing, we shall soon hurl our white striped and four star spangled banner of the Nepali Congress on Singha Durbar of Kathmandu".[69] The political developments in

65. *The Hindu*, January 8, 1951, p. 1.
66. *The Hindu*, January 10, 1951.
67. *The Voice of Prajatantra Radio*, Kartik 20, 2007 (Nov. 1950), E. No. 6, *Poka* No. 3, File No. 454 of 1950; also A Press Note issued by NG, Kathmandu, January 16, 1951. *Ibid.*
68. A Statement given by the Nepali Congress to PTI reporter at patna, December 25, 1950. See *The Hindu*, December 26, 1950, p. 6.
69. *Ibid.*

Kathmandu after the first week of November gave birth to a new wave of violence in Kathmandu. It was on Marga 11, 2007 (November 1950) a procession of about 500 in number paraded through the streets of Kathmandu shouting slogans against the Fascist Rana Government. As the slogan *"Rana Sahi Murdabad"** became louder and the state para-military police force became increasingly paranoid and being overpowered by anger and nervousness replied the protests with the sounds of bullets.

As a consequence a sixty three year old Congress activist, Nuche Bahadur Udas, was mortally wounded who subsequently passed away the next day. The mood of Kathmandu, thus, became very bitter, grim and tense. Accordingly, a massive funeral procession defined the curfew orders of the Government as the Kathmanduites poured forth in unprecedented numbers from the numerous *chowks, gallis* and *bahals* to bid farewell to their fearless friend who had sacrificed his dear life so that others may learn to live with honour and dignity that was denied to him. The tears that trickled from their eyes were not idle tears but a fountain of determination to uproot the ugly Rana oligarchy from the face of the earth.[70]

However, the Press Communique issued by the Government on November 9, 1950 relating to the death of Nuche Bahadur, though very interesting, is highly deceptive. The official version of the episode, which was clearly an attempt to hush up everything, in part ran :

> Nuche Bahadur Udas, an inhabitant of Asan Tole, Kathmandu, of age 60 to 65 died a natural death last night. But mischiefmongers have spread a false rumour that he was a brutal victim of the police assault. This story is far from the truth; and the government has thought it necessary to place the real fact before the people. The Government also urges the people to remain calm and not be swayed by such malicious propaganda.[71]

* The slogan may be literally translated as "Death to Rana Regime".

70. Interview with Gautam Ratna Udas, an eyewitness during the beating of Nuche Bahadur Udas on Marga 11, 2007 (November 1950).
71. A Press Communique issued by GN, November 9, 1950, E. No. 6, *Poka* No. 3.

The ability of Kathmanduites to organize themselves into a huge protest rally against the Rana oligarchy is also seen when about 25,000 Kathmandu folks shouted against the arrival of a British Mission to Kathmandu with slogans like "We want Democracy! Nepali Congress Jindabad!! Rana Sahi Murdabad!!!" The Mission led by the British Roaving Ambassador Sir Esler Denning with Frank Roberts, the Deputy British High Commissioner for India arrived at Gauchar airport, Kathmandu, on December 3, 1950 to study the political situation in Nepal.[72] But had to return with the conviction that the political climate in Nepal was unfavourable to the Ranas. Even the conservative estimate of the government put the strength of the crowd from ten to fifteen thousand. A section of the violent demonstrators even succeeded in encircling the car of the British Ambassador.[73] Demonstrations were organized in Kathmandu on almost a day to basis throughout the month of December. As the year 1950 was drawing to a close, even members of the Rana family, including the sons of Ex-Rana Premier, were seen taking active part in the anti-Rana demonstrations. It was on December 24, 1950 a reputed Rana poet, artist, essayist and playwright, Balakrishna Shumsher addressed an open gathering urging the people to help replace the Rana regime by a democratic form of Government. The result was he along with ten other Ranas were arrested, including the three sons of the ex-Rana Premier Juddha Shumsher and a nephew of the Nepali Councillor at Calcutta.[74]

As law and order situation deteriorated in Kathmandu due to frequent demonstrations before the Premier's residence, *thanas* and the prisons, the Government was compelled to

72. *The Hindu* , December 4, 1950, p. 4.
73. The police force at Kathmandu was totally unprepared to handle such a surging crowd that had assemble in defiance of the prohibitory orders of the Government. The police were mocked and jeered by the demonstrators. Some had their caps snatched away; while other had their arms broken. For a detailed account of the official version on the incident on December 3, 1950 see the report by Colonel Chandra Bahadur Thapa to the Police Goshwara on Poush 3, 2007 (December 1950). E. No. 6, *Poka* No. 3.
74. *The Hindu*, December 26, 1950, p. 4.

impose curfew orders from 8 a.m. to 6 p.m. during the concluding weeks of the month of December. It was on December 27 at about 2.30 p.m. a huge procession demonstrated near the central jail demanding the release of political prisoners. The police in an effort to disperse the mob which was moving in the direction of the prison, resorted to firing that killed six persons and wounded many.[75] Thus, as the year 1950 came to a close the political atmosphere in Kathmandu became extremely volatile and precarious. Soon the storm of "revolution" enveloped the Valley of Kathmandu and as the four star spangled revolutionary banner fluttered from house to house and from prisons to prisons the militant slogan of *"inkalab jindabad"*, in a pitch louder than the temple bells, announced to people the arrival of liberty at their threshold.

Decisive Developments in New Delhi

While "the armed struggle" against the Rana Oligarchy was plodding along slowly, but, surely from one height of success to another in the cold mountain terrain of Nepal, yet, more decisive developments were taking place with relative ease and swiftness under the warm tropical sun of New Delhi. Once King Tribhuvan had arrived in the nation's capital India became so involved in Nepali politics that she found herself thrust at its very center; and began to control the direction and momentum of the "revolution" itself. Premier Pandit Nehru then "took time by the forelock" to determine the course of events in the Himalayas. Nehru clearly saw that Chinese sovereignty over Tibet was a foregone conclusion; so the communist infiltration across the Himalayas into Nepal had to be prevented. To achieve that the violent upheaval, which an "armed revolution" could bring in Nepal had to be checked. Any radical departure with the past would, thus, besides bringing chaos and anarchy to Nepal would also pave the way for the

75. See *The Hindu*, "Disturbance in Kathmandu: Police Resort to Firing", December 29, 1950, p.1. However, the Communique issued by Nepali Embassy, New Delhi, on December 28, 1950 asserted that the firing by the police on bands of unlawful persons who were indulged in unlawful activities led to the killing of two persons and wounding several others, E. No. 1, *Poka* No. 3.

communist take over of the country. Nehru, thus, decided to crib and curb the wings of Nepali "revolution" or to use it only as a leverage to bring the needed compromise between King Tribhuvan and the Rana oligarchy. It was national interest and national security that convinced Pandit Nehru that the continuation of a constitutional monarchy in Nepal under the every grateful King Tribhuvan would serve best the interests of India as well as the democratic forces in Nepal than the stubborn unyielding Rana oligarchy or the Government by incompetent, impractical and dangerous neophytes.

Indian national interest and national security were two overriding factors that determined the way Nehru guided the path and momentum of events in Nepal in 1950-51. The speech Nehru delivered before the House of People on December 6, 1950 clarifies the foreign policy of the Government of India during this turbulent period. The important speech of the Premier in part ran:

> We are interested in our own country's security and our own country's border. We have had from the time immemorial a magnificient frontier—the Himalayas.....We are not going to tolerate any person coming over that barrier. Therefore, much as we appreciate the independence of Nepal; we cannot risk our own country's security by anything not done in Nepal which permits that barrier to be crossed or otherwise leads to the weakening of that frontier.[76]

It is interesting to see how Nehru like an experienced juggler was able to convenience at least momentarily, that the interest of the three diametrically opposite groups was best secure in the middle path rather than moving too far to the left or to the right. The restoration of King Tribhuvan to the throne of Nepal was the central path of his middle path hypothesis. To quote the Premier "We continue to recognize the King. We do not see why we should do anything else". He then warned the Rana oligarchy that if negotiation drags on it would be more and more difficult to find the middle path and that "is not good for Nepal".[77]

76. For the speech of the Indian Premier see the (Indian) *Parliamentary Debates*, Vol. VI, No. 17, Cols. 1285-86.
77. *Ibid.*

By the end November negotiations between Kathmandu and New Delhi had commenced on the question of the future political developments of Nepal. Even at this initial stage there was accord and harmony between the two governments on the concept of the democratization of the Nepali polity and society. Two hurdles did prevent an early settlement: the first was the nature of the office of the Premier (was it to be hereditary or elected?) while the second was the position of the baby monarch. The Nepali side maintained that the restoration of King Tribhuvan was a "closed chapter" hence it afforded no room for compromise.[78] Another aspect of the negotiation tangle was the sharing of power between the traditional forces represented by King Tribhuvan and *Maharaja* Mohan and the forces of modernity represented by the political parties, in particular the Nepali Congress. As India argued that if there was a danger in making a radical departure from the past then there was also an equal danger from inadequate reforms. She, thus, believed that wisdom dictated the middle course. However, to strike a neat balance between the forces of modernity and the forces of tradition so as to produce a happy compromise is always a delicate and a difficult problem. The failure of such a modus vivendi can always lead to a far more dangerous national consequences than even the excesses of a revolutionary era known better as the "reign of terror".

It was on November 27 the Nepali Defence Minister Kasher Shumsher and Foreign Minister Bijaya Shumsher arrived at New Delhi, where they were joined by the Nepali Ambassador Singha Shumsher, to open the stage for negotiations on the Nepali political crisis. New Delhi acquainted Kathmandu with her twin propositions: constitutional reforms and the recognition of King Tribhuvan as a legitimate sovereign. The Nepali delegates, however, could not see an eye to eye on both the propositions. They found the Indian position difficult to swallow for if the return of King Tribhuvan was an anathema to the stubborn Rana oligarchy, then the progressive constitutional reforms would diminish the power of the Prime Minister and subsequently a stage would reach when the hereditary Premier would be

78. *The Hindu*, December1, 1950, p.1.

replaced by an elected one.[79] Thus, the first round of negotiations ended in a stalemate leaving no room for a quick and an easy solution. So no official statement was issued by either side. However, the Nepali side was not prepared to accept that the first round of discussions was a "breakdown of talks".[80] The tactics adopted by the Ranas was dilatory.

After ten days of hectic discussions, the Nepali side returned to Kathmandu on December 8 with a text of "Memorandum of Advise" from New Delhi. The Memorandum contained three important features. First, a properly elected Constituent Assembly was to be convened as soon as possible to draw up a new constitution for Nepal. Second, the Interim Government was to consist of a cabinet headed by a Rana Prime Minister with persons representing "Popular opinion and enjoying the confidence of the people",* and the Rana nominees were to rule the country on the basis of collective responsibility; and finally in the interest of peace, stability and progress King Tribhuvan was to continue as the monarch of Nepal.[81] The Rana Oligarchy found that the progressive reforms as envisioned in the memorandum were worse than the return of King Tribhuvan for it would ultimately close the story of the Rana Oligarchy to the pages of history books. Further, the logic of Pandit Nehru, that is, the progressive reforms "involve no sudden break with the past".[82] was only a wishful thinking that was so remote with the reality of life.

The reply of *Maharaja* Mohan to the Indian "Memorandum of Advice" was a reflection of gloom and despair that enveloped the Rana bureaucracy. The memorandum had called for "momentous changes", which the Ranas could not undertake without destroying the edifice of the Oligarchy they had nurtured for more than a century. In the reply, the *Maharaja* only asked for more time to consider the proposals, which were of

79. *The Hindu*, December 9, 1950, p. 9.
80. *Ibid.*
* The popular representation which Nehru had in mind was no other than the Nepali Congress, under whose dynamic leadership the armed struggle against the Ranas had been launched.
81. *The Hindu*, December 23, 1950 , p. 4.
82. *Ibid.*

fundamental importance.[83] It was only on December 24 that the Government of Nepal replied to the "Memorandum of Advice" of the Government of India.[84] Accordingly, the Oligarchy accepted the formation of a fourteen membered cabinet with popular representation; and the convening of a Constituent Assembly within the next three years, during which the Constitution of 1948 was to operate.[85] However, the reply made no compromise on the issue of the baby monarch. Thus, when General Bijaya was asked by the press reporters whether the reply of the Nepal Government was in harmony with the Indian Memorandum the Nepali Foreign Minister curtly replied "I have brought our reactions."[86]

But as the time passed several developments, both at home and abroad, compelled the Rana regime to compromise on the issue of the baby monarch, thereby paving the way for the restoration of King Tribhuvan to the throne. These developments in brief were: the fall of more than 50 per cent of the Nepali territory to the Liberation Army, the acute internal dissension within the Rana family,[87] the low morale of the state troops and finally the inability of the Oligarchy to muster international support, in particular that of India, on the recognition of the new monarch. So in an address to the nation on January 8, 1951 Premier Mohan announced that King Tribhuvan would be restored to the throne of Nepal and an Interim Government with popular representation would be formed. His speech in part ran:

> It is our fervent home these far reaching reforms which have been announced in the spirit of pure patriotism and goodwill will be welcomed by the people of Nepal in the same spirit and they will render wholehearted cooperation....We are confident that the Great

83. Reply of *Maharaja* Mohan to the Memorandum, December 18, 1950, *The Hindu* , December 22, 1950, p. 4.
84. *Ibid.*
85. *The Hindu*, December 26, 1950, p. 1.
86. *The Hindu* , December 26, 1950, p. 1.
87. Seventy Ranas, who were not in direct line of succession, including the four sons of Premier Juddha Shumsher had resigned on block on December 24, 1950. See The Hindu, December 26, 1950; p. 4.

> Step forward which has been taken for liberalization of administration will be appreciated in its magnitude by every patriotic Nepali citizens.[88]

Reactions to the New Schemes of Reforms

The reactions to the new scheme of reforms, both at home and abroad was a mixed one. India welcomed the proposed reforms for it was in complete accord with her memorandum. In short, it was a triumph of Nehru's statesmanship. He was happy for the reforms would end the authoritarian regime and King Tribhuvan could return home to occupy his honoured place in the new arrangement. He further hoped that all the attempts of the revolutionaries for a "violent change" would cease and give place to peaceful cooperation and progress.[89] He then took this occasion to congratulate the Nepali people for taking a substantial stride forward.[90] A spokesman for the British Government also welcomed the new constitutional reforms as being constructive but reserved its judgement on the issue of the return of King Tribhuvan to Kathmandu.[91]

King Tribhuvan, who emerged as the central figure in the new scheme of reforms, was more than happy and he appealed to all sections of the Nepali people to cast away their rivalries and personal sentiments to make the proposed scheme a success. The mood of the monarch is perhaps best illustrated in his own words: "a great step forward has been taken and new responsibilities have been cast upon us all".[92] The immediate reaction of the Nepali Congress can be summed up in one word "disillusionment". The President of the organization then went on to say:

88. *Gorkhapatra,* Poush 24, 2007 (January 8, 1951), p. 1. Also *The Modern Review,* January 1951, pp. 4-6.
89. For India's reaction see *The Hindu,* January 12, 1951, p. 4.
90. Statement by Pandit Nehru, January 9, 1951, The Hindu, *Ibid.*
91. For more on the Comment by the British Government see *The Hindu,* January 10, 1951, p. 4.
92. The text of the statement of king Tribhuvan on January 10, 1951, see *The Hindu,* January 11, 1951, p. 4. also January 20, 1951, p. 5.

> The present struggle, which the people of Nepal are waging under the Nepali Congress is aimed at the liquidation of the feudal regime and the establishment of full democracy in Nepal..... No interim arrangement is acceptable to the people unless there is an effective transfer of power to the people of Nepal. The so-called proclamation does not contemplate such a transfer of authority in the hands of the people of Nepal.[93]

The Nepali leaders at this crucial juncture of history sincerely believed that had the "armed struggle" continued for a few more weeks, the Rana regime would have been toppled. But India, which had provided the base for the operation of the "revolution" was strongly against the "violent overthrow" of the Rana regime. Thus, the Congress High Command was compelled to dwarf their revolutionary zeal against the wishes of their comrade-in-arms as well as their own sentiments and feelings. The inner conflict in their mind did float into the surface when the spokesman for the Nepali Congress pointed out:

> The King's statement of accepting the reforms has placed us in an awkward position. We will have to decide how far can we follow the King's advice in satisfying the democratic aspirations of the Nepali people.[94]

The top-ranking leaders of the Nepali Congress did hold a Conference at Gorakhpur on January 12, 1951 to discuss the issue of the acceptance or the rejection of the new scheme of reforms.[95] The absence in this conference of the revolutionary comrade-in-arms like Dr. K.I. Singh, G.B. Yakthumba and Kasi Prasad Srivastav was an index to the direction the decision of the Congress decision would go. The deliberations of the Congress at Gorakhpur showed that the Congress High Command was not materially and psychologically prepared to go against the compromise formula of New Delhi. At this moment of history, circumstances compelled the Nepali Congress to make its own position secure in the "happy compromise" rather than muster

93. Statement by the President of the Nepali Congress, M.P. Koirala, *The Hindu* , January 11, 1951, p. 4.
94. *The Hindu* , January 12, 1951.
95. The leaders who attended the Gorakhpur Conference on January 12, 1951 were: B.P. Koirala, MP. Koirala, General Subarna Shumsher, Mahendra Bikram Shah and Gopal Shumsher, *ibid.*

up its courage and determination to go against it. The statement made by the President of the organization after the Gorakhpur meeting was on the whole more or less in harmony with the new scheme of reforms, though he did make it a point to point out three glaring defects in the announcement. First of all the announcement should not have come from the lips of the Prime Minister but from the mouth of the King. Second, the question who was going to nominate the seven popular representatives of the interim cabinet and the mechanics associated with the distribution of the portfolios were undecided; and finally the reference to political parties in the Kingdom in the announcement was misleading for there was only one political party in Nepal—the Nepali Congress.[96] The thing that really disturbed the Congress was the idea of sharing of the seats of the popular members in the interim cabinet with the other political parties. As the President of the Nepali Congress clearly stated that "if the deadlock (concept of political parties) is not resolved the fight for freedom will continue both violently and non-violently as the situation demands".[97] The use of the term non-violence in the statement is very significant for it was in keeping with the political climate of the time. The leaders of the Congress further felt that they had been at best left behind in the Delhi talks so its top ranking leaders—B.P. Koirala, Subarna Shumsher and M.P. Koirala rushed to New Delhi to present thier case on January 14. Upon arrival, they were quick to unfold their fourfold demands before Pandit Nehru :

(i) that all the seven popular representatives in the interim cabinet should be nominated by the Congress.
(ii) that the key portfolios should be given to popular members so that they could control the administration of the state.
(iii) that the cabinet should be responsible to the King as long as a duly elected parliament does not come into existence.
(iv) That the reforms should be proclaimed by the King.[98]

96. Statement of the Congress President, *The Hindu*, January 14, 1951, p. 7.
97. *Ibid.*
98. *The Hindu*, January 20, 1951. p. 5. A good number of Ranas had also sent a collectively signed memorandum to Pandit Nehru, which asserted that the Rana nominees in the interim cabinet should not be nominated by the Rana Premier but filled through an election process.

Thus, after receiving a verbal assurance from Pandit Nehru and King Tribhuvan the Congress President issued a cease-fire order to all the fighting units of the revolutionary army on Magh 16, 2007. To strengthen the orders of the Congress President, B.P. Koirala, with whom the revolution of 1950-51 is often identified, further added that the cessision of hostilities on both the sides was indispensable for the generation of a proper climate for negotiations at New Delhi. He also took this occasion to give a clear message to Nehru by asserting that the Congress had always stood for "unadulterated democracy" and it was that spirit that would continually guide them during all the phases of negotiations. He then congratulated the Congress Freedom Fighters for their untold courage and unflinching devotion to duty of their motherland; but asked them to remain calm during the fateful moment of history. To quote:

> The new Nepal of our dreams will be built on the foundations of their sacrifices of their sufferings and this in itself will be a matter of pride and joy for all of us who have been comrades in the perilous and noble undertaking. I would urge my comrades to be disciplined, firm and calm in mind in this fateful revolutionary phase of history.[99]

However, during its initial phase, the cease-fire order of the Congress President fell on deaf ears for the decision to cease all hostilities had been taken by the Congress High Command without consulting their comrade-in-arms. Thus, twenty comrades-in-arms took an unanimous decision on January 22, 1951 to continue the armed struggle as before until all leaders fighting in different fronts, in particular the Western Front; had an occasion to discuss with the Prime Minister of Nepal about the reforms of January 8.[100] But this attempt to continue the

99. *The Hindu*, January 22, 1951, p. 6.
100. Among those who attended the meeting were the top-ranking Congress leaders like Mahendra Bikram Shah, the General Secretary of the Nepali Congress, Kasi Prasad Srivastav, the Prime Minister of the Provisional Government of Western Nepal. The Guiding Spirit was, however, Dr. K.I. Singh, Who emerged as the strongest symbol of the appoint of the 'Delhi Accord'. See *The Hindu*, February 12, 1951, p. 1.

struggle was doomed to fail for it could either muster up internal support or external assistance. Above all, it ran contrary to the future of the Himalayan politics which Nehru had in his mind. An agreement was finally reached on February 7, 1951 which later became popular as the "Delhi Compromise" or the "Delhi Accord". In short, the "Delhi Accord" consisted of the drafting of the future constitution of Nepal by a constituent assembly elected on the basis of adult franchise. But an interim cabinet, consisting of ten members, equally divided among the Congress and the Ranas under the Premiership of Mohan Shumsher, was to administer the country during the interval. The official statement on the Delhi Accord came on February 11 from the Nepali Director General of Foreign Affairs who stated that a happy settlement for Nepal would soon be announced, which will end the hundred days of turmoil in Nepali history.[101] Thus, the protracted negotiations during the Delhi talks concluded. The Indian news media took the occasion to voice the triumph of India's statemanship for if on one hand it closed the door of Rana autocracy than on the other it checked the sanguinary hydra-headed monster of revolution, which could have benefitted only the communists.[102]

It was on February 18, 1951, King Tribhuvan dressed in his favourite blue coat and "churidar pyjama" read a proclamation before the microphone amidst over 200 Congressmen assembled before him. The proclamation created a Council of Ministers under the Premiership of Mohan Shumsher. The ten membered cabinet was equally divided among the Congress and the Rana members.[103]

101. The Statement by the Director General, Bijaya Shumsher, February 11, 1951, *The Hindu*, February 12, 1951, p. 1.
102. See *The Hindu*, February 7, 1951, p. 5; also in February 10, 1951, p. 4.
103. The five popular representatives were: B.P . Koirala (Home), Subarna Shumsher (Finance), Ganesh Man Singh (Trade and Commerce), Bhadra Kali Mishra (Communications) Bharatmani Sharma (Transport)), Those representing the Rana Oligarchy were: Mohan Shumsher (Prime Minister and Foreign) Baber Shumsher (Defence), Nripa Jang Rana (Education), Chuda Shumsher (Forests), Yagna Bahadur Basnyat (Health), See the Royal Proclamation *Gorkhapatra*, February 18, 1951, p. 1.

Thus the Rana Era came to an end, though there was a Rana Prime Minister.

An Anatomy of the "Delhi Accord"

It is needless to emphasize that the "revolution" of 1950-51 was not all fighting. No big armies were involved on either side and there were few pitched battles. The battle casualties were also small for the fighting was basically confined to what we would today call gurellia warfare. Fighting, though an essential and a significant component of the "revolution", was, however, not the most important. What was more fundamental was what was going in the minds of Nepali and Indian leadership at New Delhi, which expressed itself in the concrete formula known as the "Delhi Accord".

The term "restoration" has been very closely associated with the principles of the "Delhi Accord". Perhaps, the word "restoration" conveys best the spirit of the historic agreement. To a student of Nepali history this restoration has double meaning. First, it suggests the process by which the baby monarch Jnanendra was dethroned and King Tribhuvan was restored to his *gaddi* from his exile in India. Secondly, it refers to the sharing of the power by the Rana oligarchy with the "people's representatives". To the Nepalis the restoration was a significant event. It marked the termination of the hundred days of turmoil, political dictatorship, and internal strife; and the return of relative peace and tranquility. The spirit of accommodation and assimilation between the forces of tradition and the forces of modernity is probably best expressed when Premier Mohan Shumsher asked B.P. Koirala and Subarna Shumsher "to forget the past and remain united in the building of a new Nepal".[104] But to forget the past was not so easy.

The Delhi compromise sharply divided the Nepali intelligentsia into two conflicting ideological blocks: the democrats and the progressive forces. To some the compromise was a "good thing", while to others it was a "bad thing". But even the sanest Congressman believed that the "Delhi Accord" had left the "revolution" incomplete. One thing was for sure: the "Delhi Accord" had crushed or at best postponed the social and

104. For the Statement by the Premier Mohan see *The Hindu*, February 18, 1951, p. 6.

economic ideals that guided the "revolution". The principal thrust of the compromise was political so the focus of the compromise was on weaving a synthesis between the forces of tradition and forces of modernity, under the constant advice of the Government of India. Thus, when the Congress President called for a cease-fire the Congress party split into two. The militant group headed by Dr. K. I. Singh opposed the agreement: and decided to continue the struggle until the feudal order was totally liquidated. K. I. Singh at the time was fighting fiercely at Bhaiswan.[105] Another important segment of the Nepali Congress Comrade-in arms at Ratnahal also decided not to lay down their arms until total victory was achieved.[106] Even after the cease-fire G.B. Yakthumba was busy capturing hills in the East.[107] The opponents of the agreement argued that the compromise with the Ranas was a betrayal of the basic spirit of the "revolution". They accused the Congress High Command for fighting for seats in the Rana cabinet while they were shedding their sweat and blood in the front line.[108]

A vehement attack on the "Delhi Accord" came from the Nepali left, which made its appearence in the concluding years of 1940's. The Nepali leftists argue that when the "revolution" of 1950-51 was taking a full swing to the left the Anglo-American imperialism, Indian capitalism, the reactionary oilgarchy, the Nepali Congress and King Tribhuvan, who was under intense mental strain rushed for a "Delhi Compromise". They have outlined two basic aims of the "Delhi Accord". The overt aim was to cripple a movement that was going ahead to undo the evils of capitalism and imperialism.* The covert aim was to

105. Ratna Dev Atre, *Nepal ko Bato* (The Road of Nepal) (Kathmandu: Ratan Deva n.d.), p.13; Kaisher Bahadur K.C., *Nepal After the Revolution* (Kathmandu: Sarda Prakasan , 1976), p. 36.
106. *Yugbani*, January 20, 1951, p. 25.
107. *Rastriya Congress Bulletin,* Falgun 12, 2008 (February 1952), p. 1.
108. *Ibid.*

* To quote Lenin "Imperialism is the highest stage of capitalistic development in which dominance of monopolies and finance capital has established itself: in which the export of capital has taken a pronounced importance; in which the division of the world has been completed". See V.I. Lenin, *Collected Works,* Vol. XIX, (ed.) Alexander Trachtenberg (New York: D. Van Nonstrand and Co. 1956), p. 60.

introduce in Nepal a puppet government that would move according to the wishes of India and thereby drive a permanent wedge between the people of Nepal and the people of China.[109] Perhaps, this feeling is nowhere more vividly conveyed that in these words of a Marxist writer Shri Mani, who laments over the fact that the "revolution" in Nepal could not take a socialist character. To quote:

> The future of Nepal is thus in the hands of India in the same way the British were in control of Canada, Australia and South Africa.[110]

Even a cursory glance at the newspaper reports from India shows that the then Indian leadership was haunted by the spectre of communism casting its ugly shadow over Nepal during all phases of the "revolution" of 1950-51. To be illustrative, *The Hindu* in its editorial made it a point to note that the agreement did "check the sanguinary revolution, which would have benefitted none but the communists".[111] Perhaps, the most virulent criticisms of the "Accord" came from the rank and file members of the Congress itself. A leaflet issued by a Congressman from Kathmandu on May 1951 entitled "Aba Hami Jagrit Chhou" (Now We are Conscious) attacked the Nepali Congress triumvirate (B.P. Koirala, Ganesh Man Singh and Subarna Shumsher) for having forgotten the interest of the nation while weaving the unhappy compromise.

Their strongest indictment is seen in these lines:

> We who welcomed them (triumvirate) with flowers and garlends are now prepared to greet them with shoes. Instead of love and affection hatred and contempt is in store for them. The fault, however, does not lie with our leaders: but in ourselves—we are underlyings....But now we have mustered up our strength so we are not going to be trapped into the net woven by our leaders. We will not allow our leaders to sell Nepal to foreign lands.[112]

109. Pragatisil Adhyayan Mandal, *Jatiya Janatantrik Samyukta Morcha Ko Ghosana Patra* (The Manifesto of the Jatiya Samyukta Morcha) (Kathmandu : Pragatisil Adhyayan Mandal, 1951), p. 45.
110. Shri Mani, *Kranti ko Bad Nepal* (Nepal after the Revolution) (Stamadi: Shri Mani, n.d.), p. 1.
111. See the editorial Column of *The Hindu*, February 17, 1951, p. 4.
112. See the leaflet titled "Aba Hami Jagrit Chhou" (Now We are Conscious) May 1951, Kathmandu, p. 1.

Another leaflet was penned by another Congressman from Palpa, Dal Bahadur Pradhan on May 1951 entitled "Ahile ko Sirkar" (The Present Government). The composition opens by saying that three months ago we were told that a government representing all the people of Nepal would be formed. What we have today is a government representing the Ranas of Kathmandu Valley and five Nepalis who had lived in foreign lands under the magic spell of the riches of a few Nepali plutocrats. Ninety percent of the Nepali people do not even know their name. They instead of being guided by their comrades in-arms in the front line were not even prepared to talk to them. The leaflet ends with a sentimental appeal to the people which in part ran:

> Dear brothers these people donot represent the nation. We did not sacrifice our lives to establish such a government. Let us, thus, remain united together to form a government that will represent all the people of Nepal and establish a real democracy.[113]

But the attempt to continue the "armed struggle" by the militant comrades-in-arms was destined to a failure. However, to suppress the violent Nepali insurgents was not easy for the infant coalition government of Nepal. Thus, the interim government sought for military assistance of India to save the "Accord". Accordingly, the Indian state troops launched a series of operations from February to April in full cooperation with the Nepali state troops to restore law and order in the Indo-Nepal border.[114] The result was Dr. K.I. Singh along with his 357 associates was taken prisoners. Besides, nine of his comrades-in-arms were killed and nine wounded. The casualties on the side of the Indian troops is not known; but the state troops of Nepal lost five soldiers and five were wounded.[115] However, the fall of the Eastern districts of Jhapa and Ilam to the supporters

113. Dal Bahadur Pradhan "Ahileko Sirkar" (The Present Government), May 1951, in Sahid Smarak Library.
114. The official Indian version indicates that the operations commenced on April 11 and closed on April 18. See the statement by B.V. Keskar, Deputy Minister External Affairs, before Indian Parliament, May 14, 1951. *The Hindu*, May 15, 1951, p. 1.
115. *The Hindu*, February 23, 1951, p. 5; also July 23, 1951, p. 4.

of the Anti-Delhi Accord was a great setback to the interim Government.* India came under a volley of criticisms both in and outside Nepal for her military action in Nepal,[116] but she defended herself on two grounds. First, it was the duty of India to preserve the infant democracy in Nepal that had just been planted. Second, India was concerned about the maintenance of peace and tranquility in the Indo-Nepal border.[117]

With the close of the Indian military operations in Western Nepal the physical challenge posed by the militant Congress comrades against the "Delhi Accord" virtually came to an end. But how two leaders of the coalition government, B.P. Koirala and Mohan Shumsher, who were poles apart in their style, thoughts and intellect, could even run a government that could be half successful is difficult to perceive. As the nation was going through a period of crisis not only of the body but also of the mind, a very strong government was the need of the hour. But the Rana-Congress coalition was, perhaps, the weakest government she ever had in her history. To a casual observer the Interim Cabinet looked like a wonderful chariot drawn by two sets of spirited horses in two different directions. Thus, one is not surprised to hear from the Congress group in the Government asking King Tribhuvan to form a homogeneous cabinet consisting of "leaders who enjcy the greatest confidence of the people,"as early as May 1951. In short, the Congress group gave three reasons[118] why the government was not functioning. First, the Rana Premier and his nominees were "tempermentally unsuited" for the working of a democratic government. In fact, their age-old autocratic sentiments prevented them from seeing eye to eye with their democrat colleagues. Secondly, the cabinet was functioning as a loose conglomerate, with little or no coordination between the Rana and the Congress

* *The Hindu*, "Trouble in Eastern Nepal", August 14, 1951, p. 1.

116. Pakistani Premier, L. Ali Khan called the invasion of the Indian troops in Nepal as "an undignified attempt to gain political control and drag Nepal in a propaganda". Radio Pakistan, quoted by *The Hindu*, July 23, 1951, p. 4.

117. *The Hindu*, February 23, 1951, p. 5.

118. *The Hindu* , May 8, 1951, p. 4.

block; and finally, the incident of April 12, when an armed mob attacked the residence of the Home Minister, B.P. Koirala had led to starting disclosures. Among others, it became clear that some Rana Cabinet members, not necessarily all of them, harbored militant hostility towards the Congress members; and were behind the raid of the official residence of the Home Minister.[119] But as King Tribhuvan was unable to bring any substantial change in the existing structure of the government, both B.P. Koirala and Mohan Shumsher accompanied by their trusted colleagues, flew to New Delhi to sort out their differences.

During his talks with Pandit Nehru, B.P. Koirala stressed the need for a "homogeneous" cabinet or "a cabinet with one mine", for the country was not only on the grip of a political crisis but was troubled by chaos and anarchy. Then when asked about the king's reaction, he told the Indian Premier that "the king is prepared to accept what the Government on India decides."[120] The Indian Premier stood aghast and listened to both sides with anguish and amazement for in spite of the painstaking efforts of the Government of India to bring the two groups together they stood miles apart. Under the existing circumstances the Indian Premier could do little but listen. He,

119. The *Yugbani* reports in its editorial that on April 12, 1951 that the dissatisfied Ranas attempted to take the life of B.P. Koirala. The whole scheme was the handiwork of Premier Mohan Shumsher and the Defence Minister Baber. But the attempt was foiled for the people were on the side of B.P. Koirala. See *Yugbani*, April 19, 1951, Year II, No. 45, p. 1. The statement of B.P. Koirala tells us that on April 12, 1950 about 150 men armed with *Khudas* and *khukuris* (traditional instruments of war) disarmed the guards of B.P. Koirala at his residence at Tripureshwar. When he asked the unruly mob to present their demands and then disperse, two of the Gorkhadal members, with flashing *khudas* and *khuris* rushed upstairs to cut the Home Minister to pieces and take his head as a trophy. When the two refused to go away B.P. Koirala was compelled to fire his revolver for self-defence. The result was one fell dead and the other was severely wounded. In the mean time trucks of troops arrived to disperse the violent mob. *Yugbani*, April 26, 1951, Year IV, No. 46, p. 32.

120. *The Hindu*, May 10, 1951, p.1.

however, could think of no better idea than float the concept of the setting up of an Advisory Assembly consisting of all the important groups in the country, which would serve as a "Little Parliament". He hoped that a convention could be established according to which the recommendations of the advisory body would be binding upon the cabinet.[121] Apart from this the only positive advise Nehru could render to both the leaders of Nepal was to go slow, shed their suspicion about their *bona fied* intentions of each other and work amicably to bring about a democratic rule.[122]

The Delhi talks had not been entirely fruitless. B.P. Koirala returned home with a promise of cooperation from his Rana colleagues, a reshuffle of the cabinet and the formation of an Advisory Assembly, but above all with the feeling of satisfaction that his trip to the Indian capital had been politically educative". According to the new mood a reshuffle of the Nepali cabinet was made on June 10 without changing the Congress-Rana parity.[123] Even the exit of the conservative Baber Shumsher and the radical Bharat Mani Sharma did little to soften the attitudes of both the groups. So frustrating was the working of the "Delhi Accord" that its linchpin. Pandit Nehru, decided to come on a three days state visit to Nepal. Though this was taken to be a courtesy visit in the official circles, yet, his mission resembled more that of a physician. He came with the sole intention to administer artificial respiration to the ailing Rana-Congress coalition that was largely his own creation. But the black flags and Mao-buttons he witnessed at Kathmandu greatly upset him and put him on the defensive. So far from being busy in administering his healing touch, he had to devote a substantial portion of his time energy in clarifying India's position of non-interference in Nepali affairs. An extract from one of his speeches can be taken as illustrative. To quote:

121. *The Hindu*, May 12, 1951, p. 4. Also may 13, 1951, p. 6.
122. More on the advise of Premier Nehru see *The Hindu*, May 15, 1951, p. 4.
123. The outgoing Congress and Rana Ministers were replaced by Surya Prasad Upadhyaya and Singha Shumsher. *The Hindu*, June 11, 1951, p. 1.

> As I have said yesterday that it is not India's policy to interfere in Nepal's affairs..... Some six months ago I had the happy occasion of serving Nepal and King Tribhuvan with my advice. Nepal, since long had been free and it is essential for the well being of Nepal, India and the world that Nepal should be free. Some people say that India wants to interfere in the affairs of Nepal. It is all wrong.[124]

In his farewell speech Nehru touched upon a very sentimental note by asserting that "Nepal is the daughter of Himalayas" and a "younsister of India" and used the background to extoll the uniqueness and the unparallel nature of the Nepali "revolution" which came to be known as "the Delhi Accord". He then went ahead to pay a glowing tribute to the Nepali genius. To quote,"What is remarkable in Nepal is the manner in which hostile and warring groups have adapted themselves to these changes and are cooperating with each other today".[125] But the spirit of unity and cooperation that Nehru had envisioned in the Rana-Congress coalition was at best a myth; and if there was any trace of unity left in, it was certainly choked to death amidsts the sounds of the Indian Airforce Dacota and the thunderous shouts and slogans of Long Live Nehru (Nehru *jindabad*) that enveloped the atmosphere of the Gauchar airport during his warm and happy send-off.

The visit by Premier Nehru was in a way triumph for the democratic forces in Nepal. This inspired the democratic forces in the cabinet to pass a series of decrees which confiscated the *birta*[*] land from the Ranas, abolished feudal dues[126] and put into effect Anti-Excess Food Hoarding Act. It also appointed a commission to report on pension and other facilities to the

124. Speech of Nehru at Kathmandu, June 17, 1951, *The Hindu*, June 18, 1951, p. 1.
125. For the text of the farewell speech of Nehru see The Hindu, May 20, 1951, p. 1.

* The term *birta* denotes land granted by the state generally on tax free basis. The birta land had been a source of lucreative income source of income for the Ranas.

126. A decree by the Finance Ministry of Bhadra 1, 2008 made null and void the various feudal dues like *dharshan vet, fatimubarak* and *balbani*. The money collected from these feudal dues went into the pocket of the Ranas. See the *Gorkhapatra*, Bhadra 1, 2008 (August 1951), p. 1.

government servants.[127] The hopes of the whole nation was now centered upon the functioning of the Advisory Assembly as a panacea to all her political evils.[128] But since it had no mandatory powers, it proved to be too frail an institution to tackle the pressing problems of the time.

The vision of the democratic forces in the cabinet to establish the reign of liberty and equality could not move forward. There was crisis not only in the cabinet but chaos all over the country. The Nepali Congress, which came to power as a champion of liberty, had to resort to "temporary dictatorship" to rescue the nation from the unparallel chaos and anarchy in her history. Thus, as early as April 1951 the Public Safety Act came into operation, which armed the government with the powers to arrest and ban public meetings. However, Biratnagar which had served as the headquarters of the Anti-Rana movement, continued to be the nucleus of the oppositional politics during the Rana-Congress cabinet. The industrial population of Biratnagar served as the venue of discontent. The factory workers, finding that their petition of demands[129] had not been met, demonstrated before the factory owners. The military Government of Biratnagar, seeing a force of 3,000 workers panicked, resorted to firing at 6 p.m. on April 16, 1951. The result of this arbitrary action left nine workers dead and 150 off them wounded.[130]

The agitation against the arbitrary use of force by the government, however, did not stop, rather it spread to other parts of the country. Clashes between landlords and peasants were also reported from various places. A notable peasant uprising took place in Rajapur (Bardia) where on May 2, 1951

127. *Yugbani*, No. 10-11, Year V, October 12, 1951, p. 23-31.
128. It was on October 2, 1951 the king announced the formation of an Advisory Assembly and nominated its thirty five members, which included the ten ministers, with M.P. Koirala as its president. See the *Gorkhapatra*, October 2, 1951, p. 1.
129. The petition of the factory workers among others demanded 35% increase in salary, three months bonus, gratuity and dearness allowances. I.B. Lama, "Koirala Sahi Ko Sirkar abam Facist Chal", (The Facist Move of Despotic Koirala Government), Gorkha, Year 7, Kiran 19, May 26, 1951, p. 305-306.
130. *Ibid.*, 306-308.

the Government took the side of the landlords. The brief encounter left six peasants dead and twenty seven wounded.[131] The killing of the innocent peasant in the rural sector in Western Nepal infuriated the industrial workers at Birganj. Here also the government fired upon the procession of workers, which killed five and wounded another 125.[132] The popular protest around the nation culminated in a *satyagraha* launched by the Nepali National Congress and a demonstration by the United Students Union at Kathmandu. It was on 5, November, 1951 the police arrested five students who were about to make a speech at the Bhugol Park. The students followed the police and clashed with them. The small contingent of the police panicked and opened fire indiscriminately. The result was a teen-ager was killed and two were wounded.[133]

The firing by the government at the innocent students brought a wave of anti-Congress sentiments in the Kathmandu Valley. The anger of the Kathmanduites is seen in the parading in the streets of the surging multitude of 75,000 individuals asking for the resignation of the Congress group of ministers in the cabinet. After this incident, the exit of B.P. Koirala, the Home Minister, from the cabinet became certain. It was on Kartik 25, 2008 (November 1952), B.P. Koirala thought it prudent to resign from the cabinet but before doing so he released all the political prisoners.[134]

The exit of the Home Minister, B.P. Koirala was a triumph of the forces of reaction in the country. It was on November 11, 1951 Premier Mohan also resign, thus, the compromised formula that was so neatly devised at New Delhi nine months ago broke into fragments.[135] The King was more than happy to receive the

131. Grishma Bahadur Devkota, *Nepal ko Rajnaitik Darpan* (The Mirror of Nepali Politics) (Kathmandu: Dhurba Bahadur Devkota, 1979), p. 99.
132. The official version of the Home Ministry put the figures as: two dead and four wounded, *ibid.*, p. 101.
133. The student who was killed was Chiya Kazi and the two wounded were: Sabuddin and Ram Man Shrestha, *ibid.*, pp. 116-117.
134. Speech by B.P. Koirala on *Kranti Divas*, Kartik 25, 2008 (Nov. 1951), Grishma Bahadur Dev Kota, *ibid.*, p. 120.
135. *The Hindu*, November 17, 1951, p. 4.

resignation from Mohan Shumsher. Thus the power surrendered by King Surendra to Premier Jang Bahadur was fully restored again to the shah dynasty. At the center of the "revolution" of 1950-51, however stood an enigmatic lawyer from Biratnagar, B.P. Koirala, with whom the "revolution" is often identified. He was at the center of the whole drama. The "revolution" in fact began when he suggested at Patna in October 1946 that an organized movement against the Ranas had become the need of the hour[136]; and his resignation from the interim cabinet as the Home Minister brought the great drama to an end.

136. Parmanand, *The Nepali Congress in Exile* (Delhi : University Book House, 1978), p. 3.

CONCLUSION

The experiences of Nepal in the first half of the twentieth century, and in particular of 1950-51, still awaits encapsulation. This is partly because of the lack of academic endeavour on the part of researchers on Nepali studies but primarily because much of the archival materials on this period falls under the "restricted period" both in India and Nepal. Furthermore, many of the actors of the Great Drama have refused to speak on the subject. The reasons are personal, political and psychological. A better understanding of this tumultuous period will only be possible when exciting evidences begins to unveal themselves in the coming century. Thus, I must beg my apology for this rough and feeble sketch of the most dramatic period in Nepali history.

The first half of the twentieth century was marked by the breakdown of the nineteenth century Western Civilization that was based upon international gold standard, balance of power and self-regulating market.[1] Thus, the European man lost faith in the ideas of progress and enlightenment on which the modern civilization is firmly anchored.[2] The Nepali society in this period was also experiencing a wave of intellectual foment and physical turmoil. But the nature of this turmoil was different from the pangs and traumas his European brethren was experiencing. It can be more compared with the intellectual and

1. More on the breakdown of the nineteenth century civilization see Karl Polani, *The Great Transformation: The Political and Social Origins of Our Times* (Boston: Becon Press, 1971), pp. 8-111.
2. The ideas of progress and enlightenment are best treated in Peter Gay, *The Enlightenment: An Interpretation, The Rise of Modern Paganism* (New York: Vintage Book, 1968), pp. 3-197.

political climate France had experienced during the days of the Grand Monarchy in the eighteenth century.[3]

Political awakening in this period went through three distinct phases: the enlightenment phase (1900-1930), the underground period (1930-1940) and the hundred days of "open armed confrontation". The enlightenment phase, which can be equated with the emergence of human liberalism, took different shades and colours. The Nepali Arya Samajists were the first to take up their cudgels against the autocratic culture of the Rana period. If their attempt to rebuild the Nepali society on the *Samajist* ideals was an anathema to the Nepali orthodox Pandits then the idea of operating an Arya Samajist school for boys and girls from the funds raised by the taxation of domestic animals of Kathmandu Valley ran contrary to the spirit of the Rana culture. The Rana oligarchy was relatively comfortable with the Vedic ideals of the Samajists, but it was their interpretation of the Vedic scriptures that perpetually disturbed the oligarchy from 1900-1940.

The Nepali *philosophes* of this period used the technique of fables, parables, and short stories to transmit their messages to the masses; and made them laugh at the absurdities of the Rana polity. The publication of the political tract entitled *Makei ko Kheti* (The Cultivation of Maize) came as a bombshell and sent shock waves at all levels of Rana bureaucracy. The book, besides being a personal attack on Premier Chandra Shumsher, also inflicted a severe blow on the domestic and foreign policy of the Ranas. It also highlighted the gravity of the increasing peasant problem in Nepal; and suggested the only possible remedy — a fair distribution of land. The revolutionary literature in the 1940s not only exposed the hollowness and hypocracy of the oligarchy at all levels, but also outlined the structure of future government of Nepal. Furthermore, a survey of the political tracts of the period shows the germination of the concept of the republic. So the slogan "Long Live the Republic of Nepal" was heard loud and clear at least among a section of Nepali intelligentsia.

3. More on the Grand Monarchy see Alfred Cobban, *A History of Modern France: Old Regime and the Revolution,* 1715-1799; Vol. I (Baltimore: Penguin Books, 1968), pp. 9-81.

The message of the Nepali revolutionary intelligentsia in the first quarter of this century did not fall on deaf ears; but helped decisively in inspiring and guiding the path and momentum of the Nepali revolutionary patriots in the 1930s and the 40s. Thus, in this period Kathmandu becomes a haven for secret clubs where revolutionary agitators breathed and multiplied. The *Prachanda Gorkha* and the *Prajaparisad* were two underground organizations of the period, which aimed in replacing Rana polity by a democratic political setup. The method they chose was one of violence and terror. But both these organizations were detected, suppressed, and crushed by the oligarchy. And their leaders were either sent to gallows or to prisons. A study of the methodology used in the prosecution symbolized the spirit of the Rana judiciary. There were no public trials, no dialogue between the government prosecutor and defence. The whole affair was simply a brutal attempt to extract confessions from the accused and the subsequent sending them to gallows or *kal kotharis* (prisons).

The suppression of the *Prachanda Gorkha* and the *Prajaparisad* did bring a temporary lull in the oppositional politics in Nepal from 1940 to 1950. This setback was not only physical but also psychological. Above all, the romantic methodology of uprooting the Rana oligarchy by a few sticks of dynamite and explosives had to be discarded. So a strong political vacuum was left behind. Further, the international situation triggered by World War II helped only to strengthen the iron grip of the oligarchy by making the Anglo-Rana alliance stronger than ever before. The result was Kathmandu ceased to be home of anti-Rana movement. But the cities of North India like Kalimpong, Darjeeling, Banaras, Patna, and Calcutta became convenient enclaves for the growth of anti-Rana agitation.

The style of oppositional politics also underwent a radical change. The secret clubs and underground societies became a thing of the past. As the decade of 1940s unfolded the Nepali revolutionary intelligentsia became increasingly convinced that no political change in Nepal was possible without going to the masses; and to go to them modern tools of political agitation like mass communication and *satyagraha* had to be used with dexterity by an organized political party. The first phase of anti-Rana agitation in India was the exposition of the evils and the atrocities of the Rana regime through the press and the platform. An attempt was even made by the Nepali revolutionaries to use the Japanese connection to liberate Nepal from the arbitrary Rana rule. But the withdrawal of Japan from the south-east theater of the war and her subsequent defeat brought this scheme to a close.

This paved the way for the *satyagraha* movement in Nepal. The ending of the rising misery of the workers in the Biratnagar industrial complex due to the exploitation of the Rana industrialists served as the immediate objective of the *satyagraha* campaign; while the long term objective was to undo the Rana oligarchy itself. The *satyagraha* movement which lasted from April to September 1947 had a nation wide effect as it fanned from Biratnagar to Kathmandu and then to the remote hills of Ilam. Kathmandu was the focus of the *satyagrahis.* A procession of 30,000 young, old, and adults marched through the downtown of Kathmandu. In addition, the civil servants of Bir Hospital, the Department of Electricity and the Nepal Mint went on strike for better pay and other ammenities. The Rana bureaucracy retaliated by the arrest of thousands of *satyagrahis,* including their leaders, Man Mohan Adhikari and B.P. Koirala. This set the stage for reform and reaction and the subsequent armed struggle of 1950-51, which led to the end of Rana oligarchy.

The "revolution" of 1950-51 had two dimensions. The first was the spread of the four star spangled banner of the "revolution" from house to house and hill to hill over fifty per cent of the Nepali territory. The second, though less dramatic, was the more decisive dimensions of quiet diplomacy between the representatives of *Maharaja* Mohan and King Tribhuvan at New Delhi under the careful "goading" of the Government of India.

The Indian perception of Trans-Himalayan diplomacy helped greatly in shaping the direction and momentum of the Nepali "Revolution" of 1950-51. The spectre of communism casting its shadow across the desolate Himalayas was a cause of deep concern to Indian leaders. This fear is perhaps nowhere better manifested than in these words of Deputy Speaker of Indian parliament, Ananta Sayanam Iyengar at the Bharatiya Vidya Bhavan of Bombay. To quote:

> Danger is lurking to India. Tibet having turned communist, democracy in South-east Asia can only be safe if Nepal and other small states are annexed to India.[4]

Nehru, though was always opposed to the idea of annexing the Himalayan frontier states, yet, made sure that Nepal did not go out of control so as to jeopardize India's national interest and security. To fulfil his objectives Nehru decided to clip the wings of Nepali "revolution" or in other words to use the "revolution" only as a leverage to pressurize the Rana oligarchy at the Delhi talks. Once the Oligarchy yielded to the compromised formula of New Delhi Nehru decided to quench the flames of Nepali "revolution" by even using his military muscles to undo the continuation of the "revolution" in Western Nepal.

Even a cursory glance at the events of 1950-51 indicates that the "revolution" did not come in the shape and size anticipated by the Nepali revolutionary intelligentsia. Even a moderate Nepali Congress worker would admit that the "revolution" had been incomplete. The unfortunate turn of the events had replaced the slogan "fight to the finish" by the cry of "accommodation and compromise." The freedom fighters after much blood and toil received only a shadow of their expectation. The feelings of Nepali freedom fighters is perhaps best expressed by these words of D.R. Regmi:

> And our situation is not a little easy for the fact is that instead of Ranacracy we have seen that its alternative has been king's autocratic rule with a shadow of democracy.[5]

The changes brought by the middle path, which dominated New Delhi talks, was of a limited nature. Yet, the revolution of rising expectation it sparked in Nepal was momentous. The psychological and social changes triggered by the "revolution" were also of great magnitude. The weekly periodical *Jagaran*

4. *Free Press Journal News*, April 4, 1950.
5. D.R. Regmi, *Wither Nepal* (Kathmandu:Publisher N.K., 1957), p. 104.

has carefully voiced the attitude of Nepali elites during the eve of the announcement of the compromise in these words:

> Now it is not sufficient for us to dream of becoming *Subbas* and *Sirdars*. But we should now be prepared to become Ministers and Prime Minister.[6]

It also warned the future Nepali ministers of the interim cabinet that they were not to be "little kings" otherwise they would be recalled.

Above all, the "revolution" did anahilate the regime that had consistently limited Nepal's contacts with the outside world. Since then Nepal's contacts with the international community has been on the increase and the evolution and growth of secular institutions like the Public Service Commission, the Independent Juidiciary and the Office of the Auditor General has been continuous and widespread. These secular institutions served as the agents of change in transforming the orthodox and the rigorously stratified Nepali society.

6. See editorial of *Jagaran* (weekly), Year I, No. 1, Falgun 4, 2007 (February 15, 1951), p. 2.

APPENDICES

APPENDIX A*

A REVOLUTIONARY PAMPHLET CIRCULATED BY THE *RAKTAPAT KOMMITTEE* (BLOODSHED-COMMITTEE) ON SEPTEMBER 7, 1940**

Nepal Under the Ranas: Atrocities over the Nepalese

The future program outlined by the high-souled members of the *Raktapat Kommittee* in *Sambat* 1997 (1940), just recently, is as follows. First, let me narrate, briefly, the injustices perpetrated by the Rana family and then go on to enumerate our major task. It is a pity that in the twentieth century there are non so unfortunate than the Nepalese sisters, who have been downtrodden since the time immemorial. In particular, what you are witnessing today is the outcome of the hundred years of Rana regime. It is true that day by day, hour by hour and minute by minute while the steps of the world is marching towards progress, we are rolling down the hill. The ignoble Rana Prime Ministers have sucked our blood to such an extent

* This pamphlet is taken from E. No. 6, *Poka* No. 11, File No. *Cha,* 1977, V.E. (1940 A.D.), FMAN.

** The records of the *Munshi Khana* (Foreign Ministry) asserts that the *Raktapat Kommittee* had posted, at least, 41 copies of this cyclostyled pamphlet to the different high-placed persons in the country. The above specimen is the one posted to the then *Maharaja* Joodha Shumsher on September 7, 1940 from Cwanpore, India, in an open cover. The language used is Nepali, but the script is Roman. The exact rendering from Nepali to English has been made more difficult due to a number of factors like faulty sentence structures, faded and obscure letters, lack of dicritical marks and the frequent shift of words and phrases from Nepali to English and Hindi.

that the nation has been deprived of not only her life fluid but also of the precious water. Whenever the eyes of the Ranas fall upon the luscious green fields and the luxuriant forest vegetation of the hills and the districts it becomes their *birta* (tax-free asset). At other times the endless tracts of the Terai land is also turned into their tax-free property. The reason for this is that the people have always remained so mute dumb. I will not give more examples. They consider such land to be their father's possessions or their mother's *dowary*. The overall result is that while the Ranas go on accumulating their wealth day by day the national treasury is being emptied. So much so that without falling into the mercy of these *Nokar Sahis* (wretched souls) it is difficult for one even to make a living. Is there any country in the world where such a thing can occur?

Our motherland has been blessed by God and nature in such a way that, given the proper administration, there would be no such thing called scarcity in this land. But it is extremely regrettable that this ignoble regime has not only impeded progress; but has made us so heavily depended upon the *Ferangis* (English). Even Tibet and Kabul, which were far behind in the path of development, have picked up momentum and is now much ahead of us. There is nothing to be astonished by their momentum of progress rather we should be surprised in our inability to recognize the long, absolute suppressive rule of these ignoble so called *Rajas*.

In Tibet and Kabul as well as the other countries of the world all their revenues are spent in their respective countries. But this not the case in Nepal. The annual income of this country is said to be three *crores,* in fact, it is only two *crores.* On the other hand the yearly expenditure in the civil and military is roughly one *crore* or even less. The previous Prime Ministers used to deposit six *lakhs* in the public treasury in an effort to hoodwink the people. But this thevish, *dacoit* and develish Prime Minister has not only abandoned this practise but has taken gold from the national treasury and sold it to the American Imperial Bank in return for paper currency. It is a pity that the real wealth of the country is fast disappearing and this old country is turning into a beggar. They, far from feeling guilty, are rather delighted in extracting every hit of her material resources and depositing the wealth that has accumulated from time immemorial in foreign banks. You can imagine for yourself! would this country be occupying such a low status today had the Rana Prime Ministers invested one *crore* of rupees, which they had stealthly looted from the people in their own country? We, however, shall nor remain aloof from sound of our wealth ringing in foreign lands. The Ranas should take lession from the history of Modern France.

This much for the first part. Now let me go into the second, that is, the narration of our duties. The time is approaching fast when the high-souled members of our *Kommittee* will be flying its flag in Singha Durbar, Lalitpur Durbar, Bhaktapur Durbar and the streets of Kathmandu, in particular, the Indra Chowk Plaza, the very hub of national life. Then we shall, with our head raised, narrate the atrocities of the Rana rule to the whole public very openly and candidly.

We shall keep you informed with our monthly activities through our news letters. If you want to strengthen the daily increasing membership of our *Kommittee,* subscribe to its membership without delay. The fee is also not high. A few *rupees* and *paisa* will give to you its life membership, and you will be contributing to its growth and evolution. The Ranas, who have many concubines, can detect us only if they unflod the peticoat of their mistresses otherwise we shall remain to them just fruits on the air. Now this underground *Samiti* will describe in a few words about this Prime Minister who not only cruely exploits us, but is also noted for his dirty designs, gambling, prostitution and above all his incestuous relations with his daughter-in-law. The dark clouds of suffering has enveloped us since this senseless butcher has been the *Raja* of Nepal. This country has been experiencing disturbances, diseases and recurrent earthquakes every year ever since the reign of administration fell into the hands of this sinner, through evil means. Previously, in the reign of *Raja* Chandra, the cost of a *pathi* of rice was one *mohar* (half a rupee) but now one *mohar* fetches only three *manas*. Rice has thus become the "salt" of the people. The *Raja,* however, is not at all concerned about this and is seen in devoting his energy in making alcohol cheap rather than salt to the people. Is it possible for the people to substitute alcohol for salt in their daily life? You can, thus, easily imagine the kind of intellect he possesses. So you should not be astonished to see the increasing turmoil and suffering in this country. Let me tell you one thing, namely, you will not be blessed with peace and tranquility in this Hindu Raj as long as the reign of administration of this country is the hands of an ignoble, outcasted and disrespectable *Raja* with whom (according to the laws of our *Shastras*) we should not even drink and dine. His private and public life is equally ugly and detestable. He is one who loves to incestuous relation with his daughter-in-law; one who after making his own daughter pregnant, secretly handed over the unwanted issue to a poor Bengali; one who lives a life of gambling, ease and comfort at the cost of the very subsistance of the thousands of his subjects; one who drives his own kith and kine through the hills and jungles without any regards to *dharma shastras* (religious canons); one who captures the buddying beautiful innocent Brahman damsels to be his concubines. If a person like him is not inflicted with leprosy who will be? You can imagine for yourself, how can we be happy in the regime of this person?

He, having snatched the orphan-children from the tearful bleeding bosoms of the Nepalese, send them as conscripts to foreign lands in this very problamatic and tumultuous period, though the Imperial Government has been repeatedly saying that they are not required. In doing so, he is either ashamed of his ox-like behaviour or does he cares to uphold the national honour of his country. This is an age of machinegun, so we are making our best effort to prevent the sending of the Nepalese contingent. It is obvious, that if the Nepalese troops enter into the battlefield, we will not even be able to locate their bones. But if we fail in our objective we will have to propagate the idea of *satyagraha* (conversion of the evil doer through self-suffering) among them, and in this we need your help.

The past provided two occasions for Nepal to send her troops to British India: the days of Premier Jang Bahadur Kuwar and *Maharaja* Chandra Shumsher. The Nepalese troops on both the occasions were under the command of excellent generals and returned in high spirit, with heads raised, and glory for their country. Do we have the same situation in the country today? Would Jang Bahadur and Chandra Shumsher send the Nepalese contingent under the present circumstances? The present Prime Minister has not even bothered to vizualize the great catastrope he is inviting for the country by sending the troops at this critical hour. Poor soul! when does he have the time to think about national welfare. His mind is rather engrossed with a host of other ideas like looting, gambling and the pleasures of amorous living with his mistresses and the sweet damsels who come and go every day. We really have pity over him. Jang Bahadur himself led the Nepalese contingent to India in 1857 and in the time of *Maharaja* Chandra the Nepalese troops had Baber Shumsher an equally able commander, as their leader; and on both the occasions the Nepalese troops returned with garlends on their neck and laurels for thier country. But on this occasion the Nepalese troops are not only being a laughing-stock in the Indian barracks but in fact putting *tikas* of shame (human excreta) on their temples.

Recently, there was much confusion in the Barog railway station in Simla, when the ill-worthy, ill-witted, senseless power-thirsty dacoit (Bahadur Shumsher) dropped to have his dinner. The state of confusion was so intense that it was fully reported by the newspapers like *Hamdam.* If this man had any senses it should have been a matter of grave concern; but this really does not at all bother him. What a disgrace?

The recent statements of Sahab Maulana Azad in Nani Tal has given us great hopes. In this connection the words of Father MacNeal is worth mentioning. To quote, "the subjects of Nepal are suffering a thousand times more than the subjects of India". How can we tolerate all this? The words of the Japanese Sahab Okamota is also equally apt. He points out that "it hurts us too much when we listen to the tales of suffering of the Nepalese people", and then goes on to assure the support of the Japanese *Kalong Samiti* to the struggle of freedom of the Nepalese people. In concluding his remark on Nepal he mentioned that when the Japanese designs in India was accomplished Nepal will also develop and prosper.

The relation of this revolutionary Kommittee is also very intimate with the politburo of Lenin's Party in the Soviet Union. When our president briefed them about the atrocities of the

Rana rule in Nepal they could hardly stop from shedding tears. Their help is also assured. We have enough friends among us who can bring disaster to thousands; but what we lack is a few revolutionary conspirators. When such distinguished souls come forward before this *Samiti* we can assassinate any day this disgrace to the Nepalese family in such a way that even his bones will have perished. The Nepalese will be greatly relieved the day in which we can destroy this outcaste leper. He always talks or giving up his high office but this is only a piece of rumour only to neutralize all plots against him. Only the absolute fool in the world will believe in his talks of resignation from a post that permits him so much loot and pleasure.

Why should't four persons sacrifice their lives for the deliverence of the whole nation? Brothers come and gird up your loins. If we can feed the vultures and the jackals upon his flesh then the valor of their deeds will be sung by the Nepalese ever after. One who sacrifices himself in such a noble cause will have a happy comfortable life in this world and supreme bliss in the next. Even if the mission is a fiasco he need not worry about his descendents. They will be provided with pensions and tenable land from generation to generation.

There are many people who are supporting our cause without revealing their identity, due the circumstances, would when opportunity arises, come forward to serve their country. It is true that the commotion and fury is turning every thing in this world topsy turvy, yet we are confident that in this process we will be able to unfurl the flag of independence in our motherland. National deliverence is not possible by stationing a representative in London, just for the sake of vanity. Consequently, the *Kalantar Mantar* (deliverence) will surely come in the opportune Oam hour.

Well Wisher

J.B. Malla
Permanent Secretary, *Raktapat Kommittee*

APPENDIX B*

A Copy of the Letter Intercepted by the British Government and Handed Over to the *Maharaja* of Nepal in January 1941

From: Kulnath, Banaras, January 22, 1941
To: Dilli Raman Joshi B.A. (Hons.), M.A. Ltt.
C/o Bansi Lal, Naya Tola, Bankipore

My Dear Dilli Raman,

I have the pleasure in imparting to you the following piece of news, which will be a cause of no little relief to you. Thus is the Jn. and a few others (about a dozen and a half) have been set free unconditionally. I was informed of it some ten days ago. There is no other news except this that things are coming back to normal and that the apprehension of many have definitely abated. Meanwhile, H here keeps a guarded reserve on all topics. I have not so far sought his advice on our future course of action. He does not seem to volunteer any.

I have been asked by V to go to Bombay to resume the work, which I had to leave this time last year. He has further written to me to ask you what you propose to do for the time being. You may intimate to him your intentions indirectly. Have you consulted H? Will you ask Bansi Lal not to bother himself with cows as 'V', has changed his mind. With Best Wishes.

Your's Sincerely

Sd/Kulnath

* Source: E.No. 6, *Poka* No. 11, A 14, *Kha*, 1945, FMAN.

APPENDIX C*

A Copy of the Letter Intercepted by the British Government and Handed Over to the *Maharaja* of Nepal in January 1941

From: Agni Prasad Sharma, December 14, 1941
To: Krishna Prasad Koirala

This is my first letter to you. You may not even have heard my name. I have heard about you for a long time and have met you in Kathmandu in Sambat 1988, but you may have forgotten. It has become very necessary that both of us should meet at Banaras for the discussion of some secret matters. When we meet I will tell you about the problem on which I seek your advice. You will kindly ponder over its merits and demerits and render advice accordingly. I want to meet you here at Banaras. Please inform me about the time and location about our meeting. I intend to go to a certain place with a specific objective within five or twenty days. If success crowns my mission I see great advantage stored up for us for the future; and that is why I want to see you before I go and take your advise and directions.

Your's Sincerely

Agni Prasad Sharma

* Source: The English rendering of the letter from Nepali is mine, E.No. 6, *Poka* No. 11, A 14, *Kha*, 1945. FMAN

APPENDIX D*

A Copy of the Letter Intercepted by the British Government of India and Handed Over to the *Maharaja* of Nepal On March 11, 1941

From : Colonel Khagendra Bikram Bahadur Rana
325 Oam Bahal Tole, Kathmandu, Nepal
March 1, 1941
To: Dr. A.P. Singh, Hewett Road, Lucknow

I had written a letter to you a fortnight ago, but I have not, yet, received a reply from you. My letter must have been miscarried otherwise you would have replied to it. A few days before my leaving Lucknow you had told me to get a fish** from Madras. Now that fish must be with you and you had promised to get the fish up to Raxaul for me. I have not heard anything about these fishes. What about that? Please let me know, at your earliest convenience. If you are ready to arrange I will send a man up to Raxaul. Hope to receive a reply as soon as possible. I hope that you are doing well.

Your's Sincerely

Khagendra Bikram

* Source: E.No. 6, *Poka* No. 11, File No. A 14, *na,* FMAN.

** The term "fish" used in the letter was a code language. The British Government of India, thus, decided to had over the intercepted letter to the *Maharaja* of Nepal.

APPENDIX E*

A Revolutionary Leaflet Issued by the *Raktapat* Committee in February 1942

Long Five the Republic of Nepal!

Generally speaking, we do not switch on our Radio to Radio Peping when Delhi broadcasts its daily news bulletin, the reason is that it always gives false and absurd news; but accidently yesterday evening at 6 p.m. one of the member of our club switched on: what we hear is that this Joodha Shumsher or Joota Shumsher our nincompoop, bastard self-made Prime Minister has donated from the public purse a check for Rs. 50,000/- rupees fifty thousand, through his drunkard imcompetent son Bahadur Rana at Delhi to Generalismo Chankaishek on the false pretext that this sum is to be utilized for the Chinese by the Chinese Red Cross Society.

We know fully well that this amount is given on the above pretext, the real reason is either for the hidden good or this hotheaded supposed Nepali Hittler Bahadur or it might be a bribe to acquire for himself or his son or his hangers some good for nothing Chinese decorations.

Is it not a pity that many Nepalese are dying in the hills and in the plains by some deadly diseases like Malaria, Cholera, Tuberculosis and other deadly diseases but this nincompoop never cares. No not even a travelling dispensary is ever set for our aid. Even in places where his predicessors have left a few built hospitals or dispensaries no medicine are available now a

* This leaflet is taken from E.No. 6, *Poka* No. 11, File No. 11 A, 14, *Ga*, 1944, FMAN.

days. It is even said almost publically that the local doctors have received a circular to administer pure water diluted with faint colours to the people coming for medical aid—such is the condition of Nepal in this Reign of Terror.

It is high time that Cromwell should arise and give this nincompoop the example of Charles I, then only can raise (sic) its head in this fast changing time. Surely Japan will help us.

How long are to bear this misrule? This mad p.m., not afraid of dharma, is allowing Bolshevikism to creep silently into our Hindu Raj by allowing our Gorkha sepoys serving in British India to mix with the Bolsheviks in Iran. Is he not aware of the fact that the Archbishop of Canterbury did resign for making alliance with U.S.S.R. No it is idle for us to expect from this Mad Man, for we can expect nothing from a man who is always in favour of a prostitute, gambling and making money by the use of force by starving the public. A man who has taken a public prostitute, the Lagan Bharadari Nani, and has made this prostitute even Kanchi Maharani, should not be allowed to hold the reign of Govt. any longer. He should be banished or shot dead at once.

Long Live the Republic of Nepal!!

APPENDIX F*

A statement given by the Government of India showing actions taken against persons connected with Anti-Rana Conspiracy Case, who are either British Subjects or those Nepalese identity could not be established on April 21, 1945.

Name	*Period of Detention*	*Present Position*
B.P. Koirala	Two years and one and a half months	Released and movements restricted to the town of Patna, Bihar under the restriction order of the Government of India, January 6, 1945.
Santa Bir Lama	One year and eleven months	Released and movements restricted to Suna Pokhari of Darjeeling district under the restriction order of the Government of India, January 9, 1945.
Jajeshwar Prasad Upadhyaya	Ten months	Released and movements restricted to Darjeeling under the restriction order of the Government of India, January 15, 1945.
S.B. Gyawali	Ten months	Released and movements restricted to Darjeeling under the restriction order of the Government of India, January 15, 1945.
Dharanidhar Sharma	One year	To be released on April 1945 and movements restricted to the Darjeeling municipal limits under the restriction orders of the Government of India.

* See a letter from G.A. Falconer, the British Minister in Nepal, to *Maharaja* Juddha Shumsher, April 21, 1945, E.No. 6, *Poka* No. 11, File No. A 14, *Kha*, FMAN.

BIBLIOGRAPHY

Unpublished Materials
Manuscripts and Governments Documents

Foreign Ministry Archives, **Kathmandu**

Manuscripts and Documents

The documents in the Foreign Ministry Archives, Kathmandu, of this period of study bears two kinds of classification. The greater majority of documents are labeled according to their position in the armorie. The numbers run from E.No. 1 to E.No. 10. However, a few bundles that were not in the *almirah,* are labeled as *bastas.*

(a) *Basta* No, Seventy Nine
(b) E. No. 2, *Poka* No. 3, E. No. 2, *Poka* No. 11, E. No. 2, *Poka* No. 79, E. No. 2, *Poka* No. 560.
(c) E. No. 6, *Poka* No. 1, E. No. 6, *Poka* No. 3, E. No. 6, *Poka* No. 6, E. No. 6, Poka No. 11.
(d) E. No. 8, *Poka* No. 3.
(e) *Poka* entitled "Membership in the United Nations".
(f) *Poka* entitled "New *Poka*", with the sub-title as "Chin Lhasa Saga Ko Lekha padi", This *Poka* has several sub-*pokas.* The sub-*poka Bho* is important for our purpose.
(g) Register of Secret Letters in the 1940s. This contains the correspondences between the Nepali Premier and the British Minister at Kathmandu.
(h) The Radio Broadcasts.

Millitary Archives, Kathmandu,
Book No. 291, Magh 15, 2007 (December 1950).

India Office Library, London
E.C. 21-26
Collection of the letters in the External, Department
National Archives, New Delhi

The Government documents may be classified as follows: Indian *Politi-Proceedings, Secret External-B, Foreign Secret Political Proceedings, Foreign Secret Consultations, Political External Collections, Nepal Residey Papers.*

Miscellaneous Unpublished Materials

Budathoki, Chandra Bikram, "History of Democratic Movement in Nepal, 1931-51". Unpublished Ph. D. Dissertation, Patna University, 1974.

Jones, Kenneth Williams, "The Arya Samaj in the Punjab: A Study in the Social Reformation, 1877-1902", Unpublished Ph.D. Dissertation, University of California, Berkeky, 1966.

————, "Identity, Ideology and the Arya Samaj in the Punjab: Acculturation in the Punjab". Paper presented at the meeting of the Association of Asian Studies, Chicago, February, 1966.

Subeedee, Raja Ram "History of Bajhang (1503-1848)". Dissertation submitted to Tribhuvan University, Kathmandu, 1986.

Upadhyaya, Nil Raman, Nila Samchhipta Jivani (Concise Autobiography of Nil), *Interviews,* 1920, unpublished manuscript. Author's collection.

The following were interviewed by the author on the dates indicated and were willing to have their remarks attributed to them by name in whole or in part.

Acharya, Tanka Prasad, April 7, 1975 (President of Nepal *Prajaparisad* and Nepal National Congress in the 1930s and 40s, October 14, 1984.

Basnyat, Khadga Man Singh, May 15, 1980 (Member *Prachanda Gorkha* founded in August 1931).

Byathit, Kedar Man (Secretary of the *Nagarik Adhikar Samiti,* founded in 1937 and one of the founders of the Shiva Samiti in 1938.

Chuda Prasad Sharma, April 5, 1976 (Member *Prajaparisad*).

Dhakal, Dharma Raj, September 12, 1980 (Guard Commander during the Birganj attack by the Nepali Liberation Army on November 10/11).

Dhakal, Chetra Pratayandra Purush, November 8, 1984 (Nepali Police Inspector posted at Thori, who was successful in capturing Ganesh Man Singh and his colleagues at Thori in October 1950).

Dhakal, Ram Babu, September 10, 1982 (A close attendant of *Maharaja* Juddha who deputed by the Primier himself to watch an report on the execution of Dharma Bhakta Mathema. He was with General Nara Shumsher during the execution).

Gyawali, Surya Bikram, August 8, 1980 (An advocate of Nepali freedom and was imprisoned by the Government of India several times for taking part in anti-Rana activities in the 1940s).

Koirala, Dharanidhar, March 10, 1975 (An advocate of Nepali freedom and was imprisoned by the British Government in India several times for taking part in the anti-Rana activities during the 1940s).

Mathema, Dhurba Bhakta, April 20, 1982 (brother of *Sahid* Dharma Bhakta Mathema).

Maskay, Chandra Man, December 12, 1978 (Member of *Prajaprisad* in the 1930s and 40's).

Poudyal, Ram Raj, February 15, 1975 (Member *Prajaparisad*, 1930s and 40s).

Rana, Brahma Shumsher, October, 1980 (He was noted for his liberal views in the Rana Period).

Regmi, Dilli Raman, April 15, 1980 (President, Nepali Rastriya Congress in the 1940s and a noted historian).

Sharma, Ram Hari, December 10, 1979 (Secretary of the *Prajaparisad* founded in August 1938).

Singh, Khadga Man, March 8, 1975 (One of the founding members of the *Prachanda Gorkha,* as radical organization that was founded in August 1931).

Singh, Narayan, October 18, 1980 (Commander of the Nepali Liberation Army which captured Udyagiri Fort during the Nepali Congress offensive of 1950-51).

Udas, Gautam Ratna, January 11, 1975 (Eyewitness during the *lathi* charge of the police on Marga 11, 20007 (November 1950).

Uprety, Puskar Nath, February 18, 1965 (Member *Prajaparisad*).

Books and Pamphlets in English

Apter David, *The Politics of Modernization,* Chicaga: University of Chicago, University Press, 1965.

Barrier, Norman Gerald, *Banned Controversal Literature and Political Control in British India, 1907-1949*, Columbia: University of Missouri, 1974.

Beer, H. Samuel, *Modern Political Development,* New York: Random House, 1974.

Black, C.E., *The Dynamics of Modernization,* New York: Harper and Row, 1966.

Bottomore, T.B. (ed.), *Karl Marx : Selected Writings in Sociology and Social Philosophy,* New York: MacGraw Hill, Book Co., 1964.

Brinton, Crane, *The Anatomy of Revolution,* New York: Prentice Hill, 1952.

Burke, Edmund, *Reflections on the Revolution in France* (4th ed.), Boston: Little Brown & Co., 1871.

Chaudhari, K.C., Anglo-Nepalese Relations (From the Earliest Times from the British Rule in India till the Gurkha War), Calcutta: Modern Book Agency, 1960.

Chauhan, R.S., *The Political Development in Nepal, 1950-1970 (Conflict Between Tradition and Modernity),* New Delhi: Associated Publishing House, 1970.

Dayanand Saraswati, *The Light of Truth: Satyartha Prakash,* trans. by Ganga Prasad Upadhyaya, Allahabad: Kali Press, n.d.

Dmytryshyan, Basil, *Imperial Russia: A Source Book, 1700-1917,* New York: Holt, Rinehart and Winston, Inc., 1967.

Embree, Ainslie (ed.), *The Hindu Tradition,* New York: Random House, 1966.

Feur, Louis (ed.), *Marx and Engles: Basic Writings in Political Philosophy,* New York: Doubleday & Co., 1959.

Gandhi, M.K., *From Yervada Mandir: Ashram Observances,* trans. from original Guzrati by Valji Govindji Desai (3rd ed.), Ahmedabad: Navajivan Publishing House, 1945.

Gupta, Anirudha, *Politics in Nepal: A Study of Post-Rana Political Developments and Party Politics*, Bombay: Allied Publishers, 1964.

Gurkha League (All India), *Freedom for All: Protect the Ligitimate Rights of the Gurkhas*, Khurseong: All India Gurkha League, 1945.

———, *Resolutions Adopted by the Seventh Session*, Lumdeng: Gurkha League, 1950.

Resolution Passed by the Open Session of the All India Gurkha League Conference, Khurseong: Gurkha League, 1945.

Hagen, Toni, The *Kingdom of Nepal in the Himalayas*, New Delhi: Oxford & IBH Publishing Co., 1980.

Haqqi, S.A.H. (ed.), *Democracy, Pluralism and Nation Building*, Delhi: N.B.O. Publisher, 1984.

Husain, Asad, *British India's Relations with the Kingdom of Nepal, 1857-1947. A Diplomatic History of Nepal*, London: George Allen and Unwin, 1970.

Jain M.S., *Emergence of a New Aristocracy in Nepal (1837-1858)*, Agra: Sri Ram Mehra & Co., 1972.

Joshi, Bhuvan Lal, Leo E. Rose, *Democratic Innovations in Nepal*, Berekely: University of California, 1966.

Kasher Bahadur, K.C., *Nepal After the Revolution of 1950*, Vols. I-II, Kathmandu: Sarada Prakasan Griha, 1976.

Kennion, R.L., *Diversion of An Indian Political*, London: William Blackwood & Sons, 1932.

Mazumdar, R.C., *History of Freedom Movement in India*, Vol. III, Calcutta: K.L. Mukhopadhyay, 1963.

MacLane, John (ed.), *Political Awakening in India*, New Jersey: Prentice-Hall 1970.

Mill, John Stuart, *Bentham and Coleridge*, London: Chatto & Windus, 1950.

Mojumdar, Kanchanmoy, *Nepal and the Indian National Movement*, Delhi: K.L. Mukhopadhyay, 1975.

———, *Political Relations Between India and Nepal*, Delhi: Munshi Ram & Manohar Lal, 1975.

Muni, S.D. (ed.), *Nepal: An Assertive Monarchy*, New Delhi: Chetana Publications, 1977.

Nepal Communist Party, *An Open Letter to Shri Nehru, the Prime Minister of India,* Kathmandu: Nepal Communist Party, 1951.

Pal, Bipinchandra, *Swadesi and Swaraj* (The Rise of New Partriotism). Calcutta: Yugyatri Press, 1954.

Paramanand, *The Nepali Congress in Exile,* Delhi: University Book House, 1978.

Pomper, Philip, *The Russian Revolutionary Intelligentsia,* New York: Thomas Y. Crowell Co., 1971.

Poorna Bahadur, M.A., *Nepal Behind the Screen,* Kathmandu: Nepal Youth League, n.d.

Powell, E. Alexander, *The Last Home of Mystery: Adventures in Nepal,* New York: The Century Co., 1920.

Prabhu, Pandharinath, H., *Hindu Social Organization: A Study in Socio-Psychological and Ideological Foundations,* Bombay: Popular Prakasan, 1963.

Prasad, Ishwari, *The Life and Times of Maharaja Juddha Shumsher Jung Bahadur Rana of Nepal,* New Delhi: Ashish Publication, 1975.

Pushkarev, *The Emergence of Modern Russia, 1801-1917,* trans. R.H. MacNeal, Tova Yedlin, New York: Holt, Rinehart and Winston, Inc., 1963.

Pye, Lucian W., *Aspects of Political Development,* New Delhi: Amerind Publishing Co., 1972.

Radhakrishna, Sarvepalli, Charles, A. More, *A Source Book in Indian Philosophy,* Princeton: Princeton University Press, 1970.

Rahul, Ram, *The Himalayas as a Frontier,* New Delhi: Vikas Publishing House, 1978.

Rana, Daman Shumsher, *Nepal: Rule and Misrule,* New Delhi: Rajesh Publication, 1978.

Regmi, D.R., *Wither Nepal,* Kathmandu: Publisher N.K., 1952.

———, *Nepal,* Banaras: Nepal National Congress, 1948 (?)

———, *A Century of Family Autocracy in Nepal,* Banaras: Nepal Rastriya Congress, 1950.

Rose, Leo E., Nepal, *Strategy for Survival,* Delhi: Oxford University Press, 1973.

———, Margaret Fisher, *The Politics of Nepal: Persistence and Change in An Asian Monarchy,* Cornell: Cornell University Press, 1970.

———, John T. Scholz, *Nepal: Profile of An Himalayan Kingdom,* New Delhi: Selected Book House Syndicate, 1980.

Russel, B., *Power—A New Social Analysis* London: George Allen & Unwin, 1957.

Satish Kumar, *Rana Polity in Nepal, Origin and Growth,* Bombay: Asia Publishing House, 1967.

Shah, Rishikesh, *Politics: Retrospect and Prospect,* Delhi: Oxford University Press, 1978.

Sharma, Agni Prasad, Shri Prasad Sharma, *An Appeal: Imparting of Knowledge is the Noble Charity,* Banaras: Shri Prasad Sharma, 1940.

Sharma, P. Narendra Keshari, *The Search for the Seven Star Kings of Nepal,* Banaras: Akhil Barga Mahasabha, 1940.

Sharma Ranganath, *Nepal ko Rajnaitik Bibechana* (An Analysis of the Politics of Nepal), Ayodhya; Publisher N.K., 1950.

Shastri, Gokul Chand, *Freedom Loving Nepal,* Kathmandu: G.C. Shastri, 1960.

Shrivastava, Kasi Prasad, *Nepal ki Kahani,* Delhi: Atma Ram & Sons, 1950.

Singh, Khadga Man, *A Retrospect on Democracy, Party and Panchyat,* Kathmandu: Khadga Man Singh, N.D.

Singh, Shiva Bahadur, *Impact of Indian National Movement on the Political Movement on the Political Development of Nepal,* New Delhi: Marwah Publications, 1985.

Stiller, Ludwig (ed.), *Letters from Kathmandu: The Kot Massacre,* Kathmandu: Centre for Nepal and Asian Studies, 1981.

Stokes, Erich T., *The English Utilitarians in India,* Oxford: Clarendon Press, 1959.

Subba, G.L., *Memorandum of the Gurkhas to Gandhiji and Jinna Sahib,* Calcutta: G.L. Subba, 1944.

Tucker, Francis, *Gorkha: The Story of the Gurkhas of Nepal,* London: Constable Co., 1957.

Upadhyaya, Devendra Raj, *A Glimpse of Nepal Under Rana Tyranny,* Calcutta: Nepal National Congress, 1948.

Uprety, Prem, R., *Religion and Politics in the Punjab in the 1920's,* New Delhi: Sterling Publishers, 1980.

———, *Nepal Tibet Relations, 1850-1930: Years of Hopes, Challenges and Frustrations,* Kathmandu: Puga Nara, 1980.

———, *Nepal: A Small Nation in the Vortex of International Conflicts, 1900-1950,* Kathmandu: Pu Gomi, 1984.

White, R.J., *Europe in the Eighteenth Century,* New York: St. Martin's Press, 1965.

William, Raymond, *Culture and Society: 1780-1950,* New York: Harper & Row, 1966.

Yadhav, Sohan Ram, *Nepal, Feudalism and Rural Formation,* New Delhi: Cosmo Publications, 1984.

Yemi, D.R., *The Study of Critical Situation in Nepal,* Kathmandu: Himalaya Press, 1958.

Articles in English

Barrier, Norman Gerald, "The Arya Samaj and Congress Politics in the Punjab 1894-1908", *The Journal of Asian Studies* XXVI, No. 3, 1967, pp. 363-379.

Budathoki, C.B., "Activities of Prachanda Gorkha", *Voice of History,* Vol. II, 1976, pp. 27-30.

Chetwode, Penelope, "Nepal the Sequestered Kingdom", *The National Geographic Magazine,* Vol. LXVII, No. 3, March 1935, pp. 319-352.

Hagen, Tony, "A Foot on Roadless Nepal", *National Geographic Magazine,* Vol. 117, No. 3, March 1960, pp. 361-404.

Hunt, L.E., "The Road to Kathmandu", *The Statesman* (Nepal Supplement), April 4, 1937, p. 3.

Hurlimann, "Remote Nepal: Land of Mystery", *National Geographic Magazine,* LXVII, No. 3, March 1935, pp. 329-336.

Kennion, R.L., "Recollections from Nepal", *Blackwood Magazine,* Vol. CXXIX, No. MCCLXXXVII, May 31, pp. 665-78.

Koirala, M.P., "Struggle Against Oligarchy", *Free Nepal,* January 15, 1951, pp. 11-12.

Louis, D. Hayer, "Political Development in Nepal", *The Indian Journal of Political Science,* Vol. 37, No. 2, pp. 22-39.

Pant, Shamba Bhakta (Bhai Sahib), "Padma Shumsher's Succession to Prime Ministership", *Kasturi,* Vol. VII, Year 8, 1978, pp. 60-67.

Redfield, Robert, "The Folk Society", *The American Journal of Sociology,* Vcl. LII, January, 1947, pp. 293-308.

Ripley S. Dillo, "Peerless Nepal — A Naturalist Paradise", *The National Geographic Magazine,* Vol. XCVII, No. 1, January 1950, pp. 1-40.

Uprety, Prem, "Nepali Bureaucratic Culture: Few Dominant Features", *The New Horizons,* Vol. II, No. 1, February 23, 1981, pp. 1-7.

Books and Pamphlets in Nepali and Hindi

A Congressite, *Aba Hámi Jagrit Chhou* (Now We Are Conscious), Kathmandu: A Congressite, 1951.

Akhil Nepal Rastriya Mahasabha, *Akhil Nepal Rastriya Mahasabha ko Dwamukhi-Congress Haruma Chetawani* (A Warning to Double.faced Congressites from Akhil Nepal Rastriya Mahasabha), Kathmandu: Akhil Nepal Rastriya Mahasabha, 2008 (1952).

Bhatta, Ananda Dev, *97 Sal* (The Year 97), Kathmandu: Nepal Bharat Maitriya Sangha, 2015, 1959.

Jatiya Janatantrik Samyukta Morcha, *Jatiya Janatantrik Samyukta Morcha ko Ghosana Patra* (The Manifesto of Jatiya Janatantrik Samyukta Morcha), Kathmandu: Pragati Adhyan Mandal, 1951.

Kharel, Agni Prasad, *Bintipatra: Prastabit Pranali ko Swarup ko Drisha* (Petition: A Glimpse of the Proposed System), Banaras: Agni Prasad Kharel, 2004 (1948), (Nehru Lai Khula Patra).

Nepal Communist Party, *An Open Letter to Premier Nehru,* Kathmandu: NCP, 1951 (?)

Nepali Congress, *Nepali Congress ra Nepal ko Pradhan Mantri* (Nepali Congress and Nepali Prime Minister, Kathmandu: Nepali Congress, 2009 (1953).

Nepali Janabadi Prajatantra Sangh, *Nepali Congress ko Akha Ugriyo re* (It is said that the Eyes of the Congress have Opened), Kathmandu: Nepali Janabadi Prajatantrik Sangh, 1951.

Nepali Prajaparisad, *Ajako Ek Matra Bato* (The Only One Road Today), Kathmandu: Nepal Prajaparisad, n.d.

Paropakar Ausadhalaya, *Paropakar ko Akhtiar Sanad* (Legal Charter for the Operation of the Paropakar), Kathmandu: Paropakar Ausadhalaya, 1947.

Poudyal, Bhupahari, *Itihasik Makei Parba* (Historical Maize Episode), Kathmandu: Dipyajoti Prakasan, 2040 (1984).

Pradhan, Dal Bahadur, *Ahile ko Sirkar* (The Present Government, Khurseong: Dal Bahadur Pradhan, 1951.

Pratham Akhil Nepal Rajnaitik Samyalan Ma Pas Bhayako Prastabharu, Banaras: Nepal Rastriya Congress, 1948.

Regmi, D.R., Aj ke Nepal ki Itihasik Pithika (The Facts of Nepali Present History), Banaras: Nepal Rastriya Congress, 1949(?)

Shai, D.K., *Sat Sal Pachi ko Sat Sal* (The Seven Years After the Year Seven) Kathmandu: Nepali Congress, 2014, (1958).

Sharma, Balachandra, *Nepal ko Itihasik Rup Rekha* (An Outline of the History of Nepal), Banaras: Krishna Kumari, 2033 (1977).

Sharma Ranga Nath, *Nepal ko Rajnaitik Bibechana* (An Analysis of Nepali Political Conditions), Ayodhya: Publisher N.K., 1950.

Shastri, Shukra Raj, *Svarga ko Darbar* (The Palace of Heaven), Calcutta: Shukra Raj Shastri, 1986.

———, *Shri Madhav Raj Joshi ka Jivan Charitra* (Biography of Shri Madhav Raj Joshi), Kathmandu: Publisher N.K., 2015 (1959).

Shri Mani, *Kranto ko bad Nepal* (Nepal After the Revolution), Sitamadi: Shri Mani, N.D.

Shumsher, Meg Raj, *Shri 3 Mohan Shumsher Jang Bahadur Rana,* Kathmandu: Megh Raj Shumsher, 2006 (1949).

Singh, Ganesh Man, *Satya Kay* (What is Truth), Banaras: Nepal Rastriya Congress, N.D.

Singh, Jaya Prithvi Bahadur, *Sichya Darpan,* (Mirror of Education), Kathmandu: Jaya Prithvi Bahadur Singh, Vol. 1, 1962 B.S. (1905), Vol. I, 1964 (1907), Vol. III, 1964 (1907).

Sing, Khadga Man, *Jail Ma Bisbarsa* (Twenty Years in Jail), Kathmandu: Ganyananda Baidya, 2040 (1984).

Singh, Uttam Bahadur, *Manabtabadi Raja Jaya Prithvi Bahadur Singh* (Humanistic King Jaya Prithvi Bahadur Singh), Kathmandu: Sabitri Singh, 2035 (1978).

Upadhyaya, Devendra Raj, *Ajaa ko Nepal* (Today's Nepal), Calcutta: Devendra Raj Upadhyaya, 2005 (1949).

Upadhyaya, Ganga Prasad, *Arya Samaj ki Niti* (Fifty Four Answers to Questions).

———, *Arya Samaj aur Islam,* Allahabad: Arya Samaj, 1967.

———, *Suddhi* (Purification), Delhi: Bharatiya Hindu Sabha, 1967.

Vidyavachaspati, Indra, *Arya Samaj ka Itihas,* Vol. I, Delhi: Sarvadeshik Arya Pratinidhi Sabha, 1957.

Yemi, Dharma Ratna, Nepal ka Kura (The Happenings of Nepal), Kathmandu: Yemi Prakasan, 1957.

Articles in Nepali and Hindi

Baral, Iswar, "Sambhu Prasad Dhungel", *Nepali,* No. 7, 2018 (1961), 3-35.

Baskota, Narayan, "Hamro Kranti" (Our Revolution, *Sharada,* Year 16, No. 9, Poush-Magh 2007 (1950), pp. 298-3000.

Bhandari, Ganesh, "Itihasik Makei Parba", (Historic Makei Episode), *Prgna,* Year I, No. 2, 2027 (1970), pp. 5-11.

———, "Pandit Shamba Bhakta Subedi", *Madhuparka,* Year II, No. 8, Poush 2026 (1969), pp. 66-75.

Bhattari, Krishna Prasad, "B.P. Koirala ra Samajbad", B.P. Koirala and Socialism *Rajdhani* (B.P. Supplement), Year I, No. 28, 2041 (1984), pp. 5-6, 45.

Budathoki, C.B., "Shukra Raj Shastri ra Unko Den" (Shukra Raj Shastri and His Contribution), *Voice of History,* Vol. IV-VI, 1978-80, pp. 24-28.

Chetri, Khadga Bahadur, "Hamro Desh Aur Jati ko Bartaman Awasta" (The Present Condition of Our Countrymen and Our Race), *Gorkha Sansar,* Year IV, Kiran 6, December, 1929.

Dikshit, Harihar Acharya, "Bidya ra Gorkha Vasapo Durdasa" (The Sad Plight of Education and Gorkha Language), in Ishwar Baral, *Sayapatri* (Collection of Nepali Prose of Essays), Kathmandu: Sajha Prakasan, 2030 (1974), pp. 86-90.

Devkota, Laxmi Prasad, "Pravuji Bhedo Banu" (God Made Me a Sheep), *Sharada,* Year 13, 2004 (1948), Nos. 1-2, pp. 30-32.

Gurung, Damber Singh, "Akhil Bharatiya Gorkha League ko Janma" (The Birth of All India Gorkha League) in Ram Krishna Sharma(Ed.), *Jaya Gorkha: Gurkha League Ismarak Patra,* 1948, pp. 4-7.

Koirala, B.P., "Mero Jivan Katha" (My Autobiography), *Pragati,* Year II, No. 2, 2011 (1954), pp. 123-132.

Lama, I.B., "Koirala Sahiko Shikar aibam Facist Chal", (The Victim of Koirala Despotism and the Facist Move), *Gorkhali,* Year 7, Kiran 19, May 26, 1951, pp. 305-306.

Merak Paras Diwan, "Samala Gharedi" (Look After Your Field Where Your House is Going to be Built), *Gorkha,* Year 7, Kiran 19, May 26, 1951, pp. 302-303.

Mishra, Yuddha Prasad, "Jabik Charo"(The Bird in a Net), *Sharda,* Year I, No. 12, 1992 (1935), p. 5.

Naupane, Kedar Nath, "Ram", "Ektantra bad ra Janatantra bad" (Dictatorship Democracy), *Free Nepal,* January 15, 1951, pp. 16-18.

Pradatta, "Nepal ma Prajatantra" (Democracy in Nepal), Gorkha, Year 7, Kiran 19, May 26, 1951, pp. 299-301.

Pradhan, Bhuvan Lal, "Makei ko Kheti ka Lekhak — Krishan Lal Adhikari" (The Cultivation of Maize and its Writer Krishan Lal Adhikari), *Madhuparka,* Year 9, No. 10, March, 1977, pp. 11-14.

Pradhan, Hridaya Singh, "Nepal ma Jana Jagriti ra Rana Sahi ko Anta" (People's Awakening in Nepal and the End of Rana Rule), *Jagaran* (Weekly), Year I, No. 1, Falgun 2007(1951), pp. 9-14.

Regmi, D.R., "Nepal Aur Jana Andolan ka Udeshya" (Nepal and Objectives of Peoples Movement), *Nepali Congress Occasional Bulletin,* unnumbered, N.D.

Satyal, Jogendra, Raj, "Hamro Samaj ko Durgati ko Karan" (The Causes of the Deterioration of Our Society), *Gorkha Sansar,* 1925, 1-19.

Sharma, Tika Ram, "Gorkha ko Afno Itihas" (The History of the Gorkha), in Ram Krishna Sharma (ed.), *Gorkha League Ismarik Patra,* 1948, pp. 17-19.

Singh, Ganesh Man, "B.P.: Mahantaka Praynadai Chhanharu" (Moments of Inspiration from B.P.), *Rajdhani Weekly,* Year I, No. 28, 2041 (1981) pp. 3-4, 57.

Subba, Ranadhir, "Gorkha League — Siddhanta ra Niti" (Gorkha League—Principles and Objectives), *Jaya Gorkha: Gorkha League ko Ismarika Patra,* 1948, pp. 20-25.

Upadhyaya, Krishna Prasad, "Makei Parba ra 2007 Sal "(The Cultivation of the Maize Episode and Year 2007), *Gorkhapatra,* Falgun 7, 2025 (February 18, 1969), p. 15.

Proscribed Tract Literature

Adhikari, Krishna Lal, *Makei ko Kheti* (The Cultivation Maize), Kathmandu: Nepal Bhasa Prakasini Samati, 1977 (1920).

Kharel, Agni Prasad, *The Seven Star Kings of Nepal,* Banaras: Akhil Barga Mahasabha, 1942.

———, *Jagriti* (Awakening), An unpublished manuscript in Nepali that was destroyed by the Government of Nepal.

Raktapat Committee, "Nepal Under the Ranas: Atrocities Over the Nepalis", A cylostyled pamphlet, preserved in the Foreign Ministry of Nepal.

Regmi, D.R., *An Appeal to the Congress,* Banaras: Akhil Nepal Barga Mahasabha, 1942.

———, *Nepal,* Banaras: Nepal National Congress, 1948.

Upadhyaya, Devendra Raj, A Climpse of Nepal Under the Rana Tyranny, Calcutta: Nepal National Congress, 1948.

Radio Broadcasts

The Radio Broadcasts have been collected by Kula Dharma Ratna Tuladhar and is now preserved in the Ministry of Foreign Affairs, Kathmandu, Nepal.

All India Radio (1950-51)
British Broadcasting Cooperation (1950-51)
Radio Pakistan (1950-51)
Radio Saigon (1950-51)
The Voice of America (1950-51)
The Voice of Prajatantra Radio (1951)

Newspapers and Periodicals in English

Blackwood Magazine
Evening Standard
Free Nepal
Free Press Bulletin
National Herald
Observer
Search Light
The American Journal of Sociology
The Hindu
The Independent
The Journal of Asian Studies
The Leader
The Modern Review
The New Horizons
The Pioneer
The Readers Digest
The Voice of History
Young India

Newspapers and Periodicals in Nepal

Awaz
Gorkhapatra
Gorkha Sansar
Jagaran
Jaya Gorkha: Gorkha League ko Samarika Patrika
Madhuparka
Nepali
Pragna
Rajdhani
Rastriya Congress Bulletin (Nos. 1-67)
Sarada
Yugbani

INDEX